D1473996

Wethersfield Institute

SIGRID UNDSET
ON SAINTS AND SINNERS

Sigrid Undset
On Saints and Sinners

New Translations
and Studies

Papers Presented at a Conference
Sponsored by the Wethersfield Institute
New York City, April 24, 1993

EDITED, WITH AN INTRODUCTION BY
DEAL W. HUDSON

IGNATIUS PRESS   SAN FRANCISCO

Cover photo: Norwegian Information Service
New York, N.Y.
Cover design by Riz Boncan Marsella

Published by
Ignatius Press, San Francisco
© 1993 Homeland Foundation
All rights reserved
ISBN 0–89870–483–9
Library of Congress catalogue number 93–80753
Printed in the United States of America

To Hannah

WETHERSFIELD INSTITUTE
STATEMENT OF PURPOSE

The purpose of Wethersfield Institute is to promote a clear understanding of Catholic teaching and practice, and to explore the cultural and intellectual dimensions of the Catholic Faith. The Institute does so in practical ways that include seminars, colloquies and conferences especially as they pursue our goals on a scientific and scholarly level. The Institute publishes its proceedings.

It is also interested in projects that advance those subjects. The Institute usually sponsors them directly, but also joins with accredited agencies that share our interests.

Msgr. Eugene V. Clark, President
E. Lisk Wyckoff, Vice President
Patricia Puccetti Donahoe, Program Director

CONTENTS

Studies

Translations

CONTRIBUTORS

DEAL W. HUDSON is Associate Professor of Philosophy, Fordham University, Rose Hill.

SUSAN T. VIGILANTE, a writer living in New York City, is working on a biography of Sigrid Undset.

EVELYN BIRGE VITZ is Professor of French at New York University.

ERASMO LEIVA-MERIKAKIS is Professor of Comparative Literature at the University of San Francisco.

PAUL EVANS is a teacher and writer living in Atlanta.

MSGR. EDWARD A. SYNAN is Director Emeritus of the Pontifical Institute of Medieval Studies in Toronto.

MITZI M. BRUNSDALE is Professor of English at Mayville State University in North Dakota.

DAVID A. BOVENIZER, the Executive Editor of *Crisis* magazine, is a veteran journalist and bookman living in Crozier, Virginia.

ASTRID O'BRIEN is Associate Professor of Philosophy, Fordham University, Lincoln Center.

LIV I. SHANK is a translator and language teacher of Norwegian and German who lives in Ardsley, New York.

REV. JOHN E. HALBORG is Associate Pastor of the Church of St. Thomas More, New York City, the Editor of *St. Ansgar's Scandinavian Catholic Bulletin*.

DEAL W. HUDSON

SIGRID UNDSET ON SAINTS AND SINNERS:
AN INTRODUCTION

> The proclamation of all heathen religions is not a longing for
> comfort, not even a longing for salvation, as much as a longing
> for clarity. The question of first and last things has engaged
> humanity more deeply than the question of their own weal
> and woe.
>
> — Sigrid Undset

Among Catholic writers there are more familiar names—
Graham Greene, Evelyn Waugh, Georges Bernanos, François
Mauriac, Flannery O'Connor—but Sigrid Undset belongs
among them. Her medieval trilogy *Kristin Lavransdatter* bears
a name more recognized than its author, and it stands along-
side *The Power and the Glory*, *Brideshead Revisited*, *The Diary of
a Country Priest*, *The Viper's Tangle*, and *Wise Blood* as one of
the great Catholic novels in this century.

Unfortunately, Undset's reputation remains confined to a
single work. This may account for the fact that relatively few
critics have attempted to account for the impact of the trilogy
itself. This volume attempts to remedy both situations. Some
of these essays ponder the enduring power of *Kristin Lavransdatter*, and others explore the larger context of Undset's spiritual
legacy, a prophetic authorship begging for rediscovery. English
versions of previously untranslated material provide an opportunity to sample portions of that legacy formerly available only
to those who read Norwegian.

Those who take the trouble to peruse her other works—the
novels, memoirs, children's books, apologetics, literary essays,

hagiography—will find that the mastery of *Kristin Lavransdatter* was not an accidental outpouring of an obscure Norwegian writer.[1] The same spiritual intelligence that gives the trilogy a potency to convert the lives of its readers is found throughout her other writings. In fact, Undset lamented the popularity of *Kristin* and worried that it eclipsed appreciation of a work she thought superior—the medieval tetralogy *The Master of Hestviken*. Without taking anything away from the earlier work, many Undset commentators, including Paul Evans in his essay on *Hestviken*, agree with the author's assessment.[2]

Sigrid Undset (1882–1949) was born at the dawning of modernity, the same year as Jacques Maritain, James Joyce, Virginia Woolf, and Igor Stravinsky. Like Maritain, whom she studied and admired, she became a Catholic by choice in a society hostile to the authority of the Roman magisterium. Maritain's foes were atheists, socialists, and avant-garde intellectuals of all stripes; Undset fought them as well, but as filtered through a Protestant sensibility. Both "Catholic Propaganda" and the "Reply to Archbishop Söderblom" reveal the degree to which Undset thought Protestantism too cozy with the modern age. But it is clear from "Progress, Race, Religion", one of the best examples of her polemical writing, that she sees godlessness as the fundamental threat.

Also like Maritain, she bore something of modernity within herself and her work. Undset's lifelong concern for the plight of women in the postindustrial age is apparent in her earliest fiction, *Mrs. Marta Oulie* (1907) and *Jenny* (1911), and remains consistent through her last novel, *Madame Dorthea* (1939). Her concern, as seen in "Some Reflections on the Suffragette Movement", takes a different trajectory from other women's advocates: Undset decries the progressive alienation of women from their own bodies, from their children, and from men. The importance of affirming an ordinate relation to nature and tradition is treated by David A. Bovenizer in his reflection "Mr. Lytle's *Kristin*". Undset's clarity on these issues remained intact in spite of her own adultery, an experience which shaped the remainder of her life. Susan Vigilante's essay provides a succinct account of Undset's sixty-seven years, cut short evidently by grief and hard work.

In an age preoccupied with the debate over "family values", it is refreshing to come across someone who unapologetically advocates the graces of family life. Her "Christmas Meditation" offers an example of her eye for the place of the child in God's economy.[3] No writer, to my knowledge, has been so successful at depicting the love of parents, especially mothers, for their children. Furthermore, Undset's depictions of this love, which are always far from sentimental, disclose how this love participates in God's own charity. As she writes, "It is by no means the commonest case for a man to turn from God because he loves something which he is determined to make his own at all costs. It is far commoner for him to allow himself to be held back by a love which has conquered him."[4] In Undset, it is children who most often hold their parents back from damnation:

> There is no getting away from the fact that very few people would be able to endure each other if they were not bound together to serve some ideal which is so great as to make them both seem equally insignificant when measured against it. And it is impossible to advocate lifelong monogamy unless one believes that every single human soul is worth God's dying to save it.[5]

It can be said that *the value of life* dominates Undset's fiction[6] insofar as the care, nurture, and sacrifice of parents for their children are the primary instantiations of that value.

Some of Undset's best treatments of familial love are found in works written the decade before her confirmation. The degree to which her early works anticipate her conversion suggests that if there ever were a natural Catholic it was Undset. However, her essay "If 2 + 2 = 5" unambiguously states that Undset saw nothing whatsoever naturalistic about her conversion. The essay by Evelyn Vitz on Undset's view of medieval female saints indicates how her understanding of female sanctity was immeasurably deepened by her Catholic faith. Still there is no denying the shattering effect of works like the short story "Thjodolf" (1918),[7] depicting the effect on a foster mother of a child being given and taken back by the biological mother.

Another early work, *Images in a Mirror* (1917),[8] portrays the unhappy marriage of a former stage actress to a man who falls well short of fulfilling her desire for companionship, much less her persistent dreams of romantic love. Uni's marriage to Kristian has long since lost the brief erotic twinge that brought them together. She has given birth to five children in ten years. The death of one of the boys has weakened her confidence in ever finding a lasting joy in her family. Falling briefly into an affair, Uni has begun to neglect her children when she unexpectedly is called back to herself by a friend who remarks that she misses the way Uni used "to sing to the children in the evening". Uni's recognition that her change of heart has been noticed leads to a confrontation and eventual reconciliation with her husband. Having broken off her affair, she recollects why she risked losing her family:

> "Happiness," she thought, "happiness—what was I doing, at my age, to go and believe in happiness—or doubt of happiness? The happiness that Kristian and I once shared. The happiness that is like a shooting star. In the brief instant that it shines one must think of one's heart's desire and wish; and in the brief space while caresses are new and thrilling, one is called to understand and determine one's life. I wonder how many there are who succeed.
>
> "And happiness in one's children is so natural that one does not think of it. All the times when our heart gleams with joy —at the odd things they say, and their comical first steps, at their beginning to take notice, at their caresses and those we give them, at the fright which proved needless and an illness which did not turn out to be dangerous. It does not occur to us that this is happiness, all these thousand little gleams. And yet it is on them that we live. No one could live without being happy now and then, but we do not think of it when it is there. We are only truly conscious of ourselves when we are unhappy.

So long as I have my children I know that I can face life—
cheerfully, in whatever way everything else may turn out."[9]

Such moments of spiritual awakening are typical in Undset's fiction, though the outcomes, as in life, are not always
as happy. Msgr. Edward Synan discusses the important role of
the awakened conscience in relation to the Church in Undset's
medieval epics. Though some might view Undset's character
of Uni as paying homage to a defunct gender role, Undset's
intention is clearly to defend it as crucial to caring for human
life and to passing on the hope of true happiness. In doing so,
Undset draws our attention to possibilities of fulfillment that
offer themselves through the very offices we so often consider
opposed to our own interests. This theme of abandonment
to God underlying all of Undset's later writing is treated by
Erasmo Leiva-Merikakis in his reflection on sanctity and culture. Another scholar has argued that Undset's understanding
of spirituality and the family came to unique fruition in her
later novels; she writes, "Undset's work is ultimately a reflection on the strength that surpasses autonomous self-expression,
the strength embodied in selfless forms of love."[10]

Children represent the opportunity for release from the preoccupation with self. In welcoming them, Undset thinks, we
overcome our yearning for hedonistic self-realization and find
joy in serving a will other than our own. Yet children in particular, and family life in general, must be seen as standing in
harm's way, given the growing disposition to self-absorption.
She castigates the cruel spread of the contraceptive mentality
in this century: "For it is notorious that no means exists . . .
of inquiring of children yet unconceived or unborn whether
they are willing to enter society and take upon themselves the
tasks that await them."[11]

The tensions of everyday domestic life, seen from this angle, take on the import of a spiritual trial, the option being
to seek ersatz redemption in the isolation of a short-lived romantic ecstasy. Mitzi Brunsdale traces the seismology of these

decisive moments in her discussion of happiness and penance in Undset's fiction. Her early one-act play *In the Gray Light of Dawn* (1908) reveals this dialectic of infidelity and regret, and its terrible effect upon children, using the most economic means possible.[12] It stands as a near-distillation of the novels about family life to come.

Undset's forty years of meditation on sin, sanctity, marriage, children, religion, power, cruelty—on the hardships of love in a secularized world—deserve, and will eventually find, a wider audience. Many of the novels and short stories, not just the medieval epics, the memoirs, the essays on sanctity, deserve to remain in print. The rest of her fiction needs to be translated, along with the rest of her apologetics. Her correspondence, of which only one volume is available, must be fascinating. Some have suggested that *Kristin Lavransdatter* itself should be retranslated to take into account her Norwegian dialect.

Whatever the fate of Sigrid Undset's work in the future, one can be sure that there will continue to be those who stumble onto her works (or have them thrust importunately into their hands) and finish reading them only to find themselves changed: some obstacle or another has fallen away—to faith, to marriage, to children, to repentance—and some new vision now seems plausible when only weeks ago it seemed absurd.

The editor wishes to acknowledge the generous support of the Wethersfield Institute, particularly President Msgr. Eugene V. Clark, Mr. Lisk Wyckoff, President of Homeland Foundation and Vice President of the Wethersfield Institute, and Program Director Mrs. Patricia Donahoe, and to thank Dr. Astrid O'Brien and Susan Baer, both of Fordham University, and Shannon Mary Bridget Polley for their help in preparing this volume.

NOTES

[1] The following is a list of Undset's works that have been translated into English: *Jenny*, 1921 [some sources give 1920—ED.]; *Kristin Lavransdatter*, 1920–1922; *The Master of Hestviken*, 1925–1927; *The Wild Orchid*, 1931; *Christmas and Twelfth Night*, 1932; *The Burning Bush*, 1932; *Ida Elisabeth*, 1933; *Saga of the Saints*, 1934; *Stages on the Road*, 1934; *The Longest Years*, 1935; *Gunnar's Daughter*, 1936; *The Faithful Wife*, 1937; *Images in a Mirror*, 1938; *Men, Women and Places*, 1939; *Madame Dorthea*, 1940; *Return to the Future*, 1942; *Happy Times in Norway*, 1942; *Sigurd and His Brave Companions*, 1943; *True and Untrue and Other Norse Tales*, 1945; *Catherine of Siena*, 1954; *Four Stories*, 1959. Much of Undset's writing remains untranslated. For the complete listing, see Ida Packness, *Sigrid Undset Bibliografi* (Oslo: Universitetsforlaget, 1963).

[2] A. H. Winsnes comments on Undset, "All her writing deals with the individual's desire to break, and his struggle to keep, the covenant set between God and man; and this is nowhere presented with greater imaginative force and power of artistic realisation than in her profoundest psychological study, *Olav Audunsson* [English translation: *The Master of Hestviken*]" (*Sigrid Undset: A Study in Christian Realism*, trans. P. G. Foote [New York: Sheed and Ward, 1953], pp. 247–48).

[3] This was previously translated and published with illustrations in Sigrid Undset, *Christmas and Twelfth Night* (New York: Longmans, Green, 1932), pp. 31–40.

[4] "The Strongest Power", *Men, Women and Places*, trans. Arthur G. Chater (New York: Alfred A. Knopf, 1939), p. 165.

[5] "Reply to a Parish Priest", *Stages on the Road*, trans. Arthur G. Chater (New York: Alfred A. Knopf, 1934), p. 257.

[6] Mitzi Brunsdale, *Sigrid Undset: Chronicler of Norway* (New York: Berg Publishers, 1988), p. 127.

[7] Originally published in *The Wise Virgins* but translated and collected in *The Four Stories*, trans. Naomi Walford (New York: Alfred A. Knopf, 1959).

[8] *Images in a Mirror*, trans. Arthur G. Chater (New York: Alfred A. Knopf, 1938). The Norwegian title is *Fru Hjelde*, which was originally only one of the two novellas published under the title *Splinten av troldspeilet* [Splinter from the troll's looking-glass].

[9] *Images in a Mirror*, pp. 225–26.

[10] Elisabeth Solbakken, *Redefining Integrity: The Portrayal of Women in the Contemporary Novels of Sigrid Undset* (New York: Peter Lang, 1992), p. 204.

[11] "Reply to a Parish Priest", p. 259.

[12] This English version of *In the Gray Light of Dawn* was first performed in an adaptation by Jay Magruder at Fordham University Lincoln Center, April 1993. The two characters were played by Carver Hudson and David Omar; the director was Michael Petshaft.

STUDIES

SUSAN T. VIGILANTE

A LIFE OF SIGRID UNDSET

Denounced as a traitor by feminists of her own day, she was praised in *Ms.* magazine years after her death as a strong, gifted woman who was faithful to her talent and never failed to stand up for what she believed in, even at great personal cost.[1]

The most practical and self-disciplined of women, her hopeless romanticism would pull her into a disastrous relationship.

A staunch defender of the sanctity of marriage, her own marriage began with an affair with a married man and ended in divorce.

A prolific Catholic apologist, she was brought up an atheist and wrote her greatest and most deeply Catholic novels before her conversion.

A Nobel Prize winner and world famous in her lifetime, her own sense of privacy and the desire of family and friends to smooth over the rough spots in a difficult and passionate life has made her a mystery to biographers and kept her almost a stranger to her fans.

But some forty-four years after her death she still has legions of readers all over the world. Her most powerful books have never been out of print, and her life is an inspiration to artists and writers, single women and working mothers, and to anyone who has ever tried to live a worldly life according to Christian principles.

Sigrid Undset was born in Kalundborg, Denmark, on May 20, 1882. Her mother, Anna Charlotte Gyth, was a Dane, the

23

daughter of a successful provincial attorney. Sigrid's father, Ingvald Undset, was a Norwegian archaeologist on temporary leave from his university post in Oslo.

Anna Charlotte was an attractive, intelligent woman. Her mother had died when she was a child; she and her five brothers and sisters were raised by a maiden aunt who chose Anna Charlotte as her clear favorite and spoiled the little girl shamelessly. People who knew her as an adult described Anna Charlotte as a reserved and proud woman given to assuming superior airs.

After her marriage, Anna Charlotte Undset took an active interest in her husband's work, often accompanying him on his expeditions. A "progressive" parent, she dressed her daughters in boy's breeches under their skirts and sent them to a coeducational school, a shockingly liberal thing to do in Oslo in the 1880s.

Some have claimed that Anna Charlotte was a cold and distant mother. Others disagree, insisting that she was as close to her children as her temperament would allow. Whatever the case, it was her father whom little Sigrid idolized.

Ingvald Undset came from a farming family in Trondelag, the region in which Sigrid would one day set her most famous work, *Kristin Lavransdatter*. Both Ingvald's parents were hard-working, deeply religious people.

But, like the ancient saga heroes his daughter loved in childhood and recreated as an adult, Ingvald seems to have had a strong sense of personal destiny that diverted him from his family's ways. He abandoned both his parents' faith and their way of life and became a scientist and an atheist.

Even his scholarship had a certain heroic flair to it. Archaeology is history for outdoorsmen. Its apostles can spend nearly as much time out of doors, frequently under rough circumstances, as they spend with the library catalogue. To uncover an ancient site is to touch the past with one's own grubby fingers. It is to know for certain that, centuries before, some mere mortal very much like oneself touched the same objects, maybe even with some of the same dirt under his finger-nails.

The year before Sigrid's birth, he published *The Beginnings of the Iron Age in Northern Europe*, a landmark study of Scandinavian archaeology that established Undset's international reputation.

For all Anna Charlotte's determined progressivism, the Undset home was permeated with the past. Like most families, they had a few knickknacks scattered about the house, but one of theirs was a terra-cotta horse from Troy, a gift from Heinrich Schliemann; Ingvald sometimes let his daughter play with it. Like other families, they had visitors, but theirs were historians and other archaeologists, colleagues of Ingvald from the University, and the children could listen in on conversations about digs and artifacts and pagan cultures. Like most fathers, Ingvald read aloud to his children, but sometimes the stories were in Old Norse or Old Icelandic, which Sigrid learned to read as a child. It was, to say the least, an unusual early education.

It was also sadly short. For much of his eldest daughter's life, Ingvald Undset's health was poor. He had contracted malaria on one of his expeditions to the Mediterranean, and, as Sigrid grew older, her father grew progressively weaker. She was just eleven years old when Ingvald died.

The little girl he left behind was a solitary and independent child. Even at school she had only one close friend, a little girl who shared her passion for botany. (The study of plant life would fascinate Undset all her life; even while escaping from the Nazis, she would stop to notice an unusual flower or plant along the refugee-thronged road.) Her chief companions, outside of her mother and sisters, were books.

All her life Undset was a voracious reader. She was blessed with a phenomenal memory and a remarkable gift for languages, so there was virtually no limit to what she could gain from the printed word. Scandinavian literature was naturally a favorite, but she devoured all European literature and had a deep love for the great English writers. Dickens and Shakespeare were favorites, but she read everything from Anglo Saxon lays to Rudyard Kipling.

She was still an adolescent when she discovered a copy of *Njál's Saga* in her grandfather's library. She would eventually describe this encounter as "a turning-point in my life".[2] This thirteenth-century Icelandic family-saga is the grim and heroic tale of two men, Gunnar and Njál. Both are men of peace, but their honor will not let them escape the destiny marked out for them by the violence of the age and the intricate web of family obligations into which they were born. They represent the classic saga-hero type: a man who is different from ordinary men, knows it, and is determined to follow his own destiny—but therefore also is willing to accept his doom.

Some critics have suggested that Undset fell in love with the saga-hero type. She herself once remarked that *Njál's Saga* gave her a premonition of how women could easily allow their own destinies to become hopelessly entangled with those of gifted but neurotic men.[3]

After her husband's death, Anna Charlotte Undset and her daughters were plunged into genuine poverty. It must have been indescribably difficult for this proud and pretty lawyer's daughter to cope with raising three children on her small widow's pension. It was certainly difficult for Sigrid, who never forgot her painful embarrassment at watching her mother shopping for cheap goods and haggling over prices.

Ingvald Undset had dreamed of a university career for his gifted daughter; Sigrid herself, as a young girl, longed to be an artist. But now for the first time she would display the rock-solid realism that would mark not only her fiction but most of her actions throughout her life. She decided that, in the family's straitened circumstances the most valuable thing she could do would be to start earning her living right away. At the age of fifteen she enrolled in the Christiania Commercial College. A year later she received her certificate and, with the help of family friends, she secured a job as a secretary at the German Electrical Company in Oslo. Not surprisingly she found the work tedious and distasteful, and she felt deeply alienated from her coworkers. She stayed for ten years.

Perhaps to kill the boredom as much as anything else, she began writing after hours. In a letter to a Swedish friend in 1902, she announced that she was hard at work on a novel set in the Middle Ages. Two years later she took the completed manuscript to a publisher. It was rejected. In one of the great literary miscalls of all time, a well-meaning editor advised her, "Don't try your hand at any more historical novels. It's not your line."[4] But he did suggest she try writing another novel with a more modern theme.

Undset took his suggestion. She went back to work, and in 1907 her first published novel, *Mrs. Marta Oulie*, appeared in Oslo bookstores.

The first sentence of *Mrs. Marta Oulie*—"I have been unfaithful to my husband"—is one of the most memorable in European literature. The novel's theme of the destructive power of untrammeled passion would appear repeatedly in Undset's fiction and in her life.

Typically for a first novel, *Mrs. Marta Oulie* was not a great commercial success. (Years later when a young American critic pointed this out, Undset primly corrected him, "[The book] attained a great deal of attention."[5]) Undset, who had already had enough of scrimping and saving to last her a lifetime, had too much common sense to rely on writing for a living yet. Only after her novel, *The Story of Viga-Ljot and Vigdis* (English trans.: *Gunnar's Daughter*), was published in 1909 did she feel secure enough to give up her job and devote herself to her literary career full time.

By this time her reputation had grown, and she was sufficiently highly regarded for the Norwegian government to award her a travel fellowship. She was then twenty-seven years old.

She traveled first to Berlin, where she introduced herself

to her German publishers. It was not a happy meeting. She formed a lifelong dislike of the Germans, who, she felt, "lived in an atmosphere of self-importance".[6] After eight weeks in Germany, she went on to Rome. She settled in the Via Fratina, not far from the Villa Borghese and a short walk to the Tiber and the bridges leading into Vatican City. She attached herself to a small community of young expatriate Norwegians, artists and writers like herself.

Here she met Anders Svarstad.

Anders Castus Svarstad was what Sigrid herself had dreamed of being: he was a painter. He was thirteen years older than Undset and far more experienced than she; he had traveled widely, studied in Paris and Copenhagen, and worked in the United States. He was almost a stereotype of the "tortured" artist, headstrong, sensitive, temperamental. He was an intelligent man with real talent—Undset was unlikely to be impressed by less—who was dedicated to his calling and whose works would one day be compared to those of Gauguin.

He was also a married man. His wife, Ragna Moe, had been a childhood friend of Sigrid. The Svarstads had three children, one of whom was mentally handicapped.

None of these considerations was enough to prevent Undset and Anders Svarstad from falling in love.

Despite her involvement with Svarstad, Undset left Rome in the summer of 1910. After a brief visit to Paris, she went back to Oslo and lived for awhile with her family. The following summer she stayed at a boarding house in Bundefjord, working furiously on the novel she had begun in Rome.

The plot of *Jenny* bears eerie suggestions about Undset's life in Rome. It is the story of a young Norwegian woman, a struggling artist, living in Rome. Engaged to be married, Jenny has an affair with her fiancé's father, gets pregnant, and bears an out-of-wedlock child, a sickly baby boy who soon dies. Convinced she is a failure not only as a mother and an artist but as a woman, Jenny falls into despair and kills herself.

Jenny was published in 1911. (It was the first of Undset's books to be published in the United States [in 1920/1921], thus bringing her at last to the attention of the American reading public.)

In Norway it placed Undset at the center of a storm. Already the most promising woman writer in Norway, Undset had naturally been something of a heroine to Norwegian feminists, who at the time were still deeply engaged in the fight for voting rights. To them, *Jenny* was a betrayal. They were outraged that Undset's heroine should be destroyed by the loss of her child rather than find solace in her work. The depiction of any woman as having a "biological destiny" to bear children and, perhaps worse, a powerful emotional need to rear them seemed to imply that women were not quite the equals of men.

Undset's own life, of course, vindicated all the feminists' important claims about the value of women to society. But the same qualities that made them want to claim her as one of their own made that claim impossible. The suffragettes were ideologues with the ideologue's longing for simplicity. But Undset was a realist. She would not surrender her tragic sense to their neat certainties. She knew that the struggle between the need to express her talents and the equally powerful imperative to love and protect her children was the central and potentially tragic contradiction in the life of every woman artist. She knew that this contradiction could never be denied or glossed over and would not be made any easier by debates or pamphleteering.

One evening in February 1912, Undset's sensational novel was the topic for discussion at the meeting of the Club for Women's Suffrage in Oslo. Undset decided to come to watch the fireworks. Although she managed to keep silent during the debate, she later remarked that it was all she could do not to burst out laughing. Things got so heated, she said, that "I sat and waited for them to start beating one another about the head with their handbags, but unfortunately it never got so far."[7]

Within a few weeks she returned to Rome and took up again with Anders Svarstad. Svarstad's marriage to Ragna Moe had foundered by now, and he obtained a divorce. Undset now had her artist lover all to herself.

To anyone who dreamed of living a creative life, Undset and Svarstad must have seemed the ideal couple: she a celebrated author, he a talented painter. Moreover, they had the great good luck to be living in Rome, surrounded by some of the world's most beautiful art treasures and some of its best cheap wine. It was the stuff idylls are made of.

Lover of art and student of history that she was, Undset naturally adored Rome, and the romantic in her must have looked forward to a long and carefree interlude with her lover. But by the spring of 1912 it must have become evident that the time had come to take some serious steps about their situation. In the late spring she and Svarstad left Rome suddenly for Belgium. On June 29, 1912, they were married in the Norwegian consulate in Antwerp.[8] Less than seven months later, on January 24, 1913, their first child, a boy, was born[9] in London.

The year she spent in England was one of the happiest of Undset's life. She was writing, she was deeply in love with her husband, she adored her son, Anders, and she was delighted to be living in London. "Except for Rome, I know no city I like so much", she wrote to a friend.[10]

But her new life, while happy, was certainly not easy. In a letter to a friend and colleague Nini Roll Anker, Undset wrote that the conflicting demands of motherhood and writing were becoming almost crushing. For the first time her phenomenal willpower, which had gotten her through so many difficult times in the past, threatened to fail her. She found the experience unnerving.[11]

Within a short time after her son's birth, it became clear

to Undset that she could not manage on her own. She was worried that the baby was not thriving properly, and she decided the best thing to do would be to go home to Oslo so she could be near her mother, who could help her care for the baby. Early in 1913, she returned to Oslo. The idyll was over.

Back in Norway, the Svarstad family grew quickly and in some ways tragically. In 1915 Undset bore a daughter, Maren Charlotte, who was called Tulla. Tulla was epileptic and profoundly retarded; she never learned to speak properly, and she was able to communicate only by touch. (When Undset's two nieces started coming to visit a few years later, their aunt happily spoiled them with gifts and clothes and pocket money. Years later one of the girls remembered, "We had the feeling that with us . . . she was experiencing everything that she had been unable to lavish on her own daughter.")[12]

Around the time of Tulla's birth, Undset learned that Ragna Moe, unable to support her three children by Svarstad, had found it necessary to place them in an orphanage. In spite of her own family's difficulties, and even though it would mean having two mentally handicapped children to raise, Undset got custody of Ragna Moe's children and brought them into her own home.

Throughout this time, her marriage was unraveling. As her family grew and her difficulties multiplied, it became clearer and clearer to Undset that the qualities that had made Svarstad so fascinating as her lover also made him completely unsuitable as her husband.

First of all there was the problem of money. "A painter's income in Norway will scarcely ever be sufficient to bring up a family", Undset commented dryly to a friend some years later.[13] Although Svarstad would eventually achieve some modest success as a painter, he was apparently not capable of actually making a living at his art. Although Undset clearly believed in art as a calling, she believed even more strongly in putting one's family first. She herself had put aside her own dreams

in order to help support her mother and sisters when she was
scarcely more than a child. The spectacle of a grown man
who could not or would not do as much for his own children
must have been more than she could stand.

Serious financial difficulty, added to the strain of raising
two retarded children as well as three others, could undo any
marriage, even one where the husband and wife were the
most perfectly compatible couple in the world. But Svarstad
and Undset were not perfectly compatible. Far from it; Undset
once remarked that Svarstad had "a talent for keeping himself
and others from being happy",[14] and even people who loved
Undset described her as "difficult".[15] And neither of them
was adept at the art of compromise.

They were both romantics, but, unlike Svarstad, Undset
was a romantic who met her deadlines and paid her bills. If
she had felt her willpower flagging during the first year of
her marriage, it was back in full force now: even in the midst
of her most severe personal difficulties, she never stopped
working. In 1917 she published *Images in a Mirror*, a novel
about a marriage at the crossroads, and a year after that she
produced *The Wise Virgins*, a story of motherhood.

In July 1919, when Undset was eight months pregnant, she
and Svarstad separated. Toward the end of that summer, she
delivered her last child, a son, Hans Benedict.

Throughout this time she never stopped writing. In 1920
Undset published *The Bridal Wreath*, the first volume of the
Kristin Lavransdatter trilogy. Within two years she would bring
out the second and third volumes of the trilogy and would
begin to see their publication in the United States. *Kristin
Lavransdatter* would eventually be translated into seventeen
languages; it would make Undset an international celebrity
and a wealthy woman. It would also help lead her into the
Catholic Church.

Set in the fourteenth century, *Kristin Lavransdatter* is the saga
of a passionate but unwise love. The well-born eldest daughter
of a prosperous family, Kristin is betrothed to Simon Darre,

a good man but one whom she finds rather dull. While she is spending a year in an Oslo convent school, she meets Erlend Nikulaussön, a handsome, dashing nobleman some years older than herself. Although Erlend is unmarried, he has a mistress of many years and several children by her. He and Kristin fall deeply in love, and they conduct a secret and passionate affair in an Oslo house of ill repute. Finally Kristin becomes pregnant. She manages to keep her condition a secret while she prevails upon her father, the saintly Lavrans, to release her from her engagement to Simon Darre and consent to her marriage to Erlend. When Erlend's mistress, Eline Ormsdatter, realizes Erlend intends to marry Kristin, she tries to murder the girl. In a dramatic confrontation, Erlend thwarts Eline's plan and forces her to kill herself instead.

All this takes place in the first volume of the trilogy, *The Bridal Wreath*, which was published in the United States in 1923. The subsequent volumes, *The Mistress of Husaby* and *The Cross* (published here in 1925 and 1927 respectively) play out the passionate and tragic story of Kristin and Erlend's life together.

The temptation to draw parallels between Undset's own life and the life of her medieval heroine is a powerful one. The fictional woman and the real one each fell in love with an older man who was already promised to another woman; each of them, however indirectly, helped to cause heartbreak and subsequent tragedy for her lover's first love: Kristin involved in Eline's death, Undset in Ragna Moe's forced abandonment of her children. Both Kristin's marriage and that of her creator were unrelievedly difficult. Kristin and Undset each wanted their husbands, men who were clearly outside the pale of everyday life, to become something they had no talent for being: steady, hard-working, dedicated family men. Each had to learn the hard way that this was impossible.

Yet, unlike her creator, Undset's heroine cleaved to Erlend Nikulaussön to the end of his life. Did Kristin represent an ideal for Undset? Was this what she wished she could have been herself? Was creating Kristin her way of sorting out her own life, making sense of it all?

The *Kristin* trilogy is loaded with learning; it is an education in medieval studies. In preparing to write her chronicles, Undset had researched every aspect of medieval Norwegian life, including the history and customs of the medieval Church in Norway and Europe. Knowing what importance their cults had in the lives of medieval Christians, she paid particular attention to the lives of the saints. The stories of St. Olav, the patron saint of Norway and one of its greatest kings, and other saints are recounted in brief but intriguing detail in *Kristin*. Reflecting on their lives helps Kristin to make sense of her own.

Studying the lives of the saints had the same effect on Undset. In 1942 she wrote, "By degrees my knowledge of history convinced me that the only thoroughly sane people, of our civilization at least, seemed to be those queer men and women which the Catholic Church calls the Saints. . . . They seemed to know the true explanation of man's undying hunger for happiness."[16] Undset knew that same undying hunger. But the Catholic saints, she realized, had discovered the secret to feeding it. From there she reasoned that perhaps there was some truth in what she called "original Christianity"[17] (i.e., Roman Catholicism) after all.

She went on reading and studying, and her efforts brought her to a place where, not many years before, she would never have imagined herself.

On November 23, 1924, Undset's marriage to Anders Svarstad was formally annulled. The following day, November 24, 1924, she was received into the Roman Catholic Church. She was forty-two years old.[18]

With the sales of *Kristin Lavransdatter* and her other books, Undset's financial situation had by now improved dramatically. She was able to buy a home for her mother as well as a small estate for herself and her children in Lillehammer, some eighty miles north of Oslo.

The town of Lillehammer is the gateway to one of the most popular skiing areas in Norway. (The Winter Olympics were held there in 1994.) Bjerkebaek, Undset's Lillehammer estate, consists of a large manor house and one or two outbuildings. Some of the structures date in part to the fifteenth century. The archaeologist's daughter now had a piece of history all her own.

Bjerkebaek meant as much to Undset as any home can mean to any woman. Her love for the place seemed to permeate the house. One of her nieces recalled years later, "Every object was stamped with Moster Sigrid's highly personal taste, every room marked by her sure sense of each thing's own beauty."[19]

Bjerkebaek was a lively place, full of children and stepchildren, and frequently Undset's two nieces. It was also a productive place: Undset published "Saint Hallvard's Life, Death and Miracles" and the first installment of *The Master of Hestviken* in 1925; *Catholic Propaganda*, a book of essays, in 1927, and the conclusion of *The Master* the same year.

The Master of Hestviken is Undset's other great medieval chronicle novel. (It was published in this country as a tetralogy.) Undset regarded it as her masterpiece. Although critical opinion on *The Master* is to this day much divided, Undset's reading public seemed to agree with her assessment: twenty-five thousand volumes were sold in Norway alone in the first two months of publication.[20]

On November 13, 1928, Sigrid Undset was awarded the Nobel Prize for Literature. She was the third Norwegian writer to be so honored, preceded by Bjørnstjerne Bjørnson and Knut Hamsun. Although she had by now written several novels with contemporary themes and settings, it was her "powerful delineation of medieval life" that the Prize Committee cited in bestowing the award.[21]

The monetary value of the Nobel Prize was $42,060 in 1928.[22] (In 1993 dollars, that amount translated to $354,187).[23] Even to a wealthy woman, this is a great deal of money, and to one who had known poverty and hardship for many years, it was a fantastic sum. Undset now displayed a quality that would characterize much of the rest of her life: her extraordinary and concrete charity to people in need. She took the prize money, and she gave it away. (The medal she kept until World War II, when she sold it and gave the proceeds to aid Finnish refugees.) Over the next ten years, Undset published ten more books: collected essays, memoirs, novels, and hagiographies. Her fiction began to take on a didactic aspect. Although her writing had always exhibited certain characteristic themes— marriage, motherhood, the crucial necessity of looking life in the eye—Undset was now in danger of becoming that most dreaded being, a novelist with a message; but before very long she stopped writing novels altogether. Perhaps she felt the world no longer had time for fiction.

In 1939 both Undset's mother and her daughter Tulla died. That same year, Hitler's armies marched into Poland.

On April 9, 1940, Germany invaded Norway. That day, while the German planes cruised back and forth above Oslo, Undset happened to be in the capital on business. When she learned that the king and his government had already left the city, she hastened back to Lillehammer, not so much out of concern for her personal safety as to make sure the three small Finnish refugee children she was sheltering in Bjerkebaek were safe. She immediately moved them to a farm where it was thought they would be better protected.

Less than two weeks later, the last of the English troops defending Lillehammer gave up their positions, and it was expected that the Germans would march into the town that day. Undset's older son, Anders, was with his unit in the Norwegian Resistance; her younger son, Hans, had joined the Medical Corps. As for their mother, she was in very serious danger herself. For several years she had been constantly writing and speaking out against Nazism, and she had actively helped refugees from Central Europe. Her books had long been proscribed in Nazi Germany. Most frighteningly, as she wrote in her memoir of the war years, *Return to the Future*, "It was said that the Germans were in the habit of taking people who had some position in the country and forcing them to speak over the radio, telling about how well the Germans behaved, and the like, or so and so many Norwegian hostages would be shot."[24] Undset, certainly a woman of "some position", was advised to leave the country immediately.

With her handbag, a small sum of money borrowed from her housekeeper, and the clothes on her back, Undset made her way out of the country. It was a tense and arduous journey. She and a handful of fellow refugees traveled by car, on foot, briefly on skis, and for a few miles on a sled. They slept in farmhouses and mountain huts, while all around them Norway's defenses collapsed. Finally they reached Lapland and crossed over the border into Sweden.

A dozen years earlier, Undset had gone to Stockholm in rare literary triumph. Now she arrived in the Swedish capital a refugee. True, she was more fortunate than most of her fellow refugees: she had a sister living in the city as well as many Swedish friends, and she was even owed some money there. But her relief at reaching safe territory was short-lived. She learned that her son Anders had been killed shortly after she escaped from Norway.

After her younger son, Hans, joined her in Stockholm, Undset left Europe. She flew to Moscow, crossed the Soviet Union by train, crossed the sea to Japan, and sailed from there to California.

"In San Francisco arrived matronly Sigrid Undset, 58, Nobel Prize winner and prolific author of chronicle novels (*Kristin Lavransdatter, The Master of Hestviken, Gunnar's Daughter*, etc.) and her son Hans", *Time* magazine announced on September 9, 1940. "Having lost home, liberty, and another son [*Time* had run an obituary for Anders on May 27] to the Nazi conquest, Refugee Undset had a brave, slim smile for newshacks. . . ."

Refugee Undset traveled across the country to New York City. After a brief stay at Manhattan's legendary Algonquin

Hotel, she moved to a hotel in Brooklyn Heights, a neighborhood of brick townhouses and cobblestone streets just across
the river from Manhattan. She lived there for most of the
next five years.

In New York, she went to work for the Norwegian government, writing speeches, giving talks, doing what she frankly
described as "propaganda work".[25] The Norwegian government was only too happy to take advantage of Undset's talents
and energy, and, characteristically, Undset greatly overworked
herself on her country's behalf. She complained to an American friend that "The people in the Norwegian Embassy
and Information Service and the Norwegian newspapers have
come to regard me as a kind of encyclopedia."[26]

In America, Undset was a celebrity, besieged by the press
and idolized by fans. It was not a role for which she was
particularly suited. Undset had the self-educated person's impatience with what she regarded as anyone else's ignorance
and/or plain stupidity. Such an attitude does not bode well
for anyone's relations with the press. And she was apparently
incapable of concealing her scorn for "newshacks": one re-
porter complained that the entire time he was interviewing
Madame Undset, she gave him a look that clearly said, "Why
are you asking me these questions?"[27]

She was interviewed by newspapers and magazines, peti-
tioned for articles and reviews, and booked on lecture tours
all over the country. She found the publicity most annoying:
she complained frequently of being misquoted, misconstrued,
and generally misunderstood by journalists. She particularly
disliked being romanticized, and in the United States she found
herself a highly romanticized figure.

She heard, for example, that some people believed that in
Europe she had spent her waking hours in the picturesque
but impractical national Norwegian costume. It irked her that
anyone could have such an image of any modern Norwegian.
Writing to an American friend about her government work,
she remarked that it gave her "an opportunity to give at least

some people some idea of what we [Norwegians] are really like—not at all the simple, honest teddy bears and national costume maidens of Mr. Steinbecks [sic]—and some dreadful movie maker's concept."[28] And when she encountered the same rumor in a young American scholar's dissertation, she noted wearily in the margin, "I have never worn one."[29]

In the same dissertation she encountered two myths she had doubtless encountered before and which she despised. The fact that Undset was a Catholic when she was awarded the Nobel Prize was a great event for Catholic artists and scholars, but unfortunately it had the effect of producing yet another myth. Undset was known to be a serious student of Catholic theology, and this no doubt was a matter of some pride to Catholic intellectuals. But the story went around that when reporters tried to interview her following the award, she told them, "I have no time to receive you. I am studying scholastic philosophy."[30] The aforementioned young scholar, a man named Willert Klass, who was a student at St. Peter Canisius College in upstate New York, reverently recounted this story in his dissertation. Undset, who very generously had agreed to read an early draft of his thesis, was flabbergasted. "You don't believe I said that?" she wrote in sprawling letters in the margin. "I'm not a perfect idiot after all!"[31]

But perhaps the most stubborn myth about Undset's life is the myth of St. Sigrid, the patient mother of six who slaved alone all day to care for her brood, completely forgetful of her own ambitions, who only sat down to pen and paper and her muse after the little ones were safely tucked in bed, dreaming the sweet dreams to which their overworked but devoted mother's lullabies had led them. Poor Willert Klass took the rap for this one, too. As to her single-handed attention to the details of running her household, Undset commented tartly, "I had two very efficient maids and a housekeeper."[32] (One can almost hear her adding, ". . . , thank you very much.") She also pointed out that writing at the "fag end" of the day was never her custom.

Although Undset loved the United States, which she called "beautiful America",[33] the war years were among the hardest of her life. She had lost her home and two of her children; and, while she remained a devout Catholic, she was particularly grieved at what she regarded as the Church's failure to respond adequately to the Nazi threat. "The undeniable lack of alertness toward fascism in many Catholic camps", she warned, "will certainly cause the Church to lose ground all over the world for generations."[34]

There were other hardships. Her lecture tour, for example, was not a success; as one of her sponsors tactfully put it, "Her brilliance was of the written, not the spoken, word."[35] Her writing became increasingly and less effectively didactic. Most of what she did write during the war had more than a whiff of homesickness about it: two volumes of memoirs (one of them at the request of First Lady Eleanor Roosevelt), translations of some Norwegian stories for children. Remarkably, this Nobel Prize winner, whose official war efforts were literary and prestigious, devoted much of her free time to sewing clothes and preparing relief packages for Europe with her own hands.

When the war was over, Undset returned to Norway. Her last years were by all accounts lonely, full of disappointment, and profoundly sad. Bjerkebaek was no longer the home she loved. The occupying Germans had commandeered her estate. Undset, with her vivid romantic imagination, could never overcome her revulsion at the thought that the hated Nazis had touched her belongings, walked across her floors, breathed the scents from her beloved gardens. Her elder son was dead, slaughtered by the same forces that had defiled her home. Her younger son, Hans, rarely came to see her.

Her literary career had deteriorated as well. The muse that had guided her fiction had disappeared, and even her non-fiction suffered: she could not avoid or resist an increasingly preachy style, and her biography of St. Catherine of Siena, contracted for before she left the United States, was rejected by her American publishers. (It was eventually published post-humously in 1954.)

Her country, to be sure, had not forgotten her. In 1947, in recognition of her war service, she received the Grand Cross of the Order of St. Olav from King Haakon VII. She was the first Norwegian woman of nonroyal lineage to be given the award. But even this honor could not restore what she had lost.

In May 1948, just three years after she returned to Norway, Undset suffered what was probably a slight cerebral hemor-rhage. A year later she was bedridden again with what was diagnosed as bronchitis. She was seriously ill, but, perhaps partly due to her stoical nature, the gravity of her condition went unacknowledged. She was alone when she died on June 10, 1949.

NOTES

¹ Article by Catherine Bancroft, *Ms.*, January 1981, pp. 35–37.

² A. H. Winsnes, *Sigrid Undset: A Study in Christian Realism* (New York: Sheed and Ward, 1953), p. 25.

³ Ibid., p. 26.

⁴ Ibid., p. 34.

⁵ Charles A. Brady, "An Appendix to the *Sigridssaga*", *Thought*, vol. 40, no. 156 (Spring 1965), p. 94.

⁶ Winsnes, p. 49.

⁷ Ibid., p. 58.

⁸ Gidske Anderson, *Sigrid Undset—et liv* (Oslo: Gyldendal Norsk Forlag), pp. 207–8.

⁹ Ibid., p. 218.

¹⁰ Winsnes, p. 58.

¹¹ Marlene Ciklamini, "Sigrid Undset", in *European Writers: The Twentieth Century*, vol. 9 (New York: Charles Scribner's Sons, 1989), p. 1022.

¹² Charlotte Blindheim, "Sigrid Undset, My Maternal Aunt", in *Scandinavian Review*, Autumn 1982, p. 49.

¹³ Mitzi Brunsdale, "Stages on Her Road", *Religion and Literature*, vol. 23, no. 3 (Autumn 1991), p. 84.

¹⁴ Letter to Hope Allen, February 16, 1947, quoted in "Sigrid Undset's Letters to Hope Allen", *The Journal of the Rutgers University Library*, vol. 33 (1968), p. 23.

¹⁵ Blindheim, p. 53.

¹⁶ Brunsdale, p. 91.

¹⁷ Ibid.

¹⁸ Authorities differ on the date of Sigrid Undset's reception into the Catholic Church. Her statement in *Twentieth Century Authors*, edited by Stanley J. Kunst and Howard Haycroft, reads: "And on the first of November, 1924, I was received into the Catholic Church."—ED.

¹⁹ Blindheim, p. 49.

²⁰ *Saturday Review*, August 7, 1926, p. 26.

²¹ *New York Times*, November 14, 1928, p. 7.

²² Ibid.

²³ U.S. Bureau of Labor Statistics.

²⁴ Sigrid Undset, *Return to the Future*, trans. Henriette C. K. Naeseth (New York: Alfred A. Knopf, 1942), p. 25.

²⁵ Winsnes, p. 228.

²⁶ Ciklamini, p. 1025.

[27] Interview with Benjamin Apfel, "Exiled Writers' Issue", *Saturday Review*, October 19, 1940, p. 3.

[28] Letter to Hope Allen, March 18, 1953, in Ciklamini, p. 1025.

[29] Brady, p. 103.

[30] Ibid., p. 108.

[31] Ibid.

[32] Ibid., p. 96.

[33] Winsnes, p. 225.

[34] Brady, p. 99.

[35] *America*, June 5, 1949, p. 375.

EVELYN BIRGE VITZ

SIGRID UNDSET AND THE
LEGENDS OF THE SAINTS

Sigrid Undset, primarily renowned as a novelist, devoted a considerable portion of her writing career to the lives of the saints —technically called "hagiography". She wrote biographies of a good many saints; I count about ten of them—they are virtually all from the medieval and Renaissance-Reformation period.

Let me try to give you some sense of how and when she came to the lives of saints and, more broadly, of the place that hagiography occupies in her work. Undset's first published novel was *Mrs. Marta Oulie*, which appeared in 1907; *The Story of Viga-Ljot and Vigdis* followed in 1909 (English trans.: *Gunnar's Daughter*); *Jenny* appeared in 1911. With these novels Sigrid Undset defined herself as a "realistic" writer, and one prepared to address, in a manner at once bold and reflective, controversial issues such as the nature of woman (including female sexuality), the role of women in society, and relations between men and women. She continued to address these themes in all her subsequent writing.

Mrs. Marta Oulie and *Jenny* were both set in the modern period. But that second novel, *Gunnar's Daughter*, was set in the Middle Ages—indeed, virtually the Dark Ages, the tenth century. And it was in fact with the Middle Ages that Undset had begun writing: it is in that period that her first, unpublished, novel was set. Only after being discouraged by an editor who read the manuscript and told her: "Don't try your hand at any more historical novels. It's not your line. But you might, you

44

know, try to write something modern. One can never tell"[1]
—only then did she turn to the modern period.

But Undset returned to the Middle Ages with her next, and
most famous, novels: the *Kristin Lavransdatter* trilogy appeared
in 1921 and 1922. Another important date here is 1924, when
Undset entered the Catholic Church. That same year, she published a work on the life, death, and miracles of the medieval
St. Hallvard. *The Master of Hestviken* came next—the first two
volumes in 1925, the last two in 1927—it, too, set in the
Middle Ages.[2]

Undset seems not to have been drawn to the medieval period, the way many moderns are, because it was remote, alien—
"other"—but, precisely, because, as she said: "When one peels
off the layers of ideas and conceptions that belong essentially to
one's own time, one steps straight into the Middle Ages."[3] For
her, the medieval period was not less but more real than today;
it was timelessly human. And she had always been interested
in Norwegian and European history. Her father Ingvald had
been a distinguished archaeologist, and she grew up thinking
and reading about the past.

In the early 1930s, she published novels set in the contemporary period, two of which—*The Wild Orchid* and *The Burning
Bush*—clearly reflect her own conversion experience, through
the character of Paul Selmer.

In 1934, ten years after her conversion, she published two
volumes of hagiography: *Stages on the Road*, largely composed
of essays she had published between 1929 and 1933, and *Saga of
Saints*. In the former, she told the lives of Bl. Raymond Lull, an
early-fourteenth-century Spanish layman and writer, martyred
by the Moors; of St. Angela Merici, the sixteenth-century Italian foundress of the Ursulines; and of Bl. Margaret Clitherow
and St. Robert Southwell: she was a housewife, he a Jesuit
priest—both martyred under Queen Elizabeth I.

Saga of Saints was devoted largely to a retelling, and reexam-
ination, of the epic and romantic legends—the great "sagas"
—of the great old Norwegian saints, the fathers and mothers

of Norwegian Christianity: St. Sunniva (a young girl martyr),
St. Olav, whom she calls "Norway's King to All Eternity",
St. Magnus, St. Eystein, and St. Thorfinn—and she incorporated into this her research on St. Hallvard. Though these are
names that do not generally roll readily off American tongues,
many of them are almost household words to any reader of, say,
Kristin Lavransdatter—especially the great name of St. Olav. It
is worth noting that Undset had long been interested in saints'
legends. When she was eighteen years old, Sigrid borrowed
from the local library a book of legends of the saints (Unger's
edition of *Heilagra manna sogur*) which apparently had not been
checked out of the library since its publication in 1877.[4] And
while she was living in Rome from 1909 to 1912—many years
before her conversion—she used to sit around with friends and
entertain and edify them with legends of the saints.[5]

In the mid- to late 1930s, before World War II, came a variety
of works including some biography with a hagiographical twist,
or at least seen in the light of hagiographical issues. In *Men,
Women and Places*, which appeared in 1938, Undset devotes a
chapter to Margery Kempe, the early-fifteenth-century vision-
ary, who wrote a sort of autobiography, *The Book of Margery
Kempe*. Now this is not, in fact, hagiography: Undset does not
give us "St." Margery Kempe, an unrecognized saint. Margery
was undeniably pious. Undset says:

> Her love of Christ is perfectly sincere, and many of the imagi-
> nary conversations she carried on with Him are of great beauty
> and show deep religious insight. But it is probable that this inter-
> weaving of piety and poetical fancy was just what made Margery
> so naïvely unsuspicious of many of her own weaknesses—her
> preoccupation with self, her love of asserting herself, her un-
> willingness to take advice from others. She never succeeded in
> ridding herself of these, although her whole conscious ego was
> turned toward God and she lived only to pray and do penance
> and to preach Christ's love and God's glory.[6]

A very shrewd assessment! Undset concludes:

What good she may have done during her long and tempestuous life no one, of course, can now say. But the rediscovered book [it had long been lost] presents us with an incomparable picture of life at the beginning of the fifteenth century, and the self-portrait of a woman whose nature was a curious compound— of piety and egoism, humility and pride, charity and hardness, talent and hysteria—but who preserved her incredible vitality even in old age (MWP, p. 104).

And this interesting woman is in curious company, as *Men, Women and Places* also contains an essay on D. H. Lawrence (whom, at least in some respects, Undset admired); another on Glastonbury Abbey. There is also a wonderful and moving piece entitled "Cavalier" on the suffering of various members of an English Catholic family—a real family, the Blundells— in the late seventeenth century. (This book is a very mixed bag!) Her last and most substantial hagiographical work was her full-scale life of *Catherine of Siena*, which she wrote in the mid-1940s. It was rejected by Doubleday; its rejection Undset clearly felt as a body-blow. This book was still unpublished at her death in 1949 and appeared only in 1954, at Sheed and Ward.

Such are the basic facts. What we see is that, starting in the late 1920s, Undset worked intermittently but persistently on, with, lives of the saints—mostly medieval—until her death. Before returning shortly to her officially hagiographical works, it should be pointed out that, in a deep sense, much of Undset's writing has strong links to hagiography. Undset was fascinated by the saints and sanctity. And when she was asked what had brought her to Catholicism, she answered: "I had ventured too near the abode of truth in my researches about 'God's friends', as the saints are called in the Old Norse texts. . . . So I had to submit."[7] She said, further:

> By degrees my knowledge of history convinced me that the
> only thoroughly sane people, of our civilization at least, seemed
> to be those queer men and women which the Catholic Church
> calls the Saints . . . [who] seemed to know the true explanation
> of man's undying hunger for happiness—his tragically insuffi-
> cient love of peace, justice, and goodwill to his fellowmen, his
> everlasting fall from grace.[8]

Let me focus for a moment on the role of saints and holiness in *Kristin Lavransdatter*. This is an historical novel in which
saints play an important role. Now not only was fourteenth-
century Norway a culture whose life, whose year was shaped by
commemoration of the saints, as well of Christ and his Mother
—Paul's Mass (January 15), St. Gregory's Mass (March 12),
Lady Day, Cross-Mass (May 3), St. Mary Magdalene's Feast
(July 22), St. Bartholomew's Mass (August 24), St. Matthew's
Mass (September 21), St. Catherine's Mass (November 25),
and so on. Norway's basic social customs were largely struc-
tured around celebrations of the saints: frequently in fairs and
"ale-feasts"! But Undset's characters pray to the Blessed Virgin and to the saints often and devotedly; they read the lives
of the saints—especially "Holy Olav"—and make pilgrimages
to their shrines. For example, after the birth of her first child,
as penance for very serious sins, Kristin makes a pilgrimage
to St. Olav's shrine at Trondheim. She arrives on a hill over-
looking the town and looks down on Christ's Church. Undset
tells us:

> Quite overcome, sobbing, the young woman flung herself down
> before the cross by the wayside, where thousands of pilgrims
> had lain before her, thanking God for that helping hands were
> stretched out toward human souls on their journey through the
> fair and perilous world.[10]

But there is yet another sense in which *Kristin Lavransdatter*
is deeply hagiographical. Undset's image of the world—and it
is a deeply Catholic view—is of a place with many joys and
pleasures, full of beauty, but also full of sorrows. Her characters

are weighed down heavily, indeed crippled, with human sin: not just lust, but shame, fear, self-interest, pride; they struggle under the burden of their own sins and those of others.

But in this great trilogy, Undset does not show us only sinners; she shows us saints—fictional saints. There is a wonderful Franciscan monk in the story, Brother Edvin, whom we meet —whom Kristin meets—early on in her life. He is presented not merely as an endearing and compassionate person but as a wise and holy monk. In the novel, after his death, he is widely venerated, and we are told that he may be canonized. Kristin sees him in a vision and is consoled by his presence. In other words, we see someone who was, and was becoming, a saint.

But it is not only religious who are saintly here. Kristin's father Lavrans is a beautiful and holy man from his youth; and we see him struggling over the years to be truly good: to be more deeply charitable, to forgive the people who have wronged him (including Kristin and his wife), to be united to God's will. Undset says that as death approached:

> Lavrans spoke much now of purgatory fire, which he looked soon to enter; but he was quite without fear. He hoped for great solacement from his friends' and the priests' intercessions, and trusted firmly that St. Olav and St. Thomas [à Becket] would give him strength in this his last trial, as he had so often felt that they had strengthened him in this life. He had ever heard that he that was firm in the faith would never for a single moment lose from before his eyes the bliss to which the soul was going through the scorching fires. . . .[11]

I think we readers are invited to believe that Lavrans was a saint, though there is no talk of his being canonized. But her work is not full of saints, by any means: Undset is—as we saw in her assessment of Margery Kempe—very shrewd and, as it were, hard-nosed about what constitutes real sanctity. Many of her characters will be doing very well to get to heaven at all, ever: to escape hell. We are not quite sure that Kristin's husband, Erlend, died in God's pardon, but we, like the characters, hope so! As to Kristin herself, though she comes closer to God by the end of the trilogy—by this time she is (for her era) pretty "old"—we know she still is no saint. All her life she has had faith; she has been at least intermittently prayerful, but she is fundamentally a self-willed, short-tempered, grudge-holding woman: someone who has wanted life her way. She is no saint. In short, like Kristin, most of Undset's characters are —it is Brother Edvin's term—"crippled with sin".

Given Undset's long-standing interest in saints and in the highly uncertain process of sanctification, it is no wonder that in the years after she wrote *Kristin Lavransdatter*, Undset turned her attention to the lives of real saints—the historical saints to whom she and her characters had referred so often in this great novel.

Now all the saints whose lives she tells had had their lives written before—some of them many times. Undset does not do extensive "original" research on these saints—that is, she does not turn up new material to add to these already-thick saintly dossiers. But I must say that I am, as a medievalist, constantly struck by how much Undset knows: she has an extraordinarily —not surprising, considering that it is Undset we are talking about!—feel for medieval private life; she has found out a lot about those saints and the texture of their lives. Let me give you just a few snippets from her chapter on St. Olav. His father, Harald Haarfagre, died before Olav was born. Actually, he was killed; he had left his pregnant wife Aasta at home with her father and was off wooing the widowed queen Sigrid Storraade of Sweden. As Undset tells it:

> Another petty king arrived at Sigrid's home at the same time
> and on the same errand, and she made both her suitors drunk
> and when they were asleep told her thralls to set fire to the guest
> house in which they lay. So both kings were burnt to death and
> Sigrid Storraade said she would teach petty kings to aspire to
> her hand.[13]

Exit King Harald! Undset says that:

> [Olav] was brought up like most princelings. . . . When he was twelve years old he . . . was sent out on Viking expeditions in the same way that parents in later ages sent their sons to the university or to a military school, or abroad, so that they might carry on creditably the tradition of the family (SS, p. 90).

He had been baptized as a baby but not raised as a Christian. But while in England, he became acquainted with the Church, and one day, on a Viking raid, he had a dream: "The legend tells us that a tall, striking and terrible man came to him and said, 'Return thou to thine estate for thou shalt become Norway's king to all eternity'" (SS, p. 91).

For Undset, he is Norway's king for eternity! In the context of Olav's, and Norway's, mixed Christian and pagan status at the time, Undset makes this interesting observation:

> There is here a similarity between the thought of the Viking period and the Christian outlook on life. To the proudest among the Vikings defeat was no disgrace if a man's fame survived him. For the Christian, death was a gain if he died for a cause which he considered immortal. . . . [T]he Middle Ages had not developed a trend of thought in any way resembling that of the prevalent Protestant mentality of the last century—that those who held the right religion would certainly receive material benefits on this earth, and that material success is a sure sign of a right religion (SS, p. 95).

She tells of a great showdown between King Olav and a heathen chieftain who told him that every day Thor "received his offering of bread and meat and . . . devoured it during the night. . . ." (SS, p. 102). The next day at the "Thing"—the great assembly—Olav managed to distract the gathering long enough for his followers to smash the image of the god: "Mice and rats and snakes came tumbling out . . ." and Olav said to the chieftain: "[N]ow you can see . . . who it was who had the benefit of all the food you took to him" (SS, p. 103).

But Undset, as always, is above all interested in Olav the man. She compares St. Olav Haraldsson with another early Norwegian Christian king, Olav Tryggveson, who ruled from 995 to 1000 and first brought Christianity to Norway. She says:

> Olav Tryggveson shines in the glory of a bygone age. From his early childhood until his last journey, the legends glitter and gleam around him who possessed all those attributes and gifts most dear to the hearts of the Vikings. Passionately he had embraced the Faith, passionately he tried to force on his people the gift which he brought to them, but he himself was altogether a child of the older age. Never do the Sagas show that a fundamental change had taken place in Olav Tryggveson's soul. . . . It seemed almost as if it never occurred to Olav Tryggveson that God demanded of him anything more than that he should plant the Cross of Christ in the land of Norway. . . . In the figure of Olav Haraldsson, on the other hand, the people stood face to face with the consequences of a new faith—in a new time (SS, pp. 113-14).

It is with St. Olav that we see the great transition to a new, a more truly Christian, mode of life. Not only did he have many parish churches built and promulgate a code of Christian laws—he actually tried to keep these laws himself. He attempted chastity; for example, he refrained from going to visit his former mistress—though Undset notes that he "was fond of women, as were most of the race of Haarfagre" (SS, p. 122), saying ". . . now it seems to me better that I should live according to God's Will and not after my own evil desires" (SS, p. 123).

Olav died in battle. Almost immediately stories arose of miraculous healings; his body was found to be incorrupt. Undset says of his cult:

> In the old heathen community the farmer's god had been Tor with the heavy hammer. He . . . watched over the cultivated districts lying between the desolate forests and the bare fields, he killed the trolls and visited the farmers as a guest. In the new Christian Norway, St. Olav took Tor's place. He was a

man in whose mind most other men could find something akin to themselves, but he had subdued his own heathen nature, had struggled in prayer and through work to give himself wholly to God, so that God might mould him as he wished. And so God had lent him the power to become a friend to mankind, just such a one as the people had created for themselves in Tor, but much more powerful (SS, pp. 144–45).

Undset says in closing:

Behind the altar in Trondhjem Cathedral lay St. Olav's body in a golden shrine as long as the Holy Sacrifice of the Mass was offered there. . . . [His body was removed during the Reformation]. But we who believe that the Church Militant on Earth is one with the Church Triumphant in Heaven, know that St. Olav still prays with us, our leader before God . . . (SS, p. 148).

Let us look now, in more detail, at what makes Undset's hagiography "Undsettian". It may be useful to compare her lives of medieval saints with texts written about these same saints during the Middle Ages themselves, or, for that matter, as penned by most traditional writers.

There are, as I see it, three major features that characterize Undset's hagiography. The first is that it is rooted in a powerful awareness of human sin. Saints' lives that were written in the Middle Ages generally suggested that the saint was not merely holy but in fact just about perfect. Rare is the medieval saint's life that even acknowledges—let alone emphasizes!—that the saint had any human failings, that the saint ever really had to struggle, that there was ever a point at which it was not absolutely certain that this person would turn out to be a saint. In medieval texts, saints are "tested", but they always pass that test with flying colors; they always get a perfect score on their holiness SATs; they are never shown to fail or to falter. I think

that can be accounted for primarily by the fact that lives of
the saints were seen then less as "biography" than as praise, as
eulogy. The author was speaking—singing a song, as it were—
in honor of the saint. And the saints are presented as models
of perfection for their audience to imitate.

But Sigrid Undset is truly interested in biography and autobiography—this is what interested her about Margery Kempe's
Book. And Undset has, as I said before, such a deep awareness
of human frailty! Although in her accounts she has to depend
on the medieval lives—on the old sagas about the saints, which
idealize them—and although Undset clearly relishes those great
stories, she is able to read between the lines and to find in all
that saintly perfection the human pulse: the holy human pulse.
Her saints struggle to be holy. We come away from her stories with a renewed appreciation of, for example, those great
Norwegian saints, such as Olav.

The second fundamental feature of her hagiography, which
sets it apart from most earlier saints' lives and marks it as Undsettian, is that it is apologetic, in the strong sense of the term.
Medieval lives are typically almost purely, simply narrative:
they tell the life of a saint. Story-tellers generally frame their
lives with prayers to the saint and often with invitations to the
readers or listeners to imitate the saint. But telling the saint's
story called for neither apologies nor apologetics; hagiography
was part of a great genre in a Catholic culture, of which the
particular life was just one example.

This is hardly the situation of a modern hagiographer, however. It had not escaped Sigrid Undset's notice that lives of the
saints were, in early-twentieth-century Protestant and secular-
atheist Norway, out of fashion literarily, part of a bygone era.
Nor were the saints part of her own personal heritage. She had
never been a Catholic child. So to write lives of the saints represented a choice. (It was similarly a choice for Evelyn Waugh
when he wrote his full-length *Edmund Campion* and his shorter
"Helena Empress".)

When Undset does hagiography, she does it not just as nar-

rative, though she is of course a great story-teller, but as part
of Catholic apologetics Undset is—she became—a more and
more outspoken defender of the Faith. This is what makes
many scholars, especially feminists, purse their lips in disapproval; since Undset spoke out so boldly on all manner of
women's issues, they could forgive her for having been Catholic if only her religious faith had remained more discreet: a
personal, private—therefore conceptually marginal, gently irrelevant—theme. But her outspokenly polemical Catholicism
sets their teeth on edge. Critics speak, with clear disapproval
in their voices, of her embracing of the "dogmatic authori-
tarianism" of the Church—as if that were what drew Undset to Catholicism! One scholar declared, condescendingly—
and in fact quite erroneously—that, in her *Stages on the Road*,
"Sigrid Undset seems to have managed to shake off, at least
for the moment, the narrower aspects of a purely Catholic
dogma in the interests of a more inclusive, universal Christian
view." [14]

Undset consistently argued for the truth—the wisdom—of
Catholicism. There are many similarities between her and another great convert, Chesterton (whom she quotes). And in
several of her saints' lives she was also attempting to show—
to demonstrate, narratively—that the Reformation had been a
tragedy: that Norway, like England, had lost something tremendous with the abandonment of Catholicism.

We can see this in two ways. First, in her interest in the old
Norwegian saints. Let us go back to the *Saga*. It begins with
a chapter on "The Coming of Christianity" (to Norway, that
is). She expresses great admiration and sympathy for the old
Norse pagans, but she has no illusions about them. She notes
that they exposed unwanted children and killed useless old people—and comments that "the regulation of the population by
the killing of new-born (or unborn) children will always to
some extent be practised everywhere outside Christendom"
(SS, p. 13). She remarks dryly that:

> . . . [i]t is only after the introduction of Christianity that [pagan
> brutality] springs suddenly into view in all its nakedness. Then
> people, terrified, protested [against Christian moral teaching]. If
> they were not to be allowed . . . to expose their own unwelcome
> children they really did not know what things were coming to.
> It was St. Olav who first put an end to the custom, though in
> Iceland they were obliged to allow the heathen to continue in
> their former ways for a generation (SS, p. 14).

Undset expresses genuine sympathy—affection!—for the
plight of those old Norsemen and women who lived in the
era of transition between paganism and Christianity. She tells
of a friend of King Olav, Hallfred Vandraadeskald who "believes in Christ but, sighing, . . . wonders whether he must
therefore hate Odin, the protector of the poetic arts in the
North" (SS, p. 50).

In this context, she also undertakes to refute the common
belief that paganism is full of joy and good cheer, Christianity
glum and joyless:

> In our days there is a great deal of talk about Christianity being a
> religion hostile to the joy of life, principally, perhaps, because it
> has attempted to command and exhort the mighty of this world
> to take less of its goods than their power would give them. We
> easily forget that real pagan joy in life was almost always strongly
> tinged with pessimism in one form or another. . . . Christianity
> will make no concessions to man's longing for the rapture of
> death and the frenzy of ruin (SS, p. 33).

She speaks of the Church's "anti-pessimism" and argues that
"optimism does not come easily to one who has delved deeply
into human nature, unless he can put his trust in something
beyond the life he knows" (SS, pp. 33–34). As to the modern
desire for a return to the old paganism of pre-Christian Norway, she once said—and it is one of my very favorite quotes
from Undset:

> Pre-Christian paganism is a love poem to a God who remained
> hidden, or it was an attempt to gain the favor of the divine

powers whose presence man felt about him. The new paganism is a declaration of war against a God who has revealed himself.[15]

Another of the ways in which we see Undset's involvement in Catholic apologetics—anti-Protestant apologetics—is in her focus on martyrs from the Reformation period, such as Margaret Clitherow and Robert Southwell, whom she treats in *Stages on the Road*. I find her life of Margaret Clitherow particularly moving and compelling, and I would like to look at it more closely with you. She originally wrote this piece as a Christmas story and as a contribution to "the Church's heroic saga in England".[16] Margaret, married to a respectable Protestant butcher, converted to Catholicism after her marriage; she had three children—two sons and a daughter. She was obviously a person of great charm—and sanctity (the two do not always go together!)—Undset says:

> It is reported of [Margaret] that "all her actions were tempered with all inward tranquillity and comfort, with mild and smiling countenance; ready of tongue, but yet her words modest, and courteous, and lowly; quick in the despatch of business, and then most pleasant when she could the most serve God, or procure the same to others" (SR, p. 189).

Margaret Clitherow was imprisoned and eventually martyred for her faith and for harboring Catholic priests. Undset tells us:

> . . . At one time she was kept in prison for over two years. She was confined in a filthy, cold, dark hole, on the poorest of prison fare, separated from her dear ones. She herself refers to this time as "a happy and profitable school"; here she learned to be patient, to live with God in solitude. . . (SR, p. 193).

She was condemned to be crushed to death—to be laid under a heavy door, more and more stones being slowly placed on top of it. Undset tells that the eve of Lady Day, Friday, March 25, 1586, was Margaret's last night upon earth. A Protestant woman, a certain Mistress Yoward, in prison for debt, was sent to keep her company.

Margaret Clitherow knelt on the stone floor and prayed in mortal anguish, and the other, Mistress Yoward, looked at her a
while and pitied her sorely—but then she grew sleepy and had
to lie down, and so she fell asleep. About midnight she woke
up—Margaret was still kneeling on the same spot, but now
she was no longer afraid—there was a radiant calm in her face.
It was not so much that she looked happy, but rather as if she
already experienced that of which all human happiness is a reflection. . . . When she awoke about six she was in her customary
cheerful humour. And then she proposed to Mistress Yoward:
"Stay with me and see me die." As anyone might say to a friend:
"Come and see me off, won't you?" But Mistress Yoward had
not the slightest desire to do so; she thought it horrible that
so young and sweet and pretty a woman was to die. But she
offered to speak to some of her friends—she would get them
to throw heavier weights upon Margaret, so that the end might
come more quickly. Margaret said she must not do that: "God
defend that I should procure any to be guilty of my death and
blood" (SR, pp. 201-2).

Before Margaret was pressed to death:

she prayed on her knees for the Church, for the Pope, for all
spiritual pastors, and then for all temporal sovereigns. Here she
was interrupted—she must not pray for Queen Elizabeth in
such company. Margaret continued undisturbed: "—and especially for Elizabeth, Queen of England, that God turn her to
the Catholic faith, and that after this mortal life she may receive the blessed joy of heaven. For I wish as much good to her
Majesty's soul as to mine own." She was urged to confess that
she suffered death for treason. In as loud and clear a voice as
before Margaret answered: "No. I die for the love of my Lord
Jesu" (SR, p. 203).

Undset tells us that after Clitherow's death

the body was . . . taken outside the city wall and buried in a
rubbish-heap. Six weeks later some Catholics disinterred it and
carried it away—no one knows whither. But one hand had been
severed from the body. A delicately shaped little hand, brown
and withered, clenched in the agony of death—this is the relic

of Margaret Clitherow which the Catholics of England venerate
to-day. It is in St. Mary's Convent, York (SR, pp. 204–5).

As to Margaret's children, Undset says:

Ann Clitherow took the veil in St. Ursula's Convent at Louvain. . . . [B]oth Henry Clitherow [her elder son] and his brother
became priests.
  So for the mother and for the three children who had been
through such bitter and cruel sufferings the story ends as a real
Christmas tale ought to end (SR, p. 206).

That is some Christmas story! And it is not just hagiography: this is Catholic apologetics at its most moving, its most
powerful.

One final feature of her hagiography marks it as Undsettian: the nature of her interest in women saints. There is a
long Catholic tradition of Lives—and veneration—of female
saints. But on the whole, in the past, what we would today
call "gender issues" were not raised about the saints. This is
not to say that these issues had no influence on the ways in
which lives were written or saints were thought about, but
these matters were not examined or "problematized". What
Undset does is to look, hard, at women saints and try to figure
out what it means to be a woman saint. This is why it is all
the more interesting that, on careful inspection, she did not
consider Margery Kempe to have been a saint. Undset was,
here as ever, interested in feminine psychology and in what it
means to be a Catholic woman—a great Catholic woman. In
other words, she was (like her contemporary Edith Stein, for
example) interested in what we might call "authentic Catholic
feminism".

She begins her life of Angela Merici with a marvelous statement:

A year or two ago I saw in a paper an account of a meeting
in which representatives of both Catholic and other women's
organizations had taken part. One of the non-Catholic ladies
had said something to the effect that she was pleased to see

that the Catholic women had now progressed so far as to be able to cooperate in social problems with other members of the woman's movement. To which a Catholic lady replied that it was we who had cause to rejoice at non-Catholic women having now progressed so far that we could meet and co-operate with them (SR, p. 69).

(When I first read this, I said, "Yes!") This is the beginning of the chapter on Angela Merici; not until page 90 does she start talking about Angela herself (the chapter ends on page 134). Those twenty-one pages of preamble are a wonderful reflection on (as we would say today) "gender"—on the handling of sex and the sexes, family life, and lots else, in the Catholic tradition. It is full of interesting observations and anecdotes. She tells the medieval story about

> the knight's lady who thought of nothing but adorning and dressing up her own mortal body—not one but ten sumptuous gowns did she possess, and each of them had cost enough to keep a poor family for a whole year. When she was dead and her soul was to be weighed in St. Michael's scales, the devil came up, dragging her wardrobe, and emptied the whole contents into the other scale—and so the lady was weighed and found wanting (SR, p. 78).

When she gets into the story itself, she is still largely interested in the ideal of female sanctity that Angela Merici embodied and preached. What particularly drew Undset, I think, is the fact that Angela did not feel drawn to the cloistered life, but she did feel called to celibacy and to the care of the poor and of children. Angela felt that she was not supposed to go into a convent, but that somehow she was called to be Christ's bride. It became clear to her in a vision that she was to found a "company of virgins" which became known as "St. Ursula's Company". (After Angela's death, it became a cloistered order.)

In the context of her discussion of the growth of Angela's new group—her band of virgins—Undset discusses the "dis-

solution of the immemorial European idea of the family" and
the decay of family life, saying:

> Girls no longer submitted to being sent to a nunnery simply
> because it suited their parents to dispose of them in this way.
> It had seemed natural enough for a medieval father to deter-
> mine that this daughter or that was to be a nun—because he
> could not find a suitable match for her, or because she was not
> very pretty, or because his forefathers had given property to a
> convent, thus establishing a tradition that the convent in return
> received and provided for a daughter of the family. . . . People
> of the Middle Ages saw nothing unreasonable in this; if the fa-
> ther could betroth one daughter while still a child to the son
> of a friend, in the assurance that he was acting for her good,
> he must feel yet surer that the daughter whom he betrothed
> to Christ would have the best Bridegroom of all, if she did
> but contribute her good will—and from the point of view of
> the family's eternal welfare it was immensely reassuring to have
> a sister who could pray for her kindred; they often had great
> need of pious intercession, as they all knew very well (SR, pp.
> 113–14).

This is one of the most interesting and persuasive defenses
I have ever read of the old custom of giving a daughter to a
convent, in the context of arranged marriage—a custom for
which Undset had quite a high (though not naïve) regard.

But Undset's interest in feminine sanctity finds its fullest expression, of course, in her full-length biography of Catherine
of Siena. Here I cannot begin to do justice to this major work.
Suffice it to say that Undset is here, as ever, drawn to a woman
at once strong and obedient to God's will, a reformer yet humble, chaste, yet not a nun, celibate but so deeply maternal: a
real saint.

To go back over the features that characterize Sigrid Undset's
hagiography, she had a deep and on-going interest in the saints
—all the greater, perhaps, because she knew how hard it is to
be, not just "pious" in some superficial sense, but truly holy;
how hard it is to want God's will, not our own; how hard it is

to rise above human frailty. She was surely drawn to the saints in part because their lives did provide such marvelous stories—and she always appreciated a good story! But also Undset clearly saw the saints as providing a wonderful vehicle for preaching what was true—and powerful—about Catholicism.

Let me close with a thought which may, at first blush, seem irrelevant to my concerns but is in fact central. It is sometimes said that Undset's work before her conversion is better —stronger, literarily—than the novels she wrote after she became a Catholic. In one sense this may be true: in her early work we see her (and her characters) struggling with ideas, realities, that were in her later work, in her mind, resolved; a certain tension has perhaps gone out of her writing, her thinking. But it could also be argued that increasingly what Undset wanted was not just to be a great writer but, herself, to be a saint: to put her art into the service of God—with some of that old Viking vigor and combativeness! If it pleased readers—certain readers—less, that was a price she was prepared to pay.

NOTES

¹ A. H. Winsnes, *Sigrid Undset: A Study in Christian Realism*, trans. P. G. Foote (New York: Sheed and Ward, 1953), p. 34.

² Undset's first, unpublished, novel had been an early version of this work.

³ Ibid., p. 42.

⁴ Carl Bayerschmidt, *Sigrid Undset* (New York: Twayne, 1970), p. 28.

⁵ Ibid., p. 30.

⁶ Sigrid Undset, *Men, Women and Places*, trans. Arthur G. Chater (New York: Alfred A. Knopf, 1939), p. 92; hereafter cited as MWP.

⁷ Mitzi Brunsdale, *Sigrid Undset: Chronicler of Norway* (New York: Berg, 1988), p. 82.

⁸ Brunsdale, p. 82.

⁹ Sigrid Undset, *Kristin Lavransdatter*, vol. 3: *The Cross*, trans. Charles Archer (New York: Vintage, 1987; orig. New York: Alfred A. Knopf, 1927), p. 139.

¹⁰ Sigrid Undset, *Kristin Lavransdatter*, vol. 2: *The Mistress of Husaby*, trans. Charles Archer (New York: Vintage Books, 1987), p. 100.

¹¹ Ibid., p. 243.

¹² Ibid., p. 65.

¹³ Sigrid Undset, *Saga of Saints*, trans. E. C. Ramsden (New York: Longmans, Green, 1934), pp. 87–88; hereafter cited as SS.

¹⁴ Bayerschmidt, p. 102.

¹⁵ Ibid., p. 45.

¹⁶ Sigrid Undset, *Stages on the Road*, trans. Arthur G. Chater (New York: Alfred A. Knopf, 1934), p. 180; hereafter cited as SR.

ERASMO LEIVA-MERIKAKIS

SIGRID UNDSET:
HOLINESS AND CULTURE

What reader of Sigrid Undset can forget the climactic grave-yard scene at the conclusion of *Kristin Lavransdatter*? I would like to recall it for us here in some detail as emblematic of my theme: the relation of holiness and culture in the thought of Sigrid Undset.

The community of nuns, grouped around their abbess, Lady Ragnhild, advance in the middle of the night at Kristin's urging into the graveyard. They are out to save the life of Tore, the poor outcast boy, who is about to be slaughtered sacrificially to the pest-ogress, Hel, by a frantic pack of men in an attempt to avert the plague.

The text reads: "Lady Ragnhild . . . tottered forward, and took up the lanthorn from the ground—no one moved a hand to hinder her. When she lifted it up, the gold cross on her breast shone out. She stood propped on her staff, and slowly turned the light upon the ring [of men] about her, nodding a little at each man she looked on." Kristin then speaks at the abbess' bidding, countering the excuse of the leader of the pack, Arntor, that Tore is an expendable victim because no one owns him, by proclaiming that "Christ owns him" and stating categorically that " 'twere better we should perish one and all than to hurt one of His little ones."

At that, Arntor breaks into a rage. He defies the abbess' authority and begins hurling filthy insults at the nuns. Then,

anger flamed up in Kristin like a new-kindled fire: "Silence!"
she cried. "Have you lost your wits, or has God smitten you

64

with blindness? Should we dare to murmur under His chastise-
ment—we who have seen His consecrated brides go forth to
meet the sword that has been drawn by reason of the world's
sins? They watched and prayed while we sinned and each day
forgot our Maker—shut them from the world within the citadel
of prayer while we scoured the world around, driven by greed
of great and small possessions, of our own lusts and our own
wrath. But they came forth to us when the angel of death was
sent out amongst us—gathered in the sick and the defenceless
and the hungry—twelve of our sisters have died in this plague
—that you all know—not one turned aside, and not one gave
over praying for us all in sisterly love, till the tongue dried in
their mouths and their life's blood ebbed away. . . ."[1]

At the novel's primary level, this scene portrays Kristin in
her own final transformation as heroic Christian woman, ready
to give her life out of love, no longer now for one of her own
sons, but for an unknown child of no account, that God's honor
may not suffer offense and human souls may not descend to
damnation. Kristin herself would soon die of the plague as a
result of this involvement with saving the life of Tore and of
her work of mercy in burying his mother, Steinunn, on the
following day. The "new-kindled fire" within her, fueling her
boldness, is now no longer the burning of self-will and lust,
but the thirst for divine charity and justice.

But the scene is as well a powerful epiphany and symbolic
dramatization of the holiness and charity of the Church in
the midst of a ruthless society, nominally Christianized some
three hundred years before yet still in the throes of the struggle
between Christianity and paganism. The concrete historical reality of the medieval Church as transforming social presence
is so personal and so palpable that only a novelist of Undset's
caliber can succeed in rendering it effectively in a scene such
as this, built up in a crescendo of interlocking symbols, ges-
tures, emotions, and soul-stirring dialogue. The unforgettable
figure of Lady Ragnhild, in her courageous stance despite her
crumbling frame, with crozier planted on the earth and cross

gleaming from her maternal breast, is an embodiment of the Church's unyielding authority and resolute charity; and she and her community of "brides of Christ" combat violence, ignorance, and fearful superstition with supernatural charity and valor, at tremendous personal cost. Undset's description of the contrast between the abbess' spiritual dynamism and her extreme physical infirmity—she is quite old, and herself convalescing from the plague—is a marvelous illustration of the Pauline doctrine of the triumph of the power of divine love through human weakness. St. Paul proclaims: "We carry about continually in our bodies the dying state of Jesus, so that the living power of Jesus may be manifested in our bodies too" (2 Cor 4:10); and Undset dramatizes Paul's vision: "Lady Ragnhild's teeth began to chatter, and her whole frame to shiver—she still sweated without cease by reason of her sickness, and the pest-boil sores were not fully healed, so that it must have wrought her great agony to walk. But she muttered angrily and shook her head when the sisters prayed her to turn, clung the harder to Kristin's arm, and plodded, shaking with cold, on before them through the garden."

The abbess' confrontation with Arntor and his "ring of desperate men" is nothing less than the ultimate showdown between a mysticism of life and joy and a mysticism of death and fear. And when Kristin raises Tore out of the open grave, we are witnessing the power of the Resurrection entering the world through the agency of an emphatically flawed person who, moreover, had throughout her life risked exposing herself to Christ's transforming action. When the abbess raises the lantern from the ground to illuminate the circle around her with both judgment and hope, in her we see the Church bringing the light of Resurrection-faith to the older Nordic grimness. Elsewhere Undset comments as follows on the medieval Church's revolutionary response to violence: "To the devastation carried out in Catholic lands by the tides of the migrations of peoples and the Viking expeditions, the Catholic Church responded by sending her missionaries right into the midst of the devastators. When monastic foundations and churches were burnt down and monks and nuns were massacred, the Church sent out Benedictines in order to convert the murderers."[2]

Sigrid Undset points out that it is a commonplace to speak of the "civilizing role of Christianity". When recalling her own process of conversion, she remarks: "We [former agnostics] did not fail to see that the Christian faith had brought with it all kinds of secondary and secular social advantages during the centuries in which Europe had professed Christianity." But, she continues, we normally forget that these social effects derive as "by-products which came about while the Church was pursuing her real aim—that of saving souls".[3]

In other words, Christianity's cultural power flows, as from its cause, from the holiness whereby the Church and her individual members partake in the virtues of her Lord, and such holiness does not exist in the abstract or generically but is always incarnated in the persons we call the saints. The transformation of pagan culture into Christian culture, surely one of Undset's central themes, may therefore be said to occur as a result of the presence and influence of individual men and women who in a multitude of ways communicate to a given society those virtues, convictions, loves, and visions—in a word, that *life*—which God has first communicated to them in and through his Church.

Sigrid Undset's views on the relationship of holiness and culture are not the direct subject of any one of her writings, because in a profound sense they are the subject of them *all*. We must look for her thought on this crucial theme, then, in the characters and situations of her novels, in her retelling of the lives of the saints, to which she devoted so much energy in her later years, and in her critical essays on the relationship of Christianity and the modern world. Here we will deal with some of the nonfiction works, seeking to cull from them examples of leading personalities, themes, and ideas which can deepen our understanding of Undset's view of how divine revelation can shape certain aspects of society through the lives of holy people, and how these examples from the past can help us discern our present situation. Most frequent reference will be made to three works: *Saga of the Saints, Stages on the Road,* and *Begegnungen und Trennungen* (Meetings and partings), a collection of essays published in German in 1931 and which features the important essay "Return to the Catholic Church", bearing in the Norwegian original the title "Catholic Propaganda".

While many have the habit of calling Sigrid Undset a "Catholic moralist", I myself prefer to call her a *mystical realist.* Like Léon Bloy, Charles Péguy, Georges Bernanos, Gertrud von le Fort, and the other great Catholic writers of our century, Sigrid Undset is interested in neither morality nor social history for its own sake, but only insofar as these are manifestations of the presence or absence in the world of *holiness,* the heart of Christian faith and life. For Undset, as for Bloy, "there is but one sadness, and that is for us not to be saints."[4]

The splendor and beauty of sanctity fascinated the young Sigrid much before the future novelist had begun sounding the depths of Christian revelation. We are told that already as a young girl, struck by the example of her grandfather's piety, "she was beginning to sense the necessity of all-consuming sacrifice that leads some to believe in Christ." She saw that "Grandfather had given himself to God without reserve, just as the old Norse warriors had flung themselves gladly into Odin's arms."[5] Undset's generous nature responded spontaneously to this prospect of reckless self-sacrifice for another; but it would take many years of study for her to realize the extent to which this initial impulse and intuition had been correct, that is, the extent to which it corresponded to the deepest vocation of human nature. Late in her life, in 1940, she gives us the following autobiographical retrospect: "By degrees my knowledge of history convinced me that the only thoroughly sane people, of our civilization at least, seemed to be those queer men and women which the Catholic Church calls the Saints. . . . They seemed to know the true explanation of man's undying hunger for happiness—his tragically insufficient love of peace, justice, and goodwill to his fellowmen, his everlasting fall from grace."[6]

Clearly, for Sigrid Undset, the saints represent the glory of mankind. She loves recalling the beautiful epithet for saints in the Old Norse writings: "God's friends".[7] When she invites us to "penetrate to the core of our civilization, to form an idea of the significance of the Catholic Church's contribution to civilization", she goes on to specify what this inquiry involves and makes us realize how inextricable the bond is between such a contribution and the interior life of holiness of individual Christians: "[We must] understand what in the intellectual life and social structure of Europe during the last 2000 years is not a fruit of natural human development, but a result of men having accepted God's revelation in Jesus Christ and worked under the grace of His Holy Spirit" (SR, p. 262).

Great as her conviction is, however, regarding the central relevance of personal holiness to Christian culture, Undset is careful not to exalt the saints artificially as if sanctity were something merely predetermined by God and bestowed unilaterally on a few perfected elect. For her, Christian holiness exhibits two impressive characteristics: it is *ordinary* (it is for everyone as the person each one is) and it is *dynamic* (it involves the transformation of the whole person and requires much cooperative hard work from the individual, simultaneously in his interior self and in the world that surrounds him).

In her life of St. Magnus Erlendsson, Earl of the Orkney Islands, Undset gives us a definition of Christian holiness which, with earthy common sense and a touch of humor, highlights both the ordinariness and the dynamic nature of sanctity:

> The saints are those men and women who have resisted the temptation of asking themselves how cheaply they can slip out of this or that obligation to God without endangering their ultimate chances of His mercy when they die. They are those who do not continually mutter to themselves, "Lord, Thou knowest how weak I am—and besides Thou knowest that it is necessary for me to consider somewhat the world in which I live."

> The saints are those who always say in their hearts, . . . "Lord,
> what can I do for Thee in the short lifetime which Thou hast
> given me? for night cometh when no man can work" (SS, pp.
> 172–73).

The particular heroism of the saint's vocation, what radically
distinguishes him from either the old Norse or ancient Greek
and Roman heroes, is that there is initially very little in his nature that promises to transform the world. Christians, in their
vocation to sanctity, are tensely poised between their certain
knowledge concerning their radical imperfection and the paradoxical command of the Gospel: "Be perfect as your heavenly
Father is perfect!" (Mt 5:48)—a saying of Christ which Undset returns to time and again. "All men more or less are moral
cripples", she reflects. "But only when we are good in the way
in which God is good, are we good enough."[8]

The roots of personal sanctity, then, and what therefore constitutes the source of the power of holiness to transform culture, lie deep in a person's struggle to overcome the downward
pull of unredeemed human nature in order finally to yield to
the transfiguring work of grace. The saint's first and enduring
struggle is with himself. The struggle of self-conquest probably
defines the moral and mystical substance of all Undset's writings. How the Beatitudes—thirst for justice, purity of heart,
poverty of spirit, joy in suffering persecution for Christ's sake
—gradually come to be *the* operative principles in a human
heart, dramatically replacing ambition, lust, arrogance, and the
spirit of self-promotion: for Undset, no other process or evolution is more worthy of man; nothing else captures her imagination more readily as a theme worthy of artistic portrayal.

When describing the colossal cultural accomplishments of
St. Olav early in the eleventh century, Undset says tersely that
he had to wrestle to convert his people "and his own turbulent
heart" (SS, p. 269), and she affirms that, "by the taming of his
pugnacious and aggressive nature, St. Olav did more in Norway
for the cause of Christianity than by all the other projects he

undertook."[9] As she describes the particulars of how this saint, who did not have much "natural holiness" about him, transformed his love of power into a force to unify the realm under Christian laws, Undset evokes this eloquent iconographic detail: statues of St. Olav traditionally represent him as crowned king, treading a dragon underfoot. The dragon no doubt symbolizes the paganism of pre-Christian Norway over which Olav triumphed; but the dragon also happens to have a face identical to the king's, and thus, in the old paganism, he is simultaneously trampling down his own previously heathen nature (SS, pp. 123–24). By personally submitting in faith and love to the rule of Christ's Law, Olav Haraldsson transformed the very texture of Norwegian society.

In the first place, he made it clear that no human overlord, even the most powerful king, derives his authority from his own person or his natural endowments for leadership: only Christ is Overlord of all by his nature as incarnate Son of God. Yet even this drastic overturning of old Norse views is not so much an eradication of error as it is a transformation of flawed social instincts which, however, have a real basis in truth. The ancient Viking conviction that loyalty to one's fellow warriors is the supreme social value undergoes rebirth in a saint like St. Olav, for whom Christian holiness flows from a covenant of loyalty with the God who is powerful love. In his view, heroic commitment to Christian *truth* has no other meaning than living in unflinching fidelity to the baptismal *troth* with one's lord, who also happens to be *The Lord*, the Creator and Ruler of the Universe and the Father of the compassionate Christ. Here we have a dazzling example of the regeneration of pre-Christian social values by the vision of the saint. The Vikings' fierce love of freedom, inseparable from their sense of *troth* (loyalty to lord and group), becomes transformed into Christian love, obedience to Christ the Lord, and faithful adherence to the Church. And the historical paradigm receives ample personal application in Sigrid Undset's own experience. Undset continually returns to this theme of the struggle between the

instinctive, unredeemed human longing for freedom, of which
the Viking ethos is the archetype, and the freedom proposed
by the Gospel: paradoxical self-realization through responsible
love, service, and self abnegation—the freedom of Christ Crucified. In her brief autobiographical retrospect, she alludes three
times to her own wildly autonomous nature: "The reason why
I hated school so intensely [was that] it interfered with my freedom."[10] "Above all things I had always desired liberty to do
what I wanted."[11] And finally:

> In a way we do not want to find Truth—we prefer to seek,
> and keep our illusions. But I had ventured near the abode of
> truth in my researches about "God's friends. . . ." So I had to
> submit. And on the first of November, 1924, I was received into
> the Catholic Church. Since then I have seen how a hunger and
> thirst of authority have made large nations accept any ghoul-
> ish caricature of authority. But I have learned why there can
> never be any valid authority of men over men. The only Au-
> thority to which mankind can submit without debauching itself
> is His whom St. Paul calls *Auctor Vitae*—the Creator's toward
> Creation.[12]

But let us return to the cultural impact of St. Olav's sanctity.
The most tangible result of his conviction that truest freedom
is attained through the obedience of faith was the *Kristenret*
or "St. Olav's Code of Laws", which in almost every way
ran against the grain of what the Vikings considered virtu-
ous.[13] Through these laws, Olav Haraldsson intended to make
Norway a visible portion of the Kingdom of Christ—an ideal
plainly capable of being perverted in the most atrocious ways by
religious fanatics and cultists but, precisely, only in the context
of our own de-Christianized society. The Code, for instance,
rejects the alleged parental right to decide whether a child is
to live or die. The fact that a child is seen to receive life from
God establishes children for the first time as social persons in
their own right, and it is with the coming of Christianity that
children first appear as characters of consequence in the sagas
(SS, pp. 13–14). The young Tore of the scene in the graveyard

with which we began is a good example of this development: it is extraordinary to see how this little, inconsequential character, emerging out of nowhere, suddenly becomes the focus of Kristin's (and the reader's) attention at the novel's conclusion, something made possible only by the nuns' vision of him as dear child of Christ.

Against the background of severe, often unsurvivable winters, in which too many hungry mouths can endanger the very existence of the whole tribe, noble souls now begin to suggest that real praise and honor of God, and the wisest thing to do, is found in the effort to collect money to bring up the children and care for the old rather than exposing them to die. One memorable nobleman, Arnorr, turns the tables on Viking tradition by proclaiming the *unmanliness* of exposing the weak. As striking proof of this, he slaughters his own horses for food and persuades others to do the same instead of murderously ridding themselves of mouths to feed. Such an action is all the more impressive when we recall that the horse was to the Vikings a sign of pride and strength in battle, now sacrificed to become an act of charity and civilization (SS, p. 16).

St. Olav's Code also enjoins on all alike—warring nobility as well as slaves and working people—the duty to observe the sabbath rest on Sundays and holy days. This statute not only restructures traditional values by affirming the primacy of spiritual affairs over work and ambition (thus introducing Josef Pieper's principle of "leisure the basis of culture"). In particular, the principle of inviolable temporal and spatial sacredness and peace gains ground with the centrality of the church building as House of God and focus of liturgical and social activity on Sunday, as focus, therefore, of cultural life as such. Under the influence of such sacred space, time, and actions, violent souls had to adapt themselves to the solemn ritual of the Church with her disciplined and regenerative rhythms, and the notion of "sanctuary" is introduced. Just as indigenous walrus tusks were now used instead of exotic ivory for the corpora on crucifixes, so too, under the formative hand of the liturgy, the native "raw material" of Viking souls and hearts began slowly to take on the shape of Christ (SS, p. 256). With its lofty simplicity, the celebration of the Christian Eucharist began to impart a taste for the Banquet of the Kingdom "in spirit and in truth", thus displacing the former "sacrificial feasts with their good smell of food" (SS, p. 107). One of the heroic epithets by which St. Olav is remembered in the *Glaelognskvida*, a laudatory poem in his honor, is *Bokamals reginnagla* (the "sacred nail of the liturgy"), because, as Undset says, "it was he who had spread the canopy of liturgical services over the land" (SS, p. 113).

Even though in this period conversion to Christianity often occurred by means of mass baptism, administered corporately to a lord and all his subjects, usually as a result of an ultimatum or defeat in battle, Undset stresses the fact that the victorious Christian king would then leave behind him priests and build churches so that, by regular attendance at the liturgy, by the reception of the sacraments, and by listening to the priest's instructions in sermons and in confession, individual Norsemen would gradually realize the real meaning of their change in religion (SS, pp. 54–55).

Another duty imposed by St. Olav was fasting, something which at first appears negligible as a cultural force until we again recall the extent to which Viking culture was based on the principle that only those in the community who are powerful are of account, and that power results from maximizing every passion in human nature, a process that fasting is precisely intended to reverse. The law of fasting also tends to effect an equalization of all people in a society, regardless of official social rank, wealth, or influence, since now the common denominator uniting them all despite superficial social differences is their interior standing before the Lord of justice and love.

Finally, St. Olav's Code enforced the indissolubility of Christian marriage. Marriage, at least in principle, could no longer be one more vehicle of ambition and power-play. The law now required that the bride must give her consent to the marriage, and that girls could not be coerced into marriage even by their

father. (Remember how Kristin willfully broke off her solemn
engagement to Simon Darre.) Most shockingly, the man, too,
was required to be faithful to the woman! We know that marriage, as the fundamental locus of Christian sanctity for Sigrid
Undset, is the social institution to which she devotes most
attention throughout her works. In fact, A. H. Winsnes says
that it was "Christianity's high esteem and sacred regard for
motherhood and its religious consecration of marriage [that]
helped perhaps more than anything else to open Sigrid Undset's
eyes to the truth of the [Catholic] faith."[14] Her thoughts on
the fortunes of this institution, both in the Middle Ages and
in modern times, offer us a striking example of how Undset
studies pagan and Christian options of the past to shed light
on the plight of contemporary civilization.

In her famous "Reply to a Parish Priest", an essay elicited
by this very issue, Undset gives us an admirable meditation
which can be read as a twentieth-century gloss on the marriage
statute from St. Olav's eleventh-century Code of Laws. Undset's words here have such synthetic force that I quote her at
some length: "Industrial capitalism", she ponders,

> and free competition [twentieth-century avatars of the Viking
> ethos!] have resulted in the majority of members of society hav-
> ing lost all security for their economic future. . . . [Such] slave
> conditions are accompanied by a renewal of the morality of slav-
> ery. This is precisely the point about "comrade-marriage" [today
> we would say "living together"] . . . , the commonest form of
> sexual intercourse among slaves. . . . Free love is for slaves, and
> marriage is for the free-born. . . . Of a slave-born concubine a
> man can demand fidelity so long as he cares to keep her for
> himself; of a wife her whole community can demand fidelity
> . . . because she shares the responsibility and the honor of the
> family with her forefathers and with her husband . . . and with
> her children. . . . The Christian Church could not recognize any
> dual morality here either—could not acknowledge class distinc-
> tions and racial disparities to be other than trifling variations in a
> human material which was fundamentally one. . . . The Church
> insisted that Christian slave-owners at least refrain from hinder-

ing their slaves' participation in the Church's means of grace, among them the sacrament of marriage. . . . Little by little the Church's view gained prevalence all over Europe . . . [that] it is criminal for other people, or social conditions, to withhold [the right of living in matrimony and founding a family] (SR, pp. 252-54).

Legislation concerning the indissolubility of marriage, first imposed on all Norwegian society by St. Olav, was essential in stabilizing the institution of the family on the basis of the fidelity and coresponsibility of both partners.

In the kingdom at large, a similar problem of stability existed in the manner of succession to the throne. Every time a king died and the throne was vacant, any man who could claim having been fathered by the previous king—regardless of the legitimacy or illegitimacy of the birth—could enter the struggle for succession and hence plunge the country into often bloody strife. Two centuries after St. Olav, the archbishop St. Eystein (Norwegian for "Augustine") worked hard to establish the exclusive right to the throne of the legitimate heir. Nor was this merely a matter of finding a workable practical arrangement to minimize strife; important Christian principles came into play involving unique appeal to God's ultimate authority. At stake, quite simply, was the peace of the land.

The ancient custom of allowing all claimants, whether demonstrably sons of the dead king or not, to enter the succession struggle derived from the heathen conception of a mystical relationship existing between the royal house and the gods. The *strongest* claimant was deemed the evident choice of the gods, since physical prowess reflected divine favor (SS, p. 221). St. Eystein's crowning of Magnus Erlingsson marked the beginning of the exclusive line of succession by the legitimate heir, and this ushered in, at least in principle, a reign of peace in Norway. In shifting the focus of authority from the personal qualities of the man to the sacred responsibility of the office, a quasi-sacramental principle of kingship is introduced that henceforth confirms the king as servant to God, his Overlord, and administrator of an earthly kingdom which, in the realistic symbolism of the age, was said to be "St. Olav's kingdom to all eternity. . . . The reigning kings in each age [were thought to] hold the land in fief from him", and after the death of a king the crown he held on loan from St. Olav was hung again over his altar in Nidaros Cathedral (SS, p. 231). Undset summarizes the particular cultural form assumed by St. Eystein's sanctity in this way: "His struggle [was] to gain for [the Church] freedom to provide peace in the land, . . . [a struggle] for a kingdom which did not stand to win through a bloody war, which could not fall to 'wicked and foolish men'" (SS, p. 259). In treating this whole question of legitimate human government, Undset has presented the very practical holiness of Archbishop St. Eystein as resulting in the establishment of political principles of long-lasting effect in European society.

Remote as such questions appear to be from our modern political concerns, Undset deftly connects this issue of succession to the throne in medieval Norway to the contemporary problem of totalitarian despots. Writing in the years of the rise of Stalin and Hitler, she points to the affinities such tyrants have to a medieval usurper like Sverre, who claimed authority on the basis of a show of pseudomystical force and private revelations in dreams. She remarks of many contemporary fellow Europeans that "they seek to save the world by various political theories in which there is a hint of mysticism, driven onwards by a blind instinctive hope that they may find leaders who can solve the difficulties of reality" (SS, p. 241).

In the collection of essays "Meetings and Partings: Essays on Christianity and Germanism", she speaks of the ominous way in which whole populations willingly surrender their freedom to the sacred theories of state proposed by a charismatic leader who then leads everyone into slavery. And she adds at once that, on the basis of the first article of the Creed, *Credo in unum Deum*, and because the one Lord of all speaks only through the authority of the apostles and their successors, Catholics must declare war on such a pseudomystical development, even if it means being decimated and driven into hiding in caves under the earth.[15] And she concludes her posthumously published study of St. Catherine of Siena with an eloquent contrast between, on the one hand, the effects of modern political pseudomysticism (according to her, a violent reaction to the pseudorealist rationalism of the last two centuries) and, on the other hand, the "atmospheric" influence of authentic Christian holiness: "We have had terrible experience of the psychic power which can produce effects such as the possession by devils of a whole people. But we have less experience of the psychic powers which console and strengthen and fill our minds with peace, which encourage the despairing and drive out hatred and envy and the will to hurt others. . . . Perhaps the power which proceeds from good men and women is too subtle for us with our limited abilities to understand. Perhaps its waves are like the light-waves and sound-waves of which our eyes and ears perceive a small part."[16]

But for Sigrid Undset it is the Law of Charity, an essential consequence of Christian holiness, that most magnificently overturns the foundations of a society based on the natural human impulse to cooperate loyally only with the members of one's tribe, and actively to despise and, if possible, destroy all outsiders, all those different from one's group. The reorganization of a society by its incorporation into the Church through baptism and the sacraments not only provides a Constantinian principle of unity; it also imposes the consciousness of the universal brotherhood and equality of all the baptized without exception before the common Father. This faith-conviction was precisely the "new-kindled fire" that impelled Kristin and the nuns in the fictional graveyard scene.

A wonderful hagiographic story illustrating the new spirit of charity in medieval Norway is that of St. Hallvard. A poor woman of no account has been accused of stealing, and she runs from her pursuers to the edge of the fjord where the young Hallvard is about to shove off in a little boat. He welcomes her aboard and begins to plan her defense. Comments Undset:

"In the picture of the young *bonde* (or free-man) from Husaby, rowing the poverty-stricken woman across the fjord, talking so seriously to her meanwhile and asking whether she is willing to prove her innocence by ordeal by fire, there is something free and lovely. A Christian man and his fellow creature, without any petty thoughts of difference in station and social worth" (SS, p. 155). In the end, the woman's pursuers approach in another boat, and Hallvard dies with an arrow through his throat, pleading that the woman be given a fair hearing. In those "two small boats [that] lay rocking on the water at a short distance from each other, on a May morning 900 years ago", Undset sees symbolized the competing social views of heathen and Christian Norway: in one boat, three "ordinary people who followed their noses"; in the other, a young man who is "straightforward, merciful and anxious to help those who need it" (SS, pp. 158–59). After he was murdered, his body was found floating on the river despite the millstone bound to it; but "it was not the miracle of the floating stone that the dead man's contemporaries found so extraordinary. . . . That which astounded them was that the young Hallvard of Husaby had given his life to shield a worthless woman who had been accused of stealing" (SS, p. 149).

This putting of oneself in the place of another human being in need, in imitation of Christ, is at the heart of the creative principle of Catholic culture: good works are not incidental to faith but of the essence for obtaining salvation. "The Church", says Undset, "taught that the Cross and suffering are necessary for obtaining eternal bliss, and that illness and poverty, rightly understood, can be counted among God's graces, and under the impulse of these words people ran out with gifts for the poor and built hospitals for the sick."[17] Teaching the necessity of suffering in the light of the Gospel leads, not to social passivity and indifferentism, but to social action and innovative institutions. Because Christ is the Son of God, his suffering is redemptive, and so must Christian charity be—charity as service to the suffering Christ in all his suffering members.

Sigrid Undset delights in surveying in detail all the new themes that enter Norse literature with the arrival of the Law of Christ requiring that all love as he loves. For instance, brutality as such only now becomes problematic. True bravery is to save exposed children and the old. Sin and repentance, illness and sorrow, create a new focus of interest. The rich now hold a responsibility for the poor, since their wealth is given them by Christ only in stewardship for *his* poor. All those who formerly were of no account are seen as enjoying the preferential love of Christ. St. Magnus Erlendsson on one occasion negotiates with his enemy Haakon, not in order to save his own life, but to help save Haakon's soul by keeping him from committing murder (SS, pp. 180–81). Above all, the tenderness and compassion of the Virgin Mary—who is *Mater Amabilis*, *Mater Dolorosa*, *Mater Misericordiae*—enter the soul and culture of Europe by virtue of her *dogmatically* proclaimed role as Mother of Christ;[18] and this irrefutable model of a human being and a woman so splendidly transformed by the divine mercy simply revolutionizes traditional civilization. The figure of the Virgin *demonstrates* that the power of God derives from his nature as love. The ferocious human longing for freedom must stop short and ponder the meaning of *this* use of freedom: the Virgin's compassion and tenderness and maternal care for her Son in all God's children.

While all would agree that these shifts in sensibility represent wonderful social gains, Sigrid Undset sternly warns us that none of the transforming benefits Christianity impressed upon society are permanent or automatic acquisitions. In her view, they are the by-products of holiness, and since holiness is achieved only by individuals at the cost of great personal struggle, Christian sanctity is directly contrary to the notion of "social evolution" as something mystical, inevitable, as if an "enlightened" (because highly organized and democratic) society could be counted on to be permanently "improving itself" without Christ as living efficient cause.

In a key passage in which she italicizes extensively, Undset gravely affirms:

We have no right to assume that any part of European tradition, cultural values, moral ideas, emotional wealth, which has its origin in the dogmatically defined Christianity of the Catholic Church, will continue to live a "natural" life, if the people of Europe reject Christianity and refuse to accept God's supernatural grace. One might just as well believe that a tree whose roots were severed should continue to bear leaves and blossoms and fruit (SR, p. 250).

Neither the fear of hell (in the Middle Ages) nor technological and parliamentary efficiency (in modern times), but only the *love of Christ*, she affirms, "could bring about the conversion of individual souls and give them the strength which enabled them to imprint the mark of Christianity on the manifold and heterogeneous elements which went to make up the culture of the West" (SS, p. 147).

Facing the prospect of cultural and religious cataclysm in our century, Sigrid Undset finds consolation in the fact that Christian regeneration, both personal and ecclesial, has never been effected except through generous individual souls. In the examples of the saints from the distant past, she witnesses the slow but irresistible growth of the seeds of holiness that transform, first an individual soul, and eventually a whole society.

And so, writing in the early 1930s, she turns her gaze to the future with sober hope in God's providential inventiveness: "The Church militant on earth", she speculates, "may be reduced to a handful of adherents, not many more than would fill an arena or a local jail. The Christians of Europe may be reduced to a little band with no power to influence social development for a long period. . . . Until Catholic missionaries, from China or South America or Africa, return to preach the faith of our fathers to the lost barbarian tribes who are living amongst the ruins of ancient Europe" (SR, p. 265).

NOTES

[1] *Kristin Lavransdatter*, vol. 3: *The Cross*, trans. Charles Archer (New York: Vintage Books, 1987), pp. 390–91.

[2] *Begegnungen und Trennungen: Essays über Christentum und Germanentum*, trans. Franz Michel Willam (Munich: Verlag Josef Kösel, 1931), p. 86. All quotations from this work are my translation.

[3] *Stages on the Road*, trans. Arthur G. Chater (New York: Alfred A. Knopf, 1934), p. 242; hereafter cited as SR.

[4] Léon Bloy, *Pilgrim of the Absolute*, ed. Raïssa Maritain and trans. John Coleman and Harry Lorin Binsee (London: Eyre and Spottiswoode, 1947), p. 301.

[5] Mitzi Brunsdale, *Sigrid Undset: Chronicler of Norway* (Oxford: Berg Publishers, 1988), p. 29.

[6] *Twentieth Century Authors*, ed. Stanley J. Kunitz and Howard Haycroft (New York: H. W. Wilson, 1942; 7th printing, 1973), p. 1433.

[7] *Saga of Saints*, trans. E. C. Ramsden (New York: Longmans, Green, 1934), p. 74; hereafter cited as SS.

[8] *Begegnungen*, p. 78.

[9] Ibid., p. 122.

[10] Kunitz and Haycroft, p. 1432.

[11] Ibid., p. 1433.

[12] Ibid., pp. 1433–34. And in the introduction to *Begegnungen* (p. 5) she says that the fundamental fear of natural man is that there may indeed be an objective truth not derived from himself: he fears total loss of personal freedom would result. Consequently, a large part of human life is expended in the effort to obscure the truth, until one realizes the unsurpassable beauty of Christ's words: "If you continue faithful to my word, you are my disciples in earnest; so you will come to know the truth, and the truth will set you free" (Jn 8:32, Knox trans.).

[13] For what follows on St. Olav's Code of Laws, see SS, pp. 110–11.

[14] A. H. Winsnes, *Sigrid Undset: A Study in Christian Realism*, trans. P. G. Foote (New York: Sheed and Ward, 1953), p. 83.

[15] *Begegnungen*, pp. 100–101.

[16] *Catherine of Siena*, trans. Kate Austin-Lund (New York: Sheed and Ward, 1954), p. 291.

[17] *Begegnungen*, p. 91.

[18] See Winsnes, p. 84, where a passage from one of Undset's articles on the women's movement ("Efterskrift", or "Postscript") is quoted. As early as 1919 we see Undset meditating on the meaning of the Blessed Virgin's titles in the Litany of Loreto. A topic of crucial relevance to Undset's view of Catholic

Christianity as shaping cultural force, and one which we can only note in passing, is the centrality of *dogmas*. In *Begegnungen* we read: "Even the concept of sanctity presupposes certain *dogmas*, if it is indeed to have a content which is distinguishable, not only in degree but in essence, from the injunctions of pre-Christian or non-Christian religions in connection with purity of mores, moral rigor, a sense of honor and justice" (p. 97). And in *Stages* she reflects: "People [in Protestant countries] are very apt to imagine that this or that social institution or moral idea—which in reality has resulted from Europe having formerly accepted the *dogmas* of the Catholic Church—has arisen quite 'naturally', in proportion as the values 'advanced' on their road from primitive barbarism to 'higher civilization' " (p. 226) [Emphasis mine].

PAUL EVANS

IN THE BLOOD:
THE TRANSMISSION OF SIN IN
"THE MASTER OF HESTVIKEN"

Ravenous as cancer, sin feeds on the lives recounted in *The Master of Hestviken*, yet so full with eruptive force is it that it drives the novel as its propulsive current—sin is the book's dark life-blood. Character, round and detailed, may seem the first strength of this fiction Sigrid Undset deemed her best, yet so individual in its manifestations is the sin she depicts that its complex "personality" is what lingers in our minds. With all the ingenuity of a great character, sin so insinuates itself that, after finishing the gigantic novel, we know it in the close ways we know only people in lesser books. Deceiver, tempter, prod: sin plays many roles, but its final one, in keeping with Christian paradox, is that of teacher. "For the marvelous mystery of guilt, of sin, of enmity against God," writes Gerardus van der Leeuw, "is that in it man discovers God: certainly as an adversary, but nevertheless in the closest proximity".[1]

It is Undset's relentless study of sin that makes *Hestviken* distinctive among modern novels—and difficult. A 994-page tetralogy, fruit of its author's eighteen-hour workdays, the book is not stylistically daunting. Published in full in 1927, thirteen years after Joyce's *Ulysses*, it has none of the language-gaming of literary modernism, no lines of Faulknerian length, none of Beckett's gnomic anomie. In nineteenth-century prose-style, Undset tells her tale straight—her eye and ear omnivorous, she gives us color, music, and odor, but she writes without flash.[2]

If her style is not at all modern, neither is her genre. Set in a medieval Norway emerging from anarchy, sorcery, and fury into Christian mystery and love, *Hestviken* is a historical novel of a kind none too common in our time. As against stories that romanticize the past (*Gone with the Wind*) or deconstruct it (*Gravity's Rainbow*), there are not many vast historical chronicles of any seriousness outside Pasternak's *Dr. Zhivago*, Powell's *A Dance to the Music of Time*, Mishima's *The Sea of Fertility*, Solzhenitsyn's *August 1914*. Indeed, the modern novel is curious in its limitations: there are books about words, the tight sadness of domestic woe, individual crisis. All too rarely (Malraux, Koestler, Mailer, Malaparte, Orwell, among others), writers open up to politics and a larger view. But, for *Hestviken* and its many mansions, most twentieth-century novels substitute circumscribed locales (suburbs, small towns, cramped rooms) and characters nursing concerns nowhere near as epic (or as intimate) as Undset's moral life-and-death struggles. Thomas Mann's *Joseph and His Brothers*, also a tetralogy, partners *Hestviken* in grappling with sin and redemption; a retelling of the Old Testament lesson, it is also, like *Hestviken*, not widely read.

We have to turn back to the 1800s, specifically to Dostoevsky, for the mix of realism and moral scrutiny Undset attempts. John Cowper Powys makes the case that Dostoevsky towers above all novelists and does so because of his compassion, psychic acuity, and thirst for God. More conventional, and no seer on the order he was, Undset still comes close to the Russian titan in worldview. For all their emancipatory appeal, Nietzsche and the cult of self, and Marx with his materialist utopianism, waged war on that religious vision, and their work in setting the limits of modern Western writing and thought has been pervasive. Even more so has been Freud's. A Dostoevsky admirer, Freud still, with his determinism, his denial of God, and his rendering of evil in terms of mere pathology, continues to prevail as the West's ideologue.

Despite their psychologizing talent and political heat (Dostoevsky's Slavophilia, Undset's anti-fascism), the Russian and the Norwegian do not see life the way Freud, Marx, Nietzsche do. For them, the world is instead fully dimensional —a moral universe extending into the soul and God. And if modern writing matches modern philosophy in its preoccupation with *doubt*, Undset and Dostoevsky struggle with *belief*. Appropriately, then, they take up incessantly, as do Undset's Catholic near-contemporaries, Greene, Mauriac, Bloy, Waugh, Claudel, and Bernanos, the theme of sin (Undset's historical canvas, however, is much larger than her peers'). They understand that human failing is less a matter of disease or history or accident than of revolt against Pascal's "God of Abraham, God of Isaac, God of Jacob, not of philosophers and scholars". With Kierkegaard, they know that sin's true opposite is not virtue but faith. As Christians, believers in the Incarnation, they know, with Ricoeur, that "sin is a religious dimension before being ethical; it is not the transgression of an abstract rule—of a value—but the violation of a personal bond."[3] And in bringing us into "closest proximity" with the ways of sin, they instruct us in the difficult knowledge of God.

Master of Hestviken, Olav Audunsson, is Undset's Adam— her Everyman. Sinner and sufferer, Lucifer and Job, he learns early that the world is ruled by "a law for men with fleshly hearts, hot blood, and vengeful minds" (MH, p. 11) and that such law counters a higher one. Exposed to the life of men of God, he reacts with longing but also rebellion, certain that he ranks among those who act out of

> self-willed love—not among these priests and monks who . . . prayed, worked, ate, sang, lay down to sleep, and got up again to begin their prayers . . . all because they loved this law and dreamed that by its means all folk might be tamed, till no man more would bear arms against his neighbor . . . but all would be quiet and willing to listen to our Lord's new and gentle tidings of brothers among all God's children. He felt a kind of distant melancholy affection for all this even now, a respect for the men who thought thus—but *he* was not able always to

bow before the law, and the very thought that they would slip
these bonds about himself filled him with violent loathing (MH,
pp. 134–35).

Ingunn, Olav's soulmate, Eve to his Adam, comes later,
through metaphor, to learn of sin as she grows pregnant with
a bastard:

> She never thought of it as her child, this alien life which she
> felt growing in her and stirring ever stronger, in spite of all her
> efforts to strangle it. It was as though some deformed thing,
> wild and evil, had penetrated within her and sucked its fill of her
> blood and her marrow—a horror she must hide (MH, p. 220).

Augustine says, "Sin is nothing else than to neglect eternal
things and seek after temporal things."[4] Aquinas says that sin
rots us so that, when riddled by it, we are "inside, a corpse,
though outside sometimes an effigy of the human remains".[5]
Pain and remorse will haunt Olav and Ingunn as they journey
toward death, but the distinctive stamp of their sins marks them
from youth. "It seemed that none could come at the heart of
this boy", his neighbors noted of Olav, and that "a healthy
paleness gave Olav's face even in childhood something of a
cold, impassive look" (MH, p. 12). His sin will be pride, the
contortion of character Aquinas deems the worst in its affront
to God; for Meister Eckhart, to whom every being is "a word
of God", pride affronts creation—it distances us from our fellow sufferers. Ingunn, whom even Olav sees as "weak and
obstinate, short of wit, alluring and tender and warm" (MH,
p. 135), will be cursed by weakness, an obstinate clutching at
the merely human that forbids her entry into the ease of God.

Foster-son of Steinfinn, whose marriage began with the stealing of another's betrothed, Olav is joined almost from infancy
to Steinfinn's daughter Ingunn; Steinfinn, drunk, and Olav's
dying father had promised the two to each other. Exiled from
Hestviken, his birthplace and home, to a line of rebels and
madmen, Olav grows up with Ingunn, a girl "neither handy
nor bold, but weak, quick to give up and take to tears when

their play grew rough or the game went against her" (MH, p. 137). At first nearly brother and sister, they fall from innocence when Olav is sixteen. "The boy's senses were tricked with a vision of corn that is as yet but milky, before it has fully ripened" (MH, p. 24), Undset writes about their fresh passion. Aware, even then, that desire has changed them, Olav is exhilarated, but frightened, too: "It seemed to him that they were as two trees, torn up by the spring flood and adrift on a stream" (MH, p. 29).

On a night of drunken revelry, of celebration after battle that mirrors the evening when, as children, they were betrothed, Olav and Ingunn consummate their love. Yet even as his flesh sings, Olav senses their action as a violation. "A betrayer he had become—but it was as though he himself had also been betrayed. They had been playing on a flowery slope and had not had the wit to see that it ended in a precipice" (MH, p. 71). Equally temptress as prey, Ingunn cleaves to Olav as her childhood crumbles, her mother dying that night, and her father soon after. Felled by henchmen of his own murder victim (the man whose lover he had stolen), Steinfinn lingers long enough on his deathbed to refuse Olav's plea to wed Ingunn. Olav's baptism into profane love is followed by his initiation into violence: insulted by Ingunn's family in his bid for her hand, he kills one of her kinsmen and discovers, as his axe tastes flesh, "a strange voluptuous excitement". His hunger for Ingunn, now forbidden, intensifies to fever: "He would go to her, he would have her now at once, he was ready to tear her to pieces and eat her up in terror lest anyone should drag them apart" (MH, p. 133).

Fearing, however, for his life, Olav flees for four years into soldiery, campaigning in Denmark and Sweden. In his absence, Ingunn reels with a sickness "so strange" that it seems "the work of some guile". She revives, but plunges deeper: charmed by a stranger who lacks Olav's moral anxiety and also his coldness, she becomes pregnant with a child who does not so much gestate as fester inside her. Returning from his forced odyssey, feeling bound by love, pity, and honor, Olav does not desert her. Still, his outraged honor must be satisfied: again he raises his axe, and Ingunn's lover dies bleeding in the snow. The secret is kept from Ingunn, but, gripped by her own shame, she is morally paralyzed:

> She would not look *upward*, and she would not look *forward*, and she recognized the justice of her perdition since she refused to receive anything that was necessary to her soul's salvation. . . . And she saw her own soul, bare and dark as a rock scorched by the fire, and she herself had set fire to and burned up all that was in her of living fuel (MH, p. 287; emphasis Undset's).

Giving in to hopelessness, she tries to drown herself, only to be rescued by Olav's best friend. *The Axe*, first of *Hestviken*'s four books, then leads into *The Snake Pit* and a marriage that, echoing our first parents' union, binds Olav and Ingunn still faster in misery as the bloom of their sin ripens. What had begun as an idyll spirals into despair.

Moving to Hestviken, the newlyweds try for a new life. Ingunn's son is sent off, but any hope for a new family is withered as, within four years, Ingunn bears three stillborn children. She comes to think that she "must be marked in some mysterious way, with something as terrible as leprosy, so that she injected her unborn infants with death" (MH, p. 451). Long-suffering Olav nurses her ("Never, thought Olav, had he seen a creature look so like a piece of broken, washed-out wreckage cast up on the beach as did Ingunn . . ." [MH, p. 363]), and their love is an agony of forbearance and explosive pity. For her sake, he brings her bastard home as his illegitimate heir: there, his deceitful genesis is reaped in his character—a compulsive liar, Eirik grows into a boy Olav scorns as "a loose-tongued chatterer, untruthful, boasting and cowardly" (MH, p. 452). Eirik yearns for love from the man he regards as his father, but Olav, drawn inward, wrestles with his own sin. He confides to a friend: "You have never known what it is to live in enmity with Christ, to stand before Him as a liar and betrayer . . . I

have—every day, for—ay, 'twill soon be eight years now . . .
I knew not that such love was within the power of man until
I myself had abandoned His covenant and lost Him!" (MH,
p. 441).

Feeling lost to God, Olav busies himself about Hestviken
and, after a fashion, prospers. But the aloofness of his youth
lingers: "No one could deny that Olav was generous in both
giving and lending, but if anyone would ease his heart and
discuss his affairs with him, there was no comfort to be had
of it in that house . . . it seemed that God's gifts did not bite
on [Olav]" (MH, p. 407). Estranged from himself, his spirits
crushed when Ingunn produces a son who soon dies, Olav
is estranged also from humanity—until he strays into passion
with his housekeeper, Torhild, a woman as strong as Ingunn
is weak. Even then, dogged by duty, he does not seize after
release but sets up Torhild and their child in a far outpost.
Finally Ingunn bears a healthy child, Cecilia, and the parents
exult, for once, together.

Yet even this happiness does not join Ingunn and Olav in
any deeper bond than strife. Ingunn, aware of his sacrifice in
tending her, had once sensed in him "the nature of Love", but
Olav, in a moment of imagining his wife dead, sees her only
as "poor and joyless and broken in health, the widow of a secret murderer and caitiff". Desperate to end their travail, Olav
suggests that they part and that he enter religious life. Ingunn
will have none of it. Their quarrel shocks Olav, at first only
because they are risking candor: "Never had he imagined he
could talk to his wife as to another person of that which had
been growing in his soul for years" (MH, p. 478). But when,
after confessing to her the killing of her lover and then pleading
that he be allowed to confess publicly and lift the weight of
years, Ingunn forbids him: "And you know not how it feels to
have to bend beneath shame and dishonor—*I* know it, *you* have
never tried what it is to be disgraced" (MH, p. 481). Startled
out of his pride, Olav is staggered that Ingunn, whom he has
considered pitiable for so long, has a moral capacity of her own

—but in granting her request for his silence, out of misguided love for her and her honor, he retreats into the arrogance of his guilt.

Away in Oslo, he learns that his sickly wife at last is dying. Hastening into a church, he confronts his ruined life, seeing that

> every sin he had committed, every wound he had inflicted upon himself or others, was one of the stripes his hand had laid upon his God. As he stood here, feeling that his own heart's blood must run black and sluggish in his veins with sorrow, he knew that his own life, full of sin and sorrow, had been one more drop in the cup God drained in Gethsemane (MH, p. 501).

He knows the "truth of what he had been told in childhood: that the sin above all sins is to despair of God's mercy. To deny that heart which the lance had pierced the chance of forgiving" (MH, p. 507).

In the Wilderness finds Olav adrift. Traveling to London for respite from grief, he seems almost mad, one time mistaking a stranger for Ingunn (and fantasizing urgently holding her close), another time attacking a band of robbers with a ferocity that recalls the periodic blood-lust of his youth. Returning to Norway, he is tempted to marry Torhild but dismisses the idea and, as years pass, continues to delay the act of confession he knows would save him. He broods on Ingunn's death:

> In that night, when his grief was such that he could have sweated blood, God had appeared to him, bedewed with the blood of the death agony and the scourging and the nails and the thorns, and He had spoken to him as friend to friend: "O all ye that pass by, behold and see if there be any sorrow like unto my sorrow!" And he had seen his own sin and sorrow as a bleeding gash upon those shoulders. Yet he had not been strong enough to come (MH, p. 583).

One night, Cecilia proves herself too much her father's daughter—knife in hand, she slashes at an insulting drunkard—and, as the third of *Hestviken*'s books progresses, Olav him-

self draws back into battle. Fighting Swedes, he is wounded—
a bolt from a crossbow crushes his jaw. In pain, he has visions
—of Ingunn "like a wave of warmth and sweetness"—but he
has nightmares, too: of "creatures that were neither beast nor
man . . . there was a beggar without feet who darted along at a
terrible pace on boards fixed to his hands and knees . . ." (MH,
p. 714). Olav, even as he ages, still, like the beggar, moves "at a
terrible pace"—unsatisfied and unconsoled, he is restless, and
for all his trial, seems no closer to his rest in God.

The Son Avenger brings him, through agony, to that rest. The
focus has shifted to his son, and in Eirik, the father's faults and
failings return. Lacking the awful weight of Olav—Eirik is
something of a fool and, hence, a little more human—he has
his father's lust, for women, glory, and yet also for God. He
attempts, for a brief, passionate hour, monastic life. Even there,
however, his family past intrudes. As a child he had been bitten
by a stoat wandering Hestviken's barnyard. Olav, with a terrible
combination of tenderness and fury, had amputated the finger.
At the monastery, Eirik learns that this blemish, this "mark
of Cain", forbids him orders. His zeal, too, a fitful version of
his father's, defeats him—wisely the holy novice master maintains that Eirik's instability, manifested in spasmodic devotion,
is not right for religious life. He returns home, in borrowed
clothes that make him look like a lampoon dandy, to his father's
scorn. There, twice disappointed in love, he finally marries a
kind older woman, a Magdalene with a scandalous past.

And Olav is consumed with yet more grief. Cecilia marries
a wastrel—another of the book's many liars (Augustine: "All
sin is a kind of lying"[6]). She determines, after suffering his
indignities, to leave. And then Eirik finds him stabbed in his
bed.

Having once joyed in her combativeness, Olav concludes,
terrified, that his daughter is a killer. And he sees his sin re-
played in hers. He hastens to confession, arranged by a monk,
the son of his best friend. Just as he is at last about to unbur-
den himself, a stroke renders him speechless. Later, Cecilia is

found innocent—her husband was slain by a man avenging an outraged daughter. But Olav's stroke has crippled him, and, even as he sees Cecilia married finally to a good soul, his life ebbs into brooding. Finally, as he dies, he enters, still with his sin only silently confessed, into God.

> For an instant he stared with open eyes straight into the eye of the sun, tried even, wild with love and longing, to gaze yet deeper into God. He sank back in red fire, all about him was a living blaze, and he knew that now the prison tower that he had built around him was burning. But salved by the glance that surrounded him, he would walk out unharmed over the glowing embers of his burned house, into the Vision that is eternal bliss, and the fire that burned him was not so ardent as his longing (MH, p. 985).

The Son Avenger is equally the tale of the son redeemer, as Eirik, after all his Oedipal struggles with Olav, enters the monastery to stay. Not only, as "a barefoot friar", does his life embody his father's deeper strivings, but his love always, if desperately apparent, lives on in his words—he bears witness to Olav with loving stories to Cecilia's children.

The Master of Hestviken is not one thousand pages of gloom. Crags and valleys, the Northern landscape lauds creation; there are many accounts, too, of human virtue—battlefield courage, family constancy, old friendship, joy in food, sleep, and animal delight. And when its characters give in to God, breaking into rapt, mystic near-poetry, the language soars. But the book remains more one of shadows than one of light, of a world seen "through a glass darkly", of horizons dimmed and foreshortened by sin. As against the light dance of David the Psalmist, Francis of Assisi, and Jesus himself in sanctifying love at Cana and in offering up children as moral exemplars, there is the tread of the wayward step in the dark.

"Sin", Bernard Häring writes, "is alienation from one's better self, loss of knowledge of the unique name by which we are called, a plunging into darkness, and a split in the depth of our existence."[7] Orphaned, reared by a contentious, lustful man, Olav is, from the first, an Ishmael, a wanderer. He inherits restlessness and an itch for vainglory, and, when he thirsts for love, he slakes it, not with Sophia or Dante's Beatrice or Francis' Clare, but with Ingunn, whose very weakness saps him of power. Augustine distinguishes between the heedless enjoyment of the things of the world and the correct employment of them for spiritual progress: Olav's sadness increases as he soon loses any delight in Ingunn while persisting in using her as a shield against God—convinced that confessing his own sin would shame her, he condescendingly takes her sin upon himself and, in a life of indulgent guilt, never trusts God sufficiently to know that he is compelled through love and the cross to forgive. His apostasy is indeed terrible:

> If we willfully persist in sin after receiving the knowledge of the truth, no sacrifice for sin remains: only a terrifying expectation of judgment and fierce fire will consume God's enemies. . . . Think how much more severe a penalty that man will deserve who has trampled underfoot the Son of God, profaned the blood of the covenant by which he was consecrated, and affronted God's gracious Spirit (Heb 10:26–30).

Undset, with orthodox insistence on personal responsibility, makes clear that Olav deserves his punishment: he is hemmed about by warriors and reprobates, his religious training is poor, but he has had, from his youth, not only the example of priests and monks, but an inborn knowledge of, and tendency toward, God. Where he is weakest is in his appalling ignorance of and trust in those "words of God", his fellow creatures and himself. Never warm, never graced with the "optimism that is common in the New Testament",[8] he knows his wife only as a victim and near child, never as a woman and partner in moral struggle; his son is less to him a boy than a hapless reminder of his own sin, a cursed symbol. Forgoing Christ, Olav inevitably cuts himself off from the human love that is, as Mother Teresa holds, always a form of Christ's love in disguise. As an old man, he ponders his life's choices, only to find that they were not so much exercises in free will as a surrender to moral blindness, moral stupidity. For all his strain, he never worked hard enough to know that he had only to give in to God. As a young man, he had felt that:

> He himself had chosen the bitter lot of Cain, and he had chosen it of necessity, since he was to be the master and protector of the frail, weak-minded wife to whom he had been bound as a child. And yet he had had to do violence to himself many a time before he should act as a hard man—gag the voice of his own conscience . . . (MH, p. 590).

Only later does he see that:

> He had said to himself he was playing for a high stake—and he had not been playing, he had merely shuffled the draughts-men like a witless child. He had not *chosen* the lot of Cain: he himself had never known *when* he made a choice. . . . Weak, hasty, short-sighted, sleek-skinned, and spiritually yet a babe . . . (MH, pp. 590-91).

Spiritually immature, with "his stubborn obstinacy and his mute, cold defiance" (MH, p. 590), he is deluded (Häring: "sin is an enemy of sanity")[9] about himself, mistaking pride for strength, and mistaking for humility and service a capitulation to the world's judgment and a carelessness for his soul. Only late in life does he discover:

> That a man should love his even Christian as himself he had always heard and seen to be right. . . . But as when a painted window is lighted up by the sun, so that one can distinguish the images in it, so did he perceive in a flash the meaning of God's command, clear and straightforward, that a man must also love himself (MH, p. 795).

There is irony in Undset's calling Olav "The Master of Hestviken". While she emphasizes that he discharges his duties capably, there is too little of love in his stewardship to mark him as a true master. Too often he acts, or fails to act, for the world's eyes. And every bond or obligation becomes less a loving work than a burden, a cross. In refusing God's love, he not only gives up joy but gives in to a form of idolatry, paying, in violation of Matthew 6:28 ("Consider the lilies of the field . . .") too much heed to the world's work. Ironically, too, this wrongheaded concern gains him neither the warmth of community nor an end to worry: Olav always frets. What he fails to understand is that, in keeping with the Golden Rule and the doctrine of the Mystical Body, we exist for one another's sake for the realizing of the Kingdom—too proud to seek help, Olav himself helps only out of duty, grudge, honor, pride.

What ultimately readies Olav for redemption is his wrestling with sin itself, with realizing how, according to Van der Leeuw, sin provides near occasions for achieving the "closest proximity" with God. Ever since interpreting the Fall from Eden as the *felix culpa* that provoked Christ's salvific life and sacrifice, radical Christian insight has held that human failing, rather than leading us inevitably to despair, can prod us to God. Paul, Augustine, Francis—none was a stranger to Luther's injunction to "Sin bravely!" before they embraced Jesus. With Christ's death on the cross, tragedy—sin unforgiven, pain without surcease —has become impossible, and it remains a Christian's work, assisted by the grace of hope, to accept that even in the face of sin, there is enlightenment, love, release. The Good Shepherd rejoices especially over the sheep that was lost. Sin need not be an end, a death, but may so break the heart open to Love that it spurs a new birth, a resurrection.

"Sin," Ricoeur writes, "as alienation from oneself, is an experience even more astonishing, disconcerting, and scandalous, perhaps, than the spectacle of nature, and for this reason it is the richest source of interrogative thought."[10] The fiercest, truest prayer emerges from "out of the depths", and it is only from those depths that Olav discovers that ". . . I know my transgressions / and my sin is ever before me. / Against thee, thee only, have I sinned . . ." (Ps 51:4). Passing through the suffering set loose by his sins, as if withstanding a long night's journey, deepens Olav—and the suffering finally breaks him of pride.

If Olav, in his arrogance, draws Ingunn's sin upon himself, misreads both his daughter's character and his son's love solely in the light of his own failings, he is also helped, many times without his knowing or against his wishes, toward redemption through their agency. Ingunn does wreak from him a pity that, for all its insufficiency, does prepare him to receive God's pity. And his children's lives develop from and improve upon his struggles. Cecilia's first marriage is indeed disastrous, but her second one is strong and real, and her fighting spirit is a more legitimate one than Olav's—she defends herself; she does not murder. Eirik's first fitful attempt at the religious life and his final peace with it magnify and resolve Olav's own journey into the peace of God; Eirik is lusty like his father, but he catches himself before disaster—his marriage is a good one, no matter how his wife's past affronts conventional society. It is, then, through the lives of characters other than *Hestviken*'s principal that the moral balance of the book's world is finally righted— and that, too, is a lesson in humility.

Perhaps the original sin in the story is that of Olav's and Ingunn's fathers making a game of marriage—promising children to each other out of whim and thoughtlessness. But what they set in motion not only comes, in a very human way, out of mixed motivations (adopting Olav is an act of true kindness on Steinfinn's part) but does provide a basis for the workings of grace. In a Greek tragedy, Olav and Ingunn would be indeed fated for each other—and fated for doom. In this very Christian tale, however, another relationship is more primary than that of Ingunn and Olav—the relationship of God to each and all of the characters. Freely given and freely chosen, God's love and each character's response to it means that there is no pre- destined end: there is hope, responsibility, choice. Olav makes a hell of his life by resisting that love, but it is in the fury of his resistance that he comes to know that he is loved nonethe- less, and that that love overcomes all resistance. The long tragic chain of sin—from Steinfinn's illegitimate marriage to Olav's and Ingunn's drastic love and the two murders Olav commits in defense of it—is broken, in the end, by surrender into love.

This historical novel then ends with the realization that history itself is neither fate nor accident. It is, rather, along the lines of Teilhard de Chardin, an ongoing act of revelation, a work of faith and of hope, a trial indeed, but one which love redeems. For, as Paul says, "The word of God is not fettered" (2 Tim 2:9) and even "If we are faithless, he remains faithful —for he cannot deny himself" (2 Tim 2:13).

NOTES

[1] Gerardus van der Leeuw, *Religion in Essence and Manifestation*, trans. J. E. Turner (Princeton, N.J.: Princeton University Press, 1986), p. 524.

[2] Sigrid Undset, *The Master of Hestviken*, 4 vols., trans. A. G. Chater (New York: New American Library, 1978); hereafter referred to as MH.

[3] Paul Ricoeur, *The Symbolism of Evil*, trans. Emerson Buchanan (New York: Beacon Press, 1969), p. 52.

[4] St. Augustine, *Free Choice of the Will*, trans. Robert Russell, O.S.A. (Washington, D.C.: The Catholic University of America Press, 1962), p. 162.

[5] St. Thomas Aquinas, *Commentary on the Gospel of St. Matthew* in *The Book of Catholic Quotations*, ed. John Chapin (New York: Farrar, Straus and Cudahy, 1956), p. 386.

[6] St. Augustine, "Against Lying", *Treatises on Various Subjects*, trans. Harold B. Jaffee (Washington, D.C.: Fathers of the Church, 1952), p. 164.

[7] Bernard Häring, *Free and Faithful in Christ:* vol. 1, *General Moral Theology* (New York: Crossroad, 1984), p. 260.

[8] Ibid., p. 399.

[9] Ibid., p. 259.

[10] Ricoeur, p. 8.

MSGR. EDWARD A. SYNAN

CHURCH AND CONSCIENCE:
THE WITNESS OF SIGRID UNDSET

Everyone will concede that artists, of whom Sigrid Undset was one of the very greatest, ought to be approached with reverence by academics. This weighs heavily on me—no master of literature, unacquainted with the very language in which Sigrid Undset wrote, and so doomed to work from translations. Excellent though the English versions seem to be, these remain translations nonetheless. *Kristin Lavransdatter*, in the Alfred A. Knopf "Borzoi Book" edition of 1988 which is cited here, has been the work of two translators, Charles Archer for the second and third component novels, but with Charles Archer and J. S. Scott for the first, whereas a single translator, Arthur G. Chater, is responsible for the four novels that comprise the Olav Audunsson matching 1952 "Borzoi Book" edition of the *The Master of Hestviken*.[1] Even the best of academics would be in an uncomfortable position in attempting to reduce an art that transcends the abstractions of the Academy to the standard conceptions of any discipline. For parallels we may think of a professor of gross anatomy faced with the Belvedere Apollo or the Venus de Milo, of a geometrician attempting to account for the marvel that is the cathedral at Chartres, of a chemist challenged to account for the portraits in the National Gallery.

And yet, and yet . . . one thinks of the precious studies that have been occasioned by that masterpiece, medieval in origin as well as in theme, the Bayeux tapestry. Those studies have illumined armor and tactics, ships and clothing; that embroidered programme suggests a justification for the cross-channel invasion and even contains an obscure whiff of scandal: Who was AELFGYVA? Who was VNVS CLERICVS? Was the gesture of that cleric a blow or a caress? Are the grotesque little figures in the border below them the key to the puzzle?

So it is with Sigrid Undset's *Kristin Lavransdatter* and *The Master of Hestviken*. Our conclusions and analyses may well be clumsy, they will hardly be worthy of those epic novels; still, time spent in the presence of such works cannot be wasted. During the next forty minutes or so, please bear with an effort to establish the poles around which turn the lives of the fictional characters she has made more real to us than are many of our contemporaries. Those poles, it will be claimed, are two: conscience and Church. What were the conscientious travails that are worked out as the narratives proceed? On what grounds did the cast of characters make the decisions that constituted their lives? In what form was the Church present to those who struggled with aspirations and temptations, with disasters, with tragedy and stupidity, with sin and remorse, with malice and charity, with the laws, both human and divine?

This is not the place to summarize—if, indeed, the thing can be done!—the procession of memorable persons, the choreography of their passage through the turnings of Sigrid Undset's narratives. Her two medieval novels are in fact seven, for *Kristin Lavransdatter* is a trilogy and *The Master of Hestviken* comprises four full-length novels. So broad is this embarrassment of choice that it seems practical to concentrate on evidence from *Kristin Lavransdatter* without, however, neglecting parallels from *The Master of Hestviken*. No attempt will be made to "cover" the wealth of these two enormous works. To choose and to pursue points of focus that may offer hope of unlocking the author's intent is my modest aim.

Omnipresent, and more than background, the medieval Norwegian Church dominated, not without opposition, the horizons, near and far, of noble and peasant, of laymen as well as of clerks. Sorrow and tragedy and disasters were interpreted, accepted, opposed, somehow lived through, in her shadow. Her

Pope in "Romaborg" could do much, but not quite everything; there was the matter of a valid marriage, for instance, that not even he could touch:

> If we besought—the Archbishop—on our knees—promised to do penance—? . . . No man can sunder the bond there is between you, so that Olav could freely take another wife—not even the Pope in Romaborg, as I believe (MH, p. 280).

Far horizons, taken for granted in the Church, staggered the imagination, not only of peasants and serfs, but of landowners, so tied they were to their farms and granges and families. Olav Audunsson was of good birth and of some wealth; where had he been in comparison with churchmen? The Scandinavian kingdoms might seem large: only ships and skis and changes of horses could traverse them. Their dynastic transitions and wars might seem to be towering historical matters, fit material for sagas; still, he reflected:

> [I]t was a very small and narrow piece of the world he knew. These churchmen, they sent letters and messengers north, south, east, and west; in less than six weeks they managed to get word. . . . In the church were books and candlesticks from France, silk curtains from Sicily sent hither by a pope, woven tapestries from Arras, relics of martyrs and confessors who had lived in Engelland and Asia . . . great schools in Paris and Bologna, where a man might learn all the arts and wisdom in the world—in Salerno one could learn the Greek tongue and how to become proof against steel or poison (MH, p. 120).

Comedy itself fell back upon the Church. Children screamed with laughter as one of them, grandson of the parish priest, parodied his grandfather's mass and marrying and baptizing. First he married the child Kristin to a young boy, then caught a piglet, anointed it with mud and poured rain water over it. Full of his success, he then ranted that the baptized "child" had been begotten in Lent—the parents must "pay penalty for their sin to the priest". Kristin all but wept at this grossness, the grandfather came upon them as he returned from visiting the sick and exploded with rage. . . (KL, pp. 7, 8). When a friar in his cups told a priest, who was equally gone in drink, that St. Thomas of Canterbury had been granted a vision of hell and had been astonished to find no rebellious priests there, the priest countered that mendicant friars came out from under the devil's tail "like wasps out of a wasp-nest". The aristocratic Lady Aashild made peace at the same feast between two priests who had come to blows because one had leveled an accusation of near witchcraft against herself and the other had undertaken her defense. She diverted them all with "a merry tale of a misadventure" in old time when a woman could be rendered a maid by a magic wash: It was used on the wrong lady and with the worst of effects. All this she capped with " 'tis best we cease before the talk grows unseemly and gross; let us bear in mind 'tis a holy day" (KL, pp. 52, 53).

There is yet another device that will lend focus to our examination. As Job has reminded all biblical believers, human life is a campaigning, a *militia* (Job 7:1). In every epoch that campaigning is against three ancient enemies: the world, the flesh, and the devil. All three play their role in Sigrid Undset's Norway, for, across her pages, all three strive against Church and God. Members of the Church, targets as we are of those three enemies, we make our imperfect responses thanks to conscience. This dual focus on Church and conscience is expressed nowhere better in the two novels than in the reflections of the young Olav Audunsson, waiting in the guest-house of the Preaching Friars for the Bishop's judgment on his questionable marital status. Goaded into a brawl, Olav had struck his tormentor a death-blow with his ax. In doubled jeopardy, for this added manslaughter to the issue that first had brought him before the Bishop's bench, Olav reflected on law and on honor, on Church and chivalry:

> Olav's mind rose in revolt against all these new doctrines . . . they were unnatural, impossible dreams. *All* men could never be such saints as to consent to submit all their concerns, great and small, to the judgment of their even Christians, always be-

ing satisfied with the law and with *receiving* their rights—never
taking them for themselves (MH, p. 134).

However deficient a theologian, a decretist, or even a civil
magistrate might find these musings, Olav in his fashion was
forming his conscience as, indeed, owing to an addled conscience he had blundered into his web of marital irregularities.
All but innocent errors of judgment had brought him into
the friars' convent to hear the Bishop's judgment. Well might
the Bishop count Olav's "conscience" incorrect; still Olav had
shown a kind of minimum good will. His marital difficulties
had arisen because his father, already ill unto death, and on that
account sober at a feast where all his friends were somewhat
gone in drink, had espoused him, well before the age of discretion, to an even younger child. In a society that gave parents
absolute control over their children's marriages, Olav, rightly
or wrongly, had been convinced that he could never marry
another—his father had confirmed the espousal the next day
when the girl's father was sober. On his father's death, Olav
was taken in as a foster-son by the family of his affianced bride.
When the two principals reached adolescence, Olav was assured
that he could never marry any other; on this ground Olav in-
ferred that he was, in fact, authorized to deal with his affianced
bride as if a formal wedding had taken place.

From this misconception of the law stemmed all of Olav's
troubles: not only his summons to the Bishop for judgment on
his case, but also his vulnerability to the unmannerly jeers of
the man who had died, thanks to a blow from Olav's ax; nor did
it end there. Like usurious interest on an evil principal, there
followed his flight into outlawry and exile (MH, pp. 139–46),
to be rectified by his payment of blood-money to the kinsmen
of his victim (MH, pp. 191, 193, 227). This episode is but a
vignette of the total working out of Olav's life. His dubiously
espoused and notably light-minded wife had been seduced and
was with child by a vagabond Icelander who could not be
counted on to hold his tongue. Olav had taken vengeance on

the seducer, killed him in a quarrel that Olav himself had provoked, burned the mountain hut in which the killing had taken
place to conceal both the body and the deed. After all, Olav
had killed in battle many a man better than this babbler (MH,
pp. 271–73)!

There followed long years of uneasy relations with Eirik, the
child his wife had borne her Icelandic paramour, years during
which Olav was counted silent and moody by his neighbors,
as, indeed, he was. Yet at the end, after Olav's death, this illegitimate son, Eirik, entered the order of the Friars Minor; Eirik's
wife took herself to the convent. Soon Eirik died as well, a
victim of the Black Death of the mid-fourteenth century. Olav
had suffered through a lifetime of conscientious malaise, concealing the murder of the Icelander who had fathered his wife's
bastard son, concealing that bastardy to the disadvantage of his
legitimate off-spring: "I had no right to do it—give away my
daughter's inheritance as amends to the child of a stranger—"
(MH, p. 480). Never could he escape into tranquillity of conscience.

So it was with Kristin Lavransdatter. She, too, felt a degree
of responsibility, but for a death she had not caused. Returning
home furtively from an imprudent, though innocent, meeting
with a life-long friend, she had been threatened by a violent
and lustful grandson of the village priest; Kristin had saved herself by stunning him with a heavy stone. When later he and
her friend became embroiled in a quarrel, Kristin's attacker
stabbed him to death (KL, pp. 67–73). If Kristin was willing
to assert her innocence in the ordeal of putting her hand into
a flame (KL, p. 81), she also sobbed "It *is* my fault that Arne
is dead . . ." (KL, p. 82).

There was worse: Kristin had been betrothed by her parents
to one Simon Darre—solid and rich, but less than overwhelmingly attractive—in accord with the law of the land and, what
was more, a law supported by the Church. Her Franciscan
friend and counsellor, the saintly Brother Edvin, assured her:
". . . them [her parents] had God set over you before you

met him" (KL, p. 141). "Him", for Kristin had fallen into a passionate love affair with the handsome, but reckless, Erlend Nikulaussön; he had rescued her, along with a flighty young woman, from two threatening German ruffians. All this took place while Kristin was still at the Oslo convent where she had been sent by her parents in the aftermath of the death she had occasioned rather than caused. Nor was this the end of the matter; she was found to be with child by Erlend. Simon Darre agreed to the dissolution of their betrothal, and her marriage to Erlend went forward. To the end, Simon, married to Kristin's sister, remained Kristin's faithful friend.

Kristin's very presence in the Oslo convent was not without its conscientious dimension, although, to be sure, nothing came of it. Her younger sister, Ulvhild, had been crippled for life in a mishap due to a runaway bull. It was understood that her destiny was to be the cloister (KL, p. 60). The thought more than crossed Kristin's mind that perhaps Brother Edvin's observation that "nowadays 'twas only marred and crippled children . . . that their fathers and mothers gave to God" might bear upon herself:

> —she strove against the thought that God would do a miracle for Ulvhild if she herself turned nun. . . . She did not love God and His Mother, and the Saints *so* much, did not even wish to love them so—she loved the world and longed for the world (KL, pp. 61, 62).

With these references to the world in its feudal form and to the perennial sting of the flesh in place, it is possible to look at the role played by evil spirits in this vision of medieval Christian Norway. The first appearance of the demonic in the life of Kristin came to her as a child in a vision of an "Elf-maiden", or "dwarf-maiden", one of the pre-Christian "mountain people", or trolls; it is a measure of the depth of this persistent conviction that her father, the saintly and commonsensical Lavrans, took it seriously indeed (KL, pp. 16–18). Kristin herself would recall the experience as an adult (KL, pp. 47, 48; p. 660). In a different context, Kristin would hear in a saint's life, read in the refectory of the convent in Oslo, a reference to the demonic as the "divine" of pagans. St. Theodora was on the way to her violation in a house of ill-fame, brought there by a pagan ruler; he offered her the alternative of joining the service of a "heathen goddess whom they called Diana". Theodora, of course, did not accept the proffered escape: "Were I to serve the devil-woman whom you call Diana . . .", her chastity, she cried, would be as a "rusty lamp without flame or oil". Theodora's rescuer was the knight St. Didymus; wearing his somewhat anachronistic "coat of mail" as a disguise, she escaped. As Didymus went to execution, Theodora joined him voluntarily, and both were beheaded on the same day, April 28, 1304—all this on the authority of St. Ambrose (KL, pp. 93–95). What counts here is the identification of a pagan divinity as a "devil-woman", an identification made standard by St. Augustine (the most celebrated convert Ambrose ever made) in his *City of God*, books 8–11. The gods and goddesses of the Pantheon, Augustine there held, are but the fallen angels of Scripture; far from unreal, they are demons.

This by no means exhausts the presence of the diabolic in the Norway of Kristin and of Olav. Lady Aashild, it has been seen, was thought by some to have used witchcraft (perhaps to have murdered her first husband by poison, but to have attracted a second by black arts) (KL, pp. 37, 38, 50, 51, 360). The official Church is represented as not overly concerned with popular conviction on such matters. Charges might lead to investigation, but such an investigation could break up in laughter and good humor, as Kristin's Erlend managed when called in for questioning that bore on gossip concerning an old man from his Wardenship (KL, pp. 527–31).

What was more serious, and it was a matter that burdened Kristin's conscience, was her desperate recourse to the occult in order to save a child of the Simon Darre to whom she once had been betrothed. Not even for her own child would she have "dared to try this last shift of all", but Simon, she knew, had taken at her "hands more than a man may take with honour unabated". Into the graveyard she had gone for a strip of turf, buried in its place her grandmother's betrothal ring, and laid the strip of graveyard earth on the child's breast. When the baby stirred to push it off, she burned the "demon-ware" in the open fire (KL, pp. 681–87; 741). The child recovered.

Simple superstitions paled beside this violation of conscience —the dew, for example, she had gathered with Lady Aashild for her crippled sister's washing, "dew that had more virtue if gathered by an innocent maid", as the child Kristin then was (KL, pp. 47, 48), or belief that yearning "sorely for another" might effect a forewarning to that other (KL, p. 677), or the conviction of neighbors that Lady Aashild and her husband Sir Björne walked after death on the land where they had lived— and so would no one live there (KL, p. 725). The same view (that such convictions did no harm) might have been thought of the three "warnings" of impending doom that Olav and a monastic cook, Brother Helge, noticed: the shaving cut Olav could not staunch, the "singing" of his fatal axe, "Kinfetch", the bird that flew in the door. Had those ominous "signs" not been followed by the journey during which the adulterous Icelander would die at Olav's hand (MH, pp. 262, 263)?

As for the world that Kristin so loved and for which she longed, it was the world of feudalism, a society in which one's oath of fealty committed reciprocally vassal and overlord, king and earl. In that world a knight wore gilded spurs, a squire silver; the gentry bore splendid arms; peasants fought with clubs or knives. Olav reminded Teit, his own bride's seducer, when he impudently offered to marry her and to acknowledge her child, that "an unmarried woman's child follows the mother" and ". . . we will never give her away outside our own rank" (MH, p. 258). Social strata must be maintained intact. It was the world in which Olav, having given his word, would not "wriggle out of my marriage", despite his bride's infidelity and attempted suicide (MH, p. 289). In that world the wildly imprudent Erlend, despite his well-developed sense of honor, came to grief. Having organized a plot to bring in Haakon, the young half-brother of the new King Magnus, to rule Norway in place of Magnus, Erlend engaged in an illicit assignation. The woman read a compromising letter Erlend had left about (KL, p. 576); "how could I have thought she could read writing? She seemed—most unlearned—" (KL, p. 622). Arrested, Erlend was racked by imported torturers ("Frenchmen doubtless", KL, p. 619), or perhaps "Moorish" ones (KL, p. 623)—in violation, it was held, of Norway's laws and customs. The other side of the coin that was his character meant that under torture he said not a word that would betray his fellow-conspirators (KL, pp. 619–38). If Kristin could endure repeatedly the pangs of childbirth, Erlend said, he would bear the rack (KL, p. 623). Friends intervened for him with the new King, and Erlend escaped with his life but not with his property; his estates went to the crown (KL, p. 597). Kristin and he and their sons then lived on her father's more modest holding, Jörundgaard, which she had inherited.

Their Norway was notably xenophobic. Germans were generally cast in a bad light. The core of the attacking forces at an assault on a bridge where Olav was grievously wounded were German mercenaries, fighting for the Duke Eirik in his 1308 invasion of Norway; two Germans had threatened Kristin and her friend, and from those louts Erlend had saved them both. Of all the Germans who appear in the two novels, only one comes off well. Claus Wiephart was a merchant who had entered into a business partnership with Olav (MH, pp. 497, 524), and it was his leechcraft—learned from Saracens, whose prisoner he had been (MH, pp. 464–66)—that helped in the partial healing of Olav's wound after the battle at the bridge (MH, p. 716). Danes Erlend knew well, thanks to his service in Denmark; he counted them cruel and relentless in warfare (MH, pp. 370, 371). The single Fleming in either chronicle was seen through by the urbane Erlend. When that Flemish knight offered service as his squire to a son of Kristin and Erlend (the boy had been urged to speak in Latin to the strange knight and was glad to parade his ability to do so), Sir Allart gave the boy a costly gift. He seemed "something too *kurteis*" to Erlend; Kristin's husband had caught the scent of the Cities of the Plain (KL, pp. 783–86). Russians and Karelians were the object of defensive fighting, and Erlend hanged eighteen of the latter; had he enjoyed a better reputation for prudence, Erlend might have headed a crusade against those northern "heretics and heathens" for the High Steward (KL, pp. 436–38). In England Olav met with an attempted seduction by a rich wife whose husband was away from home; to Olav's indignation, he recognized the husband as a blind man with whom, some days before, he had tried with small success to speak Latin (MH, pp. 567–82). On the way to his ship in her berth by Thamesside, Olav was all but caught in a forest by English robbers (MH, pp. 594–97). We have seen that when King Magnus had rackmasters "put Erlend to the question by torture", they were either Frenchmen or Moors (KL, pp. 619, 620, 623).

For Sigrid Undset's medieval Norwegians, the Church in her full extent was, of course, all who believed, all who had been baptized; everyone is "even Christian". Within that vast and all but universal community, some Christians represented faith and morals in a special mode. These were the clergy, the friars, nuns, monks, and, above all, the bishops. The Bishop of Rome presided over an enormous, sacred analogue to kingdoms and empire that was more than merely a bureaucracy. For most Christians the first point of contact was also the most permanent and the most influential. This was the parish priest. Often loved and admired, his virtues and vices, his education and talents, were known intimately and routinely discussed. Sira Eirik, for instance, was parish priest of Kristin's Jörundgaard and a great friend of her pious father. His parishioners were not much disturbed by the fact that this former man-at-arms had a slaying in his past, to say nothing of "three children by the woman who tended his house". The Gregorian Reform with its law of celibacy for priests had come late to Norway; people easily made allowance for a pastor as knowledgeable as

Sira Eirik. They were realists all the same, and his avarice escaped the notice of none (KL, pp. 76, 807, 808). Sira Eirik's
grandson Bentein, also a priest, was another matter. Sly and
avaricious, forward with women, he was the one who had
threatened Kristin one winter's night on a lonely road and, in
the end, stabbed to death her childhood friend with whom her
meeting had been innocent; for this he would surely hang (KL,
pp. 67–75). The Bishop, who had noticed Eirik's aptitude for
learning while still a man-at-arms under ban for a slaying, had
not been wrong to forward his preparation for the priesthood.
In addition to the learning required by his liturgical functions,
Sira Eirik was a most skillful leech—the first to be called in
when Kristin's sister, Ulvhild, met with her crippling accident;
somewhat reserved on their calling in the Lady Aashild with
her reputation for witchcraft, he was willing to hold his tongue
on the matter (KL, pp. 38–40).

Such a parish priest might be enlisted to instruct children.
Sira Eirik had instructed Kristin: "had taught her her books
and writing. . ." (KL, p. 57). So too, "Erlend's house-priest at
Husaby had taught the three elder sons their books. . . ." Later,
in a monastery, two of Erlend's sons did even better with an
"aged monk":

> [They] became so skilled that the monk had rarely need to speak
> to them in the Norse tongue, and, when their parents came to
> fetch them, they both could answer the priest in Latin, glibly
> and without many slips (KL, p. 782).

Their education led to the collecting of books: five from
Jörundgaard, three from Erlend's parents and another from his
Dominican brother—one that he had commissioned himself.
This last contained materials on St. Olav and his miracles, other
saints' lives, and, what must have been of enormous interest to
Kristin, a submission from the Oslo Franciscans to the Pope,
requesting the canonization of Brother Edvin Rikardsson. This
considerable library was rounded out with a prayer-book, given
to Erlend by Sira Eiliv. Kristin had less success with the educa-

tion of her younger sons, despite her efforts: she felt a degree of learning would be "fitting for men of their birth" (KL, pp. 782–83).

Olav, too, had a striking and virile parish priest, Sira Hall-björn. Impressive at the altar, thanks to his resonant voice, he was even more impressive as a warrior. When the Duke Eirik threatened the countryside, Sira Hallbjörn was in his element: "easier for him to mix with worldly lords and knights than with priests and countrymen" (MH, p. 696). With Olav he went to the defense of their countryside, helmeted and in his hauberk, wearing baldric and sword; he carried for good measure an English longbow and a quiverful of arrows over his shoulder. This priest was "arrayed", Olav joked, "to sing a man's requiem"— to this the priest answered with the words of Qoheleth: *Tempus occidendi, et tempus sanandi*, "A time to kill and a time to heal" (Qo 3:3), and he glossed his text with the judgment that "Ecclesiastes—'tis one of the bravest books in scripture" (MH, p. 682). He and Olav scouted the enemy positions (MH, pp. 683–86). Olav took the priest to task for having given away their presence to the enemy with an incautious bow-shot, but, when Sira Hallbjörn gave his analysis of the tactical options open to the defenders, Olav announced: "I say the priest is right . . ." (MH, p. 701). In the end, Sira Hallbjörn left his naked, plundered corpse on the field (MH, p. 713). When the fighting was done, however, Olav felt an unaccustomed joy; wounded he was, but: "No pain could take from him the joy of having had the chance to stand up and act and fight for his home and his native soil against the strangers who poured over it. . . . He was glad, deeply and cordially glad, as he had not been since he was young" (MH, p. 715).

The presence of the Church, thanks to her parish priests, was supplemented by religious, by friars and monks. Although a number of other orders file across Sigrid Undset's pages, Franciscans and Dominicans are understandably the most visible. It was the era of the mendicant orders. Chief among the Franciscan "Minorites" is Brother Edvin, an artist who traveled through the country-side painting and carving altar pieces and the rest, but also generating an awed veneration for his holiness. From her childhood Kristin had known him. When her father took her to Hamar where he had business to transact, after Mass in a church so huge that it seemed to her as though she had gone "into a mountainside" (KL, p. 23), Lavrans left her with Brother Edvin, who, said Canon Martein, "draws to himself all the children he can. . . . 'Tis in this wise he gets someone to preach to—" (KL, p. 26). His "preaching" to Kristin was to take her into the church building on which he was working, having first handled with good humor the peevish complaints of some undeserving poor (KL, pp. 27–28; there is a parallel to this, late in Kristin's life, p. 1015). Edvin took the child up to the scaffolding, from which she could see, for the first time in her life, a stained glass window. He showed her the altars dedicated to St. Olav and to St. Thomas of Canterbury. He answered her childish questions, amused her with his imitations of animals speaking Latin: "—all the beasts could talk Latin in those days . . ." (KL, pp. 29–33). It was then he made the remark she was to remember long years later:

> Tis thus that folk deal with their children now. To God they give the daughters who are lame or purblind or ugly. . . . And then they wonder that all who dwell in the cloisters are not holy men and maids— (KL, p. 33).

Poor in the extreme, infested with lice, Brother Edvin was often under disciplinary restrictions from his superiors—when Kristin consulted him years later on her involvement with Erlend, Brother Edvin "had been strictly forbidden to hear confession" (KL, p. 140). He counselled her without absolution; he did not count it against his restriction to reverse the prohibition and to confess to her on his own part that "God's mercy alone have I to thank that I am not called manslayer. . . ." In a quarrel between the begging friars and the Bishop over a church building on which Edvin had been working, the Bishop's men destroyed his work and he had struck at a man with his hammer; "I could not contain me. . . ." (KL, pp. 142–43). In the end, Brother Edvin died with a serious reputation for sanctity on all sides; this reputation was such as to generate a pious warfare between the Preaching Friars, among whom he died, and the Barefoot Friars, of whose number he had been, over whether Dominicans or Franciscans had the right to keep his body. He was venerated by all under the name of St. Evan (KL, p. 236). His own brethren did not neglect to send an appeal to Rome for a more official status of Friar Edvin as a saint.

Bishops appear frequently in the pages of these chronicles. Only in the case of Brother Edvin's passage with a Bishop's man is it possible to infer an unfavorable estimate of these spiritual lords in the polity of medieval Norway. When the Archbishop Eiliv Korten summoned Erlend on the matter of witchcraft in his Wardenship mentioned above, the old and feeble Archbishop matched the roaring laughter of the lay lords at Erlend's reference to the well-known difficulties in love of one of their number with an old man's response: "The Archbishop tittered a little, coughing and shaking his head. It was well known that Sir Ivar's will had ever been better than his fortune in certain matters" (KL, p. 531). The investigation then came to nothing. Matters of this sort would be handled with less percipience three or four hundred years later in Paris and in Salem.

No prelate who appears in this shelf of novels is more sympathetic than Bishop Torfinn, the Dominican Bishop of Hamar. It was before him that Olav was summoned in the matter of his espousal and of his somewhat summary interpretation of what its consequences might have been. Owing to this Bishop's reputation for guarding the laws of the Church, Olav was not anxious to put the case in his hands: "In Bishop Torfinn's? I trow not *I* can look for much mercy of *him*." On "whether marriage be marriage or not . . .", his friend Arnvid assured him, "none has the right to judge but the fathers of the Church" (MH, p. 98). Thinking of all that he had been told of Bishop Torfinn, Olav was afraid of the Bishop (MH, pp. 98–102). Yet he was received kindly by the "little young man . . . clad in a greyish-white monk's frock which was a little different from that of the preaching friars . . . not so young after all. . . . It was impossible to guess his age" (MH, p. 103). When the Lord Torfinn heard that Olav had been orphaned in childhood, his words are worth citing at length:

> You know well, Olav, that motherless and friendless you are not —no Christian man is that. You, as we all, have the mightiest brother in Christ our Lord, and His Mother is your mother— and with her, I trust, is she, your mother who bore you. I have always thought that the Lady Sancta Maria prays yet more to her Son for those children who must grow up motherless here below than for us others.—True it is that none should forget who are our nearest and mightiest kin . . . (MH, pp. 107–8).

There was another side to the excellence of Bishop Torfinn, and it would seem that this meant more to Olav than did that prelate's canonical expertise and holiness of life:

> Olav thought he had never seen a man who sat his horse more freely and handsomely than the lord Torfinn. And in every way a lordly house was kept, though the Bishop himself lived so strictly—every guest who came to the palace was sumptuously entertained; every serving-man was given strong ale every day and mead on holy-days. At the table in the Bishop's guest-hall wine was served, and when the lord Torfinn himself ate with the guests he specially wished to honour, he had a great silver tankard set on the board before him. During the whole meal his cup-bearer stood by his high seat and filled the tankard as often as the Bishop gave him a sign. It was a fine sight, thought Olav, to see Lord Torfinn take the cup, sip it, bowing with graceful courtesy toward him with whom he drank, and give it to be borne to him whom he honoured thus (MH, p. 111).

If, as it seems, Church and conscience are the poles around which these accounts turn, then in what does the art of Sigrid Undset consist? This is not an easily answered question, since it is the *proprium*, the essential characteristic, of art to conceal itself—and this too is an art. To begin with the form, every medievalist will recognize that she has adopted and adapted the form used by medieval chroniclers, their effort to provide a straightforward and factual account, in the main without patent editorializing. One passage will make a number of points on this side of Sigrid Undset's work. When, at the end of her life, Kristin was fulfilling a kind of novitiate with the nuns she hoped to join, she heard read in the convent refectory, a book

> in the Norse tongue of the life of Christ, made by the general of the Minorites, the most learned and godly doctor Bonaventura. And while Kristin listened to it, and her eyes filled with tears as she thought how blessed they must be who could love Christ and His Mother, pains and afflictions, poverty and humility, in such wise as was there written—yet all the time she could not but remember the day at Husaby when Gunnulf and Sira Eiliv had shown her the Latin book from which this was taken. 'Twas a thick little book, written upon parchment so thin and shining white that she had never believed calfskin could be wrought so fine; and there were the fairest pictures and capital letters in it, the colours glowing like jewels against the gold. And while she looked, Gunnulf spoke laughingly, and Sira Eiliv gave assent with his quiet smile—of how the buying of this book left them so penniless, they had to sell their clothes and get them meat along with the alms-folk in a cloister, till they came to know that some Norse churchmen were come to Paris, and made shift to raise a loan from them (KL, p. 1011).

This mention of a Bonaventurean "life of Christ" (and indeed of the Mother of Jesus) is an extreme instance of how deeply Sigrid Undset has entered into the spirit of medieval chronicles. Is such a work to be found among the authentic writings of the Seraphic Doctor? Could the reference be to his *Lignum vitae*?[2] No doubt, too, with ingenuity one might manage to paste together such a compilation from his devotional, as distinguished from his technical, theological, works. What is much more probable, and it is tempting to think that this is the work our author had in mind, is a *Meditaciones de passione Christi olim sancto Bonaventurae attributae*, more than once translated into modern languages and now ascribed to a Franciscan from Italy, contemporary with Kristin and the rest.[3] Whatever the identity of the work may be, the description of the manuscript book of Kristin's memory is impeccable.

Is it necessary to remark that these long fictional works have a value that outstrips questions of whether an obscure book can be identified? Sigrid Undset has provided us with an unparalleled vision of medieval Norway, above all, of how Christians formed, then violated or followed, their consciences under the pervasive influence of the Church.

In our day, it has been said, the Christian religious perspective is concerned so exclusively with the figure of Jesus that the Father and the Holy Spirit are absent from Christian consciousness. What is worse, it is averred, they are not missed. Whatever the truth may be concerning our time, the Norway of Kristin and Olav offers ground for this unfavorable view. Above all, the sufferings of the Incarnate Word, of his Mother, of the martyrs, moved Christian hearts as did no other consideration. The thirteenth and fourteenth centuries were, after all, the centuries of the mendicant preachers, Franciscan and Dominican, both strongly committed to the humanity of Jesus. It must not be thought that this option entailed a nonintellectual orientation, for those precise centuries were the golden age of theological analysis, based, to be sure, upon a biblical perception that was cruelly limited. If in the near future there looms the fifteenth-century *Imitation of Christ*, with its apparently anti-intellectual: "I had rather feel compunction than know how to define it,"[4] let us recall a parallel assertion by a thirteenth-century Master of the Sacred Page: "The love of God is better than the knowledge of God". That Master was St. Thomas Aquinas.[5]

NOTES

¹ Sigrid Undset, *Kristin Lavransdatter*, 3 vols., trans. Charles Archer and J. S. Scott (New York: Alfred A. Knopf, 1988), and *The Master of Hestviken*, 4 vols., trans. Arthur G. Chater (New York: Alfred A. Knopf, 1952); hereafter referred to as KL and MH respectively.

² Found in the Quaracchi edition of the saint's *Opera omnia*, vol. 8 (1898), pp. 68–86.

³ See Sr. M. J. Stallings (The Catholic University of America Press, 1965). There is another modern English translation under the title: *Meditations on the Life of Christ, An Illustration of the Fourteenth Century Paris*, BN MS Ital. 115, trans. Isa Ragusa, Rosalie Green (Princeton: Princeton University Press, 1961), and a German translation, *Die Betrachtungen über das Leben Christi vom heiligen Bonaventura ins Deutsch übertragen*, J. J. Hausen (Paderborn: Bonifacius Druckerei, 1896).

⁴ Thomas à Kempis, *The Imitation of Christ*, 1,1.

⁵ *Summa theologiae*, I, q. 82, a. 3, in corp.

MITZI M. BRUNSDALE

A LIFETIME OF PENANCE FOR
AN HOUR OF HAPPINESS: THE LIFE
AND FICTION OF SIGRID UNDSET

Sigrid Undset's youth, the matrix of her artistic message, was far from the carefree "happy age" that many people today consider the privilege, if not the right, of adolescents. Like many poor Norwegian girls of her generation, Sigrid Undset in 1898 took up the responsibilities of maturity at sixteen years old. For ten years she worked in an Oslo office and immersed herself in books until late at night, driven by the unquenchable desire she voiced in 1908 through one of her earliest heroines, Charlotte Hedels, narrator of the short story Sigrid Undset ironically titled "The Happy Age":

> I wanted to write about the town . . . all these half-lovely districts we respectable drudges live in. The wet dirty streets and the worn paving-stones, small apartments and small shops,—I should really like to write about the windows of such shops, —you know, shops selling chemists' sundries, and toy-shops with dolls and sewing-boxes and glass necklaces, where children stand outside in clusters and say 'Bags I that one'. Oh, when I now know how many tiny pathetic longings outside such shops have sprinkled their dew over every pennyworth of happiness bought in them . . . I could love and make use of all the worn-out little words which we all let fall so carelessly— words we use when we drop in on someone, words that go with some sign of love, words whispered in grief or in the surprise of some small joy. . . . I could write a book about you or myself or about any of us office-worms. We carry on and find a job which allows us to live—we can't live *for* it.[1]

In her mid-twenties, Sigrid Undset thus announced the techniques and themes that would reverberate throughout her life's work. The "half-lovely" realistic setting of her fiction would be "the town", no more and no less a scrupulously realized community of all-too-human beings than an exquisitely delineated collection of buildings and possessions, perceived through that female consciousness sometimes dismissed as "intuition". The old Vikings, like their Germanic Iron Age ancestors, knew better, ascribing intuition to woman's capacity to marshal myriad tiny details into near-supernatural insights.[2] Sigrid Undset's ability to create unforgettable characters with a saga-simple flash of her pen, like her portrait of poor Oslo children yearning outside dingy toy-shops, is intimately connected to her skill at realistically depicting the sights and sounds and feels and smells of "the town"—the good and bad in any group of dwellings that mattered to her stories—a farm in a remote Norwegian valley, or a cluster of wooden buildings huddled at the feet of Nidaros Cathedral; the bustle and swarm of medieval London, or the cold grey early twentieth-century Northern villages where lonely women loved and lost. Her vehicle would be the "worn-out little words which we all let fall so carelessly", the understated conversation of ordinary Scandinavian people which in her hands resonated with profound religious and historical overtones; words, as Lermontov put it, whose sense is obscure or trivial—yet one cannot listen to them without tremor.

Beyond setting, characterizations, and style, however, Sigrid Undset's literary achievement derives from her early realization of the somber truth of human life: if we want something, we must pay for it, and, as the Old Norse sagas relentlessly insist, once the thrill of the chase and the joy of the prize are gone, the price often seems too high. After her father's death when she was eleven plunged her family into poverty, Sigrid Undset herself likely stood outside little Oslo shops without the pennies to buy childish extravagances—all the more bitterly because earlier, when things were better, she probably had taken them for granted.

Sigrid Undset as a young woman also stood on the outside of a fulfilling career, looking longingly inward to a future that seemed impossible for her to reach. In her late adolescence, she confessed to her Swedish friend Dea Forsberg that "at a desperate moment in her lonely and self-centered youth [she] . . . once contemplated suicide while gazing at her image in the water."[3] Much later, in 1941, Sigrid Undset also recalled, "I wanted to become a painter—I had been drawing and painting ever since I was a baby. But we had no money for art studies."[4] The money was one thing; but even before she left Ragna Nielsen's progressive school at fifteen, the noted Norwegian painter Theodor Kittelson had warned Sigrid Undset about the perils of art, which he called "a journey that leads to no goal", since the work an artist creates never matches the dream that sparked it. The traveler bent on a life dedicated to art, Kittelson told her, "experiences nothing but humiliation, poverty, and intrigue . . . [because] Talent may be a gift, but it is also a curse."[5] Circumstances forced Sigrid Undset to give up her dream of becoming a painter, but for a decade as a secretary at the German Electric Company in Oslo, she stubbornly invested her free time in reading and writing, spending the supposed "happy age" of a woman's life in drudgery and earning the moral right to create fiction that unflinchingly depicts the hardships men and women and even children must face.

Sigrid Undset's announcement that her work would be "about you or myself or any of us office-worms" confirms her intention to root her work solidly in her own hard-won experience.[6] Sigrid Undset was notoriously reticent about her private life; at fifty-eight, she stated unequivocally, "I have always hated publicity about myself."[7] Her major autobiographical statements, all made well after her religious conversion in 1924, were her record of her childhood, *The Longest Years*, 1935; her account of her flight from Norway, *Return to the Future*; and her children's book *Happy Times in Norway*, these last two written in 1942.[8] In early 1940 she also provided a brief but illuminating sketch of her life for *Twentieth Century Authors*, and her uncharacteristic revelations there suggest she felt she was making a statement on the deathbed of the European civilization to which she had devoted her life; ". . . as things are looking", she wrote, " . . . we may all be swallowed up and deported somewhere in Siberia by the Russian aggressors if Finland does not get the necessary support in her fight for independence—I have come to the conclusion that I may just as well tell something about myself whilst I can."[9]

Though we cannot know with certainty exactly how much of her own life Sigrid Undset shaped into her fiction, her niece Charlotte Blindheim observes that "since we apprehend her [Undset's] books as realistic, written from her own experience or action, it makes us who have known her read her books in our own way . . . we always look for her own part."[10] From her earliest short stories through her last novels, Sigrid Undset's most characteristic "own part" was her insistence that humanity exists for more than the necessity of earning one's daily bread. At first she defined this desire as love of self, speaking through Charlotte Hedels in "The Happy Age": "We all want the same thing, to live for one moment with our whole being turned inward . . . into our own burning hearts."[11] As Narcissus discovered in the old myth, though, those instants of egoistic passion have their cost—death by drowning.[12] After Sigrid Undset faced and rejected suicide in her adolescence, her stories reveal successive stages of an individual's progress toward maturity; from "The Happy Age" onward, the crux of each piece of her fiction is a choice freely made in one glorious, vulnerable, and self-absorptive moment, while the successive prices her protagonists pay for a bit of transitory happiness trace Sigrid Undset's own developing relationships to her human family, to her art, and, ultimately, to her God.

After her father's death and her family's descent into poverty, Sigrid Undset experienced a late and controversial courtship, a problematic marriage, and then separation and divorce; she was left to support six children, three of whom were her husband's from a previous marriage, and two, her husband's son and her daughter Maren Charlotte (Tulla), were severely mentally handicapped. In these demanding circumstances, Sigrid Undset wrote eleven novels, four collections of short fiction, a play and a collection of verse, three autobiographical works, twelve collections of essays, several translations and adaptations from Old Norse and other medieval literature, and numerous miscellaneous pieces of prose. The great majority of her readers today know and cherish *Kristin Lavransdatter*, her re-creation of life in fourteenth-century Norway, above all her other work, but Sigrid Undset herself deplored "such a hubbub of praise for Kristin" and insisted that the story of Olav Audunsson's crime and punishment, known in English as *The Master of Hestviken*, was her finest work;[13] evidently a significant gulf exists between her public's devotion to Sigrid Undset's best-known novel and her own estimate of her fiction.

Sigrid Undset's creative life falls into two halves. The first includes her earliest attempts at fiction, beginning with a rejected draft of *The Master of Hestviken* that she wrote between 1902 and 1905, and it extends through *Kristin Lavransdatter*, whose three novels were published in 1920, 1921, and 1922, a period coinciding with the breakup of her marriage. The great watershed of her career seems to have been the annulment of her marriage on November 23, 1924, and her reception into the Roman Catholic Church on the following day. (The feast of the Carmelite mystic St. John of the Cross was at that time celebrated on this day.) Soon afterward, in 1925 and 1927, she published the two volumes of the Norwegian version of *The Master of Hestviken*. She had been expected to win the Nobel Prize for Literature in 1925,[14] that is, prior to the appearance of *The Master of Hestviken*, but at the last moment the Nobel Committee awarded it to George Bernard Shaw, and Sigrid Undset did not receive her Nobel Prize until 1928, a year before Germany's Thomas Mann became a Nobel laureate. From then until 1941, when the Nazis drove her from Norway, she wrote contemporary novels where, as in her tracts and lectures of that time, she sought to convince European civilization of its need for a neothomist religious reformation.

Looking back upon her personal and literary development in her autobiographical works, Sigrid Undset revealed the thematic common denominator integral to all of her work and its source in her early life: betrayal and all its heavy consequences. When her beloved father Ingvald Undset was still able to help with her home schooling, he introduced her to resounding ancient tales of Greek and Roman heroism, stories that probably had inspired him to take up his own study of archaeology. When she was around eight years old, Sigrid learned at her father's side that not only "the great figures who were to thrill her imagination must always do what was noble and right, unconditionally, even if it meant ruin and death", but that she was expected to bind herself with the same moral imperative (LY, p. 191).

The inexorability of fate and the necessity of suffering that Aeschylus holds out to humanity's gaze and the stern lessons of moral rectitude taught by the Roman Republic mesh almost seamlessly with the uncompromising ideal of individual responsibility presented by the old Scandinavian saga literature that Sigrid Undset also encountered as a child. She first read the greatest of the sagas, the thirteenth-century Njál's saga, on a visit to Trondheim, the ancient seat of Norway's kings, the year her father died, and she later called it the book that changed her life. She had, however, already discovered the painful discrepancy between noble ideals and the pragmatism of the here-and-now, when adults with good intentions betrayed her childish trust; they gave away her puppy, lied to her about the dangers of the world, and sent her to a school where she was ridiculed for their views, deflating her self-image and driving her to take refuge with her books. Worse, she knew she had also betrayed herself: "My schoolmates found me out from the very beginning—that I imagined myself to be somebody, to be 'different'. And they set about to make me see how unpleasant life ought to be made for anybody who is different from other people."[15]

Even as a child, Sigrid Undset defied the pains of being "different", and, in Odin's pale warrior Skarpedhin, an unforgettable figure in the Njála, she recognized as unyielding a fellow spirit as her own, a spirit that rejected everything and everyone that failed to meet his own high standards: "He was so impatient of everything in the world about him that he wanted to put an end to it all" (LY, p. 282). Skarphedin's ringing laughter as he brings his destiny of flaming death down upon himself probably contributed to her adolescent suicidal impulse, which seems more likely a manifestation of her extreme exasperation with the world than a surrender to its pressures. A few months later, Ingvald Undset died, a parent's ultimate betrayal, it might seem to a child who had had no teaching about the Resurrection; and when he was gone, in a strange way Sigrid felt free, because "there was no one on whom she cared to be dependent" (LY, p. 329).

Raised in a rationalistic home with no significant experience of Christian contrition, penance, or absolution, Sigrid Undset as a child had not learned to be sympathetic with or truly to forgive either her own failings or anyone else's, a position she seems to have shared with her strong-willed mother, who Charlotte Blindheim feels was the major influence in her aunt's youth.[16] Sigrid Undset also clung to the inflexible idealism that Classical literature and her Norwegian heritage had instilled in her. Allowing herself to be dependent would be the most valuable gift she could give someone, and, because she would not allow herself to be hurt again, as a young woman she refused to give it. In that kind of self-destructive independence, she was one in spirit with her ancient countrymen whom the sagas celebrated; for them the keeping of their sworn word was the measure of a human being, and breaking it was the worst offense imaginable, by which they would forfeit the pleasures of Valhalla. The pagan Norse warriors longed for a heroic death in battle that their skalds could immortalize as much as they dreaded "a straw death" from disease or old age at home, and perhaps the discrepancy Sigrid Undset perceived between the

Old Norse ideal of fidelity to an oath and the reality of humanity's moral weakness alerted her to a flaw in Norway's national character: "Very many Norwegians are melancholy at heart and by nature prone to distrust both their fellow-men and God himself" (LY, p. 202). Even her earliest fiction shows that she did not exclude herself from that grim assessment.

Nearly all the stories Sigrid Undset wrote while she was a secretary in Oslo hinge upon a moment of deceptive happiness that is achieved by the selfish breaking of a vow and that results in the breaking of a woman's life. All her early heroines

> gaze repeatedly at their own reflection, find the image too exquisite for such common surroundings, and wonder where the perfect "other" might be whose eyes will return the same idolatrous reflection they see. But the endings of their stories suggest different levels of growth in self-knowledge, leading to different resolutions of the problem.[17]

Sigrid Undset's first known work was an unpublished draft of *The Master of Hestviken*, whose plot hinges upon the theme of betrayal: when thirteenth-century Norwegian fathers bind children to an arranged marriage, they betray their offspring's freedom of choice, ensuring fatal consequences for the protagonist when his orphaned young wife is later attracted to an itinerant outsider. After an Oslo publisher rejected this project, telling Sigrid Undset that she should give up historical fiction and devote herself to contemporary subjects, she immediately began her next novel, *Fru Marta Oulie*, with the words, "I have been unfaithful to my husband", which, she felt, "ought to be modern enough";[18] in fact, however, a woman's marital infidelity was nothing new, as Sigrid Undset knew very well from the medieval sagas. Neither was its aftermath, the physical or emotional anguish that a straying wife inflicts on herself, usually just as painful, if not more anguishing, as society's judgment of her. What Sigrid Undset's readers would have found disquietingly "modern" when *Fru Marta Oulie* appeared in 1907 was that Marta confessed in her retrospective diary not to directing

her love outwardly, toward her lovers, but to selfishly loving
love itself—and being fatally proud of doing so:

> Love—there was nothing else in life worth living for! I loved so
> fanatically that it seemed I could never dive deep enough into
> my passion. And day by day I felt how this love was making me
> beautiful and fresh and brilliant, how it gave me an unsuspected
> understanding of life and made me brave and gay and infinitely
> superior.[19]

To enhance her own self-image, Marta first chose her husband and later took his best friend as her lover; but only after
her husband died, never suspecting her infidelity, did she realize that love directed inward consumes its object: "It seems
indeed that we have no soul outside the life of our bodies—it
lives in us like the flame in something burning."[20] Marta lost
husband, family, and lover, and she had to live on with the
realization that her choice, a flaming love of self, had reduced
her to a burned-out shell.

Before leaving her secretarial job in 1909, Sigrid Undset
looked again to medieval Norway. Even though she claimed
that her major preoccupation in *Gunnar's Daughter* was the
theme of the avenging son,[21] she created another female protagonist who loved selfishly and lost her world. The pagan
priestess Vigdis loves the Icelander Ljot but hesitates to accept
him because he has quarreled with her family; patience does
not seem to have been a Viking virtue, and after Ljot rapes her,
she raises Ulvar, the son of their union, to slay him. Uneasy
about the old pagan code of vengeance but unable to accept
the new forgiving faith being implemented in Norway by Olav
Tryggvasson, Vigdis receives Ljot's grey head from Ulvar's
bloody hands and bitterly names the fate she chose and must
live out: ". . . it was the worst of all, that I would rather have
loved him than any man."[22]

For ten grueling years in Oslo, Sigrid Undset, like the heroines she was creating, had sustained herself with dreams of
personal freedom.[23] "Above all things I had always desired lib-

erty to do what I wanted. But ever since my seventeenth year I have always had to consider somebody else's interests, whatever I have been doing."[24] Sigrid Undset's writing finally freed her from economic bondage, and at twenty-seven, with her two sisters at last able to support themselves and a modest literary success behind her, she reached out "to do what she wanted". Fatally vulnerable, she seized exactly the moment of deceptive happiness for which she would do penance for the remainder of her life.

In one of the novellas Sigrid Undset wrote during the First World War—the most difficult phase of her marriage—her character Uni Hjelde reminds all women of a sobering truth: "In that brief moment when love's caresses are new and make the blood flutter, you must understand and take control of all your life."[25] Striking parallels exist between figures and events in Sigrid Undset's personal life and her fiction from 1909 onward. She went to Rome that fall on a study grant and lived among expatriate Scandinavian artists and writers; that Christmas she sat for the brilliant and erratic Norwegian artist Anders Castus Svarstad, and suddenly he made her blood flutter; he was thirteen years older than she was, already married to Sigrid Undset's schoolmate Ragna Moe, and father of three children.

So far as can be determined today, a major problem in Sigrid Undset's marriage seems to have been the issue she described in the summer of 1910, inspired by the feminists' demand that St. Paul's words, "Wives, be submissive to your husbands", be dropped from Norwegian marriage services. She felt that natural law demanded that women choose men somehow superior to themselves: "For these selfsame words carry nature's own legal prescription for marriage: that a woman shall marry the man whom she can call her lord—and no one else."[26] At that time some quality in Svarstad, perhaps his success at painting which she had been denied, as much as his experience and personal magnetism, must have convinced Sigrid Undset that he possessed an innate superiority to which she could yield in marriage. She tried to keep her feelings for Svarstad hidden during the two and a half years it took for him to be divorced, but her family and friends in Oslo knew and disapproved, a factor which may have paradoxically contributed to her determination to marry him. After Sigrid Undset married Svarstad in the Norwegian consul's office in Antwerp in the spring of 1912, they lived briefly in England, the only "moment of happiness" in her married life, then moved to a dank wintry Rome and finally returned to Norway with Anders, their first child, where despite grinding poverty and the pressures of her three pregnancies and her writing, Sigrid Undset did her best to make a home for Svarstad. She did even more: after Ragna Moe had to put her children into an orphanage because she could not support them, Sigrid Undset took Svarstad's children—and a burden of guilt—into her own home.[27]

One of the few known comments Sigrid Undset made about her married life reveals the degree of her disillusion with the man she had thought she could "call her lord". On February 16, 1947, she wrote to her American friend Hope Emily Allen:

> Well, our marriage did not turn out a success,—he had a gift for making other people, and himself, unhappy, and to turn friends and admirers into enemies, which did much to prevent him from being recognized as the great artist he really was, as long as he was living. . . . When he arranged his own exhibitions he always dragged in a lot of his worst things to give it the most prominent places and swear they were his very best. I am really proud of Hans [Undset's only surviving child] . . . and I like his loyalty to his father, whom he admired always without having any illusions about what life with him would have been like. To my stepdaughters it was sometimes rather like hell.[28]

Eventually Sigrid Undset and Svarstad separated amicably, and her marriage was annulled on November 23, 1924.[29]

The fiction that Sigrid Undset wrote during her initial infatuation with Svarstad and the unhappy early years of her marriage displays her preoccupation with the powerful tension between a woman's physical needs and her spiritual being, a revolutionary concern for a woman novelist in the early 1900s. *Jenny*, which she wrote in the summer of 1911, was "a profound psychological study, written with painful intensity";[30] it exploded upon the European literary scene that fall and became the most widely read novel in Norway, and in it Sigrid Undset uncannily foresaw the pain her marriage would cost her. The tall attractive Norwegian artist Jenny, Sigrid Undset's autobiographical protagonist, "did not want a lover, because she was expecting a master".[31] Looking for the perfect "other" who would reflect her own impossible ideals, she gives herself to a young archaeologist, then to his father, but she refuses the one man who might have brought her true happiness; and, after Jenny's death, that man muses over her grave: "No woman has given birth to the child she dreamed of when she bore it—no artist has created the work he saw before him in the light of his inspiration. . . . And no love is what lovers dreamed when they kissed for the first time."[32] Before she had lived it, Sigrid Undset was describing the priorities that exist in a woman artist's life—motherhood, art, and romantic love. Throughout her life, she placed motherhood first, over her artistry; and last, romantic passion with its inevitable and profound regrets. Out of her ordering of her emotional and artistic priorities eventually came the message of Sigrid Undset's great medieval novels: that those things humanity, with its limited earthly vision, wants so badly that it often betrays what it loves best to possess them inevitably fade to insignificance in comparison to the needs of the immortal soul.

Before she could write *Kristin Lavransdatter*, Sigrid Undset published *Spring* in 1914, possibly her weakest novel. Svarstad was in Paris, and Sigrid Undset left her sickly first son, Anders, with her mother to stay in an Oslo boarding house and write. *Spring*, like *Poor Fortunes*, the collection of short stories she wrote in 1912, fictionally advances the social and moral position Sigrid Undset had announced in her speech "The Fourth Commandment", given to the Oslo Students' Union in March of 1914. By this time, Sigrid Undset had acknowledged that a human "other" could not provide the uplifting reflection of human aspirations necessary to spiritual progress. She now identified God as the symbol of all good, and she saw the innocent gaze of children as the earthly demonstration of his love toward their parents. In *Spring* and *Poor Fortunes*, she envisions the family as civilization's primary cohesive force, and culture as a product of the individual's responsibility toward his fellow men in the pursuit of "strength, wisdom, justice, truth, compassion, chastity, moderation, courage"; but this was the brink of World War I, and she had had to leave her baby to write; Sigrid Undset could not help but tell the truth as she saw it, that at this crucial time in her life and Europe's, these human ideals were "all bright and ancient words . . . halfway to becoming ridiculous".[33] While she was facing Norway's hardships and her own predicament, more difficult than ever because prices were high, food was scarce, and a painter's income, as she said, hardly sufficed to bring up a family of six,[34] Sigrid Undset, raised in a rationalistic home and from her childhood a champion of seeing things as they really are, was approaching traditional Christianity.

In the Oslo *Aftenposten* for February 7 and February 19, 1920, Sigrid Undset published two pieces both titled "Gymnadenia", which together comprise word for word the first chapter of *Gymnadenia*, in English *The Wild Orchid*,[35] one of the two novels in which she chronicled her conversion. Those 1920 articles record her disillusionment with everything earthly in which men and women place so many hopes. Undset, herself a master gardener, made the small woods orchid her symbol for a rationalistic life devoid of the perception of God. At first when Paul Helmer, his sensitive young spirit rebelling against his father's remarriage and his mother's liberalism, helps his mother with her wildflower garden, he is filled with youthful hope; " 'Gymnadenia,' he whispered, as though it were something that awaited him at some point of his life." When the plants bloom a little later, however, "There stood a little vase with some small green-looking flowers in it. . . . Frail stalks, with a few insignificant whitish little flowers." Paul's rationalistic mother is delighted with them, but "He was frightfully disappointed. Was that what they called gymnadenia?"[36]

Paul's disillusion with a world of purely human values reflects Sigrid Undset's own spiritual condition after 1914. In her most revealing account of her conversion, written on the threshold of the Second World War, she connected her passion for realism with what her reason had taught her of human needs:

> The war and the years afterwards confirmed the doubts I always had had about the ideas I was brought up on—[I felt] that liberalism, feminism, nationalism, socialism, pacifism, would not work, because they refused to consider human nature as it really is. Instead, they presupposed that mankind was to "progress" into something else—towards their own ideas of what people ought to be. Being fostered on pre-history and history I did not much believe in progress. An accumulation of experience and expanding knowledge does not improve man's intellect or moral qualities even if it ought to improve his ways of using his intellect and solving his moral problems. Yet it will not produce finer brains than Aristotle's or St. Thomas Aquinas', for instance, a greater or more versatile mind than St. Paul's, a humanity nobler than St. Louis of France's or Sir Thomas More's. . . . By degrees my knowledge of history convinced me that the only thoroughly sane people, of our civilization at least, seemed to be those queer men and women which the Catholic Church calls the Saints. Even their offending eccentricity offended mostly the fancies and wishful thinking of contemporary smugness. They seemed to know the true explanation of man's undying hunger for happiness—his tragically insufficient love of peace, justice, and goodwill to his fellowmen, his everlasting fall from grace. Of course I knew the historical role of the Church as a civilizatory power, and I had never looked on the religious revolt of the sixteenth century as anything but a revolt against the humanly unpalatable teachings of Christianity—the liberal Protestantism of my education left me an agnostic. . . . But I had ventured too near the abode of truth in my researches about "God's friends", as the Saints are called in the Old Norse texts

of Catholic times. So I had to submit. And . . . I was received into the Catholic Church.[37]

Sigrid Undset had to struggle to submit to the divine "other" that her reason, her general knowledge of history, and her research into Norway's medieval period had taught her to recognize. Leaving *Gymnadenia* for the time being, she fought out her spiritual battle in the three volumes of *Kristin Lavransdatter*, a novel dominated by "her own part", the record of her loyalties, her betrayals of them, and that choice she seems to have made in a few heartbeats in Svarstad's arms—the choice for which she already had begun to pay such a heavy price.

The manuscript of the second volume of *Kristin Lavransdatter*, titled in English *The Mistress of Husaby*, bears Sigrid Undset's hand-written dedication, "In memory of my father Ingvald Undset".[38] The story of Kristin's life—and at least to some extent Sigrid Undset's—parallels Norway's abandonment of paganism and its adoption of Christianity. It balances a woman's betrayal of her father, who represents the bonds of family, against her spiritual betrayal of her vow to the husband she chose as a demonstration of her individuality, fictionalizing the eternally problematic position of Woman, who must leave her father in order to marry and raise her children, and who emotionally must abandon her dependency on her husband in order to achieve genuine individuality. Sigrid Undset had already treated these themes realistically, but *Kristin Lavransdatter* exhibits two important new dimensions of her work: the insights into erotic love, marriage, and family life that emerged from her relationship with Svarstad and the children, and the setting of a moral universe where God and his Church reign supreme.[39]

Erlend Nikulaussön is every young woman's dream of love, handsome, dashing, brave in the tradition of the old pagan Tronder chieftains that Sigrid Undset, despite her hard-won Christianity, still stubbornly celebrated in her *Saga of Saints*, 1934: If a man fought on in spite of destiny, "he had won the

only thing a man is capable of winning—honor and fame . . .
his life [was] worthy of high stakes."[40] Erlend's life and death
exemplify the fatal discrepancy Undset saw in the Norwegian
character, the ideal of fidelity forever beyond the reach of realistic human weakness. An inexperienced maiden like Kristin in
The Bridal Wreath forgets that a noble warrior focuses upon the
noble act, so that he may ignore necessary but to him less con-
sequential details of day-to-day life. Similarly, a young mother
intent upon maintaining a secure home for her children, like
Kristin in *The Mistress of Husaby*, forgets that the warrior pays
his taxes in blood, and she fatally expects him to be what he
never can become, another Lavrans Björgulfssön. Not until
she has lost him can many an older woman, like Kristin in
The Cross, wholeheartedly forgive the failings and celebrate
the virtues of the warrior she chose so long before, the man
she had blamed for being what he had to be—and for what
she finally recognizes as her own inadequacies.

Kristin expected Erlend to reflect back to her her own self-
love; and because she denied him the individuality she demanded for herself, she had to learn through suffering that she
alone was responsible for the fate of her immortal soul, passing through religious experiences paralleling the early stages of
Sigrid Undset's own road toward faith.

The Bridal Wreath begins with a powerful evocation of Norway's pagan past. Thirsty for berries, the child Kristin leads
her father's red stallion, Guldsveinen, down a hillside where
she comes upon a black forest pool, "the finest of mirrors",[41]
gazes at her own reflection, and glimpses an elf-queen offering
her a golden garland. Undset's lyric scene cloaks a premonition of Kristin's future. The horse-symbol is closely connected
in Norse myth to the fertility gods Freyr and Freyja;[42] Freyja
was said to have introduced *sei r* to pagan Scandinavia, a sooth-
saying rite connected with the horse-cult and involving death-
dealing magic.[43] Kristin, not the horse, leads the way, sug-
gesting her strong will, which pursues physical gratification;
and she chooses to gaze into the water to see if she resembles

her father, that is, to see if her father reflects her own self-admiration. She then decks herself in a pink valerian wreath "like a grown maid who goes a-dancing" and proudly gazes again.[44] This wreath symbolizes her honor, tinged with self-chosen sin, which she will bring to her wedding, and the pagan vision confirms her wish with a golden wreath, foreshadowing Erlend's noble aunt Lady Aashild, reputedly a sorceress, who, resembling the elf queen, "defines for her [Kristin] the beauty and peril of a secular life".[45]

Although Kristin ran away in terror, the memory of that golden wreath of selfishness lay in her mind and heart like a festering splinter from a troll's looking glass, the symbol Sigrid Undset had chosen for her two 1917 novellas which treat opposing views of marriage. Not long afterward, saintly Brother Edvin offers Kristin a different garland, a pristine wreath of Christian doctrine: " 'Tis because our hearts are divided twixt love of God and fear of the devil and fondness for the world and the flesh, that we are unhappy in life and death." Brother Edvin also tells Kristin that Christ came "to taste in the flesh the lures of the devil . . . as well as the menace of the world . . . In such wise did He show us the way and make manifest His love."[46] Kristin, like most of humanity, listens but fails to hear. Brother Edvin suggests the nun's veil to her: "How would you like to offer up this bonny hair and serve Our Lady like these brides I have figured here?" But Kristin replies evasively, "We have no child at home but me. . . . So 'tis like I must marry",[47] as if the pious Lavrans would not have given his daughter to the Church if she had desired it with all her heart.

For most of the novel, Kristin's heart is unhappily divided between ideal and reality, the love of God she knows she ought to feel and the prideful love of the flesh she cannot resist. In denying Erlend his right to be himself, Kristin's pride costs him his life, for, though she spurned him, he keeps his bridal oath and dies defending her honor. After Erlend is gone, Kristin's children grow away from her, and she is forced to realize that the only "other" who can reflect a forgiving image of herself is humanity's selfless Savior. Her last act on earth, relinquishing Erlend's gold ring with its blood-red stone, is her first act of Christ-like love; and at last through Christ's mercy Kristin rids herself of the last vestige of the pagan golden wreath of pride she, like all humanity, had chosen in her youth. In her final moment, Kristin realizes that the marriage she had chosen was not her lifelong torment but God's instrument of her salvation.

In *Ida Elisabeth* (1932), one of Sigrid Undset's characters observes, "If a man can put up with remaining the same as he has always been and yet undergoing a ceaseless transformation—continuing to be the same in another way—then I can assure you that it's exciting to grow old. . . . One gets round things, is able to see them from one new side after another." [48] This statement justifies Sigrid Undset's preference for *The Master of Hestviken* over *Kristin Lavransdatter*, for, after she had completed *Kristin Lavransdatter*, her burgeoning religious sensibility opened new artistic vistas that she incorporated into the book she considered her masterpiece. During a visit to Monte Cassino in 1925, she felt she received an illumination of the great paradox of the Crucifixion; she saw humanity as "untold souls who have lived through the ages, each of them imprisoned in the ravelled net of his own self, from which no doctrine can set us free, only God, and He only by dying on a cross". [49] By realizing that forgiveness requires and makes sense of suffering, Sigrid Undset had also "learned why there can never be any valid authority of men over men. The only Authority to which mankind can submit without debauching itself is His whom St. Paul calls *Auctor Vitae*—the Creator's toward Creation." [50]

In Olav Audunsson, master of the old Viking stronghold of Hestviken, [51] Sigrid Undset depicted mankind trapped by its pagan values; by committing his son under oath to an arranged marriage, Olav's father betrays his child's freedom of choice, and the marriage eventually leads to the risk of Olav's immortal soul. Viking pride demands that Olav in a moment of self-satisfying vengeance kill the youth who had been the lover of Olav's weak-willed wife, Ingunn; but, by concealing the crime and rejecting God's merciful forgiveness throughout his life, Olav, "caught in his own snares",[52] fatally sets himself above his Lord. Olav has to suffer for most of his life to earn an understanding of a purpose beyond his own will: "He saw now that it was not his suffering that destroyed the happiness of his life . . . sufferings that are of some *avail* [italics in original], they are like the spear-points that raise the shield on which the young king's son sits when his subjects do him homage."[53] Olav's recognition fictionally represents the core of the Roman Catholic faith to which Sigrid Undset had come. For her, Catholicism offered the sole explanation of life which men and women cry out so desperately to hear;[54] as she later put it in *The Burning Bush*, Catholicism gave her "sober information about absolute truths. Even if the truths in themselves are not sober but fairly wild, and the absolute is infinite and inexhaustible."[55]

In her great medieval novels, Sigrid Undset often framed a character's realization of a profound spiritual truth with the imagery and the symbolism of the pagan Vikings; she used the resonance of Northern myth to reinforce the Christian message that had become her wholehearted preoccupation. *Kristin Lavransdatter* explores the price of getting what one most desires in "that moment when the blood flutters", but *The Master of Hestviken* inverts the relation of happiness and suffering: devastating disillusionment with self precedes genuine sorrow for sin and the desire for atonement so that God's gift of illumination may follow. Until one grasps all facets of human life as necessary elements of divine purpose, Sigrid Undset now believed, no spiritual growth is possible: "Is there something which we ought to have known and have never been told, and is that why we do such terribly stupid things with our lives?"[56] For Sigrid Undset, seeing divine intention was not merely enough, it was everything:

> Our spirit, looking for causes and effects in the eternal play of transformation, has felt certain that this play is directed by persons or a person whom our thinking and searching ego re-

semble in some way or other and was related to. So it has been as far back as we know anything of human history on earth, and religion is our relation to these causes or this cause which stands above matter and deals with it as it pleases. Religion is our relation to the supernatural.[57]

After *The Master of Hestviken* and her Nobel Prize, Sigrid Undset turned her attention to contemporary fiction, in which she hammered home the truths of the Church she had claimed as her own, belaboring them so forcefully that, like many of her contemporaries, today's readers frequently find her last novels unpalatable, if not unreadable. Her spiritual sanctuary was the scholasticism of Aquinas as she found it in the neothomism of Jacques Maritain, a leader of Catholicism's reaction to the moral vicissitudes of the early twentieth century. Maritain unequivocally called for safeguarding the dignity and rights of man by activist attacks upon the modern totalitarianism which threatened them and advocated the reconciliation of human conflicts through Christian wisdom. According to Maritain, "from the end of the Middle Ages—a moment at which the human creature, while awakening to itself, felt itself oppressed and crushed in its loneliness—modern times have longed for a rehabilitation of the human creature. They sought this rehabilitation in a separation from God. It was to be sought in God."[58]

Sigrid Undset's Norwegian nature never admitted much compromise. Charlotte Blindheim remarks that in the Catholic Church her aunt found "a tried and tested intellectual authority over her brooding, earthbound mind and her innate arrogance".[59] In her own life and in her medieval novels, Sigrid Undset had already unforgettably depicted the price of selfish separation from God, the oppressive loneliness Maritain described, and from the early 1930s she fought as savagely as any Viking warrior against any element of modern society, from Lutheranism to Nazism, that she believed was selfishly seeking relief by breaking with the God of Christian tradition. The policies of the Church Sigrid Undset embraced in 1924, however, were not quite those of today's Church. "Undset lived in the era of the 'triumphalist' Catholic Church. Its members were taught that it represented 'Absolute Truth', and that there was no salvation outside of it. As a neophyte member of that Church, she was especially zealous about propagating such doctrines."[60] Usually Sigrid Undset was morally in the right; frequently she stood alone; and often, too, her Viking refusal to grant mercy to her enemies brought heavy criticism down upon her for subordinating her literary talents to her religious aims. In 1941, one of her contemporaries harshly observed, "It may as well be said frankly that Sigrid Undset's novels . . . written since her conversion, are her poorest work from a literary standpoint. They are long and tedious, many of them little more than sugar-coated tracts, and . . . 'her unprincipled and purposeless moderns never come to life at all.' "[61] Some admirers of Undset's work now share Margaret Mary Dunn's opinion that Undset's later novels are impossible to teach today, because of the tone of unbending rectitude with which she tried to spread her faith,[62] but J. C. Whitehouse looks beyond Undset's occasionally peremptory tone to the salvific function of the faith she promulgates: "Catholicism, she maintains, is a religion for life (*Wild Orchid* 83), not an opiate or a substitute for erotics (*Burning Bush* 166), but a realistic and to some degree a materialistic religion (*Burning Bush* 102), bringing to the believer a kind of peace."[63]

Evidently Sigrid Undset herself came to see that much of her later work had been "Catholic propaganda", a phrase which she herself had used as the title of her 1927 essay collection. Most commentators believe that the war and the loss of her elder son, Anders, exhausted her and destroyed her artistry; but Arne Skouen, Director of the Norwegian Information Agency during World War II, when Sigrid Undset was battling Hitler from the United States, believes that she "fell silent not only because she was tired. . . . I believe she reached a new awareness that was much more painful. Writing was a moral act for Sigrid Undset; it derived from unimpeachable motives. In her letters she had broadcast her hatred of the enemy, whom she did not even have the authority to forgive. . . . It is my belief that she fell silent in a moral crisis."[64] Sigrid Undset's Christian faith, based upon the doctrine of forgiveness, could not withstand her consuming hatred of Nazi Germany and her thirst to avenge their crimes against her: defilement of her home, imprisonment and torture of her friends and relatives, above all the death of her older son, Anders, killed by German invaders a few hundred yards from their home at Lillehammer;[65] and her faith yielded to self-destructive hate.

The dark night of Sigrid Undset's soul lasted for the final four years of her life, when, back in Norway, "She worried about the things she had sacrificed because she had prioritized others, and was plagued with shame at the thought of how often she had defended her standpoints on life's problems with unyielding intensity, even anger."[66] In her last work, a biography of St. Catherine of Siena, Sigrid Undset like her creation Kristin Lavransdatter finally confessed how hard she had found it to live as Catherine had died, "seeing God in everything and everything in God".[67]

Undset's great contemporary D. H. Lawrence cautioned twentieth-century readers, "Never trust the artist: trust the tale", cutting to the heart of the relationship between great literature and the men and women who create it by transforming their human frailty and the pains it brings them into eternal art. Lawrence's statement implies that a literary work possesses a life independent of its maker's; that the creative gift makes the artist inherently incapable of avoiding deception in accounting for the creative process and its results; and that therefore the worth of the work incontrovertibly outweighs the human failings of its creator. The roots of human creativity lie far beneath the surface of human consciousness, and, like the Old Norse world-tree Yggdrasil, they are continually menaced by serpents working to devour both the artist and his gift. Sigrid Undset knew that pride gnawed at the roots of her artistry,[68] and it eventually brought her literary art crashing about her own stubborn Norwegian head, tragically demolishing her cre-

ativity. The painful record of her life and her spiritual quest
remains clear in her fiction: the realistic liberalism of her early
stories about Norway's poor; her Christian vision, filtered first
through Christian mysticism and later through the neothomism
which suited her stern view of life so well; her brief flowering
of Christian humanism, an antidote at the close of her life for
the scrupulosity and pride and hatred she at last realized had
marred it; and pervading all, the stern values of the old pagan
Norsemen from whom she and her art had sprung. Her re-
wards and their price in Sigrid Undset's life and literary works,
inextricably intertwined with her quest for God, remain best
described in the words she gave Kristin on her deathbed, words
in which all Christians might hope to share:

> A handmaiden of God had she been—a wayward, unruly ser-
> vant, oftenest an eye-servant in her prayers and faithless in her
> heart, slothful and neglectful, impatient under correction, but
> little constant in her deeds—yet had he held her fast in his ser-
> vice . . . owned by the Lord and King who was now coming
> . . . to give her freedom and salvation. . . .[69]

NOTES

[1] This passage appears in translation in A. H. Winsnes, *Sigrid Undset: A Study in Christian Realism*, trans. P. G. Foote (New York: Sheed and Ward, 1953), p. 37; italics in the translation. Winsnes' book is the first authorized biography of Sigrid Undset, who read the manuscript in Norwegian not long before her death in 1949.

[2] In Old Norse tradition, the particular kind of divinatory witchcraft practiced mostly by women was known as *sei r*, the province of the fertility goddess Freyja, sister-wife of the Vanir god Freyr. In the Prose Edda Snorri Sturluson indicates that Freyja was the most renowned of the goddesses and that she still lived; the implication is that the early Scandinavians revered women for their intuitive capacities, which seemed to link them in a special way to divinity. Tacitus claimed that the Germanic tribes regarded women as endowed with the gift of prophecy and thought of them "even as goddesses" (*Histories* IV, 61). Scandinavian seeresses originally traveled about the land in groups, visiting farms and predicting the progress of crops and the destinies of young men and women of the area. See Hilda Ellis Davidson, *Gods and Myths of Northern Europe* (New York: Penguin, 1964), pp. 114–16. Lady Aashild in *Kristin Lavransdatter* fulfills a similar function. Also note the misogynist perspective of the ninth- or tenth-century Havamal ("Sayings of the High [Wise] One [Odin]"): "No one should trust the words of a girl or married woman, for their hearts have been shaped on a turning wheel and they are inconstant by nature" (translated in Johannes Brondsted, *The Vikings*, trans. Kalle Skov (New York: Penguin, 1965), p. 251.

[3] See the collection of Undset's letters edited by Christiane Undset Svarstad, *Kjaere Dea* (Oslo, 1972), pp. 32–33.

[4] "Sigrid Undset", autobiographical sketch in *Twentieth Century Authors*, ed. Stanley J. Kunitz and Howard Haycroft (New York: H. W. Wilson, 1942), pp. 1432ff.

[5] Quoted in Carl Bayerschmidt, *Sigrid Undset* (New York: Twayne, 1970), p. 26.

[6] The connection between Undset's life and her art has not yet been authoritatively and exhaustively explored, and relatively little material is available in English. The standard biography is considered Borghild Krane's *Sigrid Undset: Liv og meninger* (Oslo: Gyldendal, 1970), not translated. Krane, Undset's friend in her old age, devotes half her book to Undset's essays and societal commentary, because Krane believes that Undset's true character is revealed in her essays rather than in her fiction. Krane had access to sources previously inaccessible because of "the savage discretion" of Undset's family and friends, as Nicole Deschamps

described their attitude in *Sigrid Undset, ou la morale de la passion* (Montreal: Montreal Presses de l'Université, 1966). The only available major collection of Undset's letters was written in her youth to her Swedish pen pal Dea Forsberg; see *Kjaere Dea* (Oslo, 1972), edited by Christiane Undset Svarstad. Undset's son Hans Benedict Undset Svarstad exercised editorial control over the notes to this correspondence. Rutgers University holds a repository of Undset's letters to her American friend and fellow medievalist Hope Emily Allen, written between February 1941 and December 1948. Norwegian biographical sources include a memoir by Undset's niece Charlotte Blindheim, *Moster Sigrid: Et familieportrett av Sigrid Undset* (Oslo: Aschehoug, 1982), and *Sigrid Undset skriver hjem: En vandring gjennom emigrantarene i Amerika* (Oslo: Aschehoug, 1982), a reminiscence by Arne Skouen, Director of the Norwegian Information Service, who worked with Undset while she was in exile in the United States during World War II. Critical work on Undset includes doctoral dissertations for Norwegian universities, such as Liv Bliksrud's *Natur og normer hos Sigrid Undset* (Oslo: Aschehoug, 1988), not translated. In English, see Harald Beyer, "Sigrid Undset", in Beyer's *History of Norwegian Literature* (New York: New York University Press, 1956); and Alrik Gustafson, "Christian Ethics in a Pagan World: Sigrid Undset", in *Six Scandinavian Novelists* (Minneapolis: University of Minnesota Press, 1968). Also see "A Centennial Tribute to Sigrid Undset", *Scandinavian Review*, vol. 70 (June 1982), pp. 39–54; Marlene Ciklamini, "Sigrid Undset", in *European Writers*, vol. 9 (New York: Scribner's, 1983), pp. 1011–40; Astrid Saether's review article, "Sigrid Undset: Revaluations and Recollections", *Scandinavica*, vol. 23 (May 1984), pp. 53–57, treating four Norwegian books issued by Undset's publisher H. Aschehoug for the centenary of her birth; J. C. Whitehouse, "Religion as Fulfillment in the Novels of Sigrid Undset", *Renascence*, vol. 38 (1985), pp. 2–12; Mitzi Brunsdale, *Sigrid Undset: Chronicler of Norway* (Oxford: Berg Publishers, 1988); and Sherrill Harbison, "Medieval Aspects of Narcissism in Sigrid Undset's Modern Novels", *Scandinavian Studies*, vol. 63 (Autumn 1991), pp. 464–75.

[7] In a 1941 letter which accompanied her autobiographical essay, Undset made the statement quoted above to the editors of *Twentieth Century Authors*.

[8] Sigrid Undset, *The Longest Years*, trans. Arthur G. Chater (New York: Alfred A. Knopf, 1935); hereafter referred to as LY. *Return to the Future*, trans. Henriette Naeseth (New York: Alfred A. Knopf, 1942); *Happy Times in Norway*, trans. Joran Birkeland (New York: Alfred A. Knopf, 1942).

[9] *Twentieth Century Authors*, p. 1434.

[10] *Moster Sigrid*, p. 56; Translations from this source are my own.

[11] "The Happy Age", quoted in Bayerschmidt, p. 61.

[12] In "The Happy Age", Charlotte's friend Uni reminds her of Narcissus' fate, but Charlotte counters, "Yes, but don't you think there are a lot of us today who are just like that?"; translated in Harbison, p. 464. "Charlotte" was

the middle name of Sigrid Undset's mother, the name by which she preferred
to be called.

[13] *Moster Sigrid*, p. 58.

[14] *Twentieth Century Authors*, p. 1434.

[15] Ibid., p. 1432.

[16] Charlotte Blindheim "asserts categorically that Sigrid's mother was the
dominant parental figure and points out that there was a character affinity between the two: those personality traits which people found difficult to cope with
in Undset also characterized her mother. Blindheim's judgment must be taken
seriously, for her mother was Undset's long-time confidant, and she herself knew
her aunt well; see Ciklamini, p. 1021. This statement reverses the commonly
held assessment, one that Undset herself encouraged, that her father, to whom
she was devoted, was the more important parental influence in her development.

[17] Harbison, p. 464.

[18] Winsnes, pp. 34–35.

[19] Ibid., p. 38.

[20] Ibid., p. 39.

[21] Winsnes refers to Sigrid Undset's October 3, 1910, interview with the
Norwegian periodical *Urd*; see ibid., p. 403.

[22] Sigrid Undset, *Gunnar's Daughter*, trans. Arthur G. Chater (New York:
Alfred A. Knopf, 1936), p. 272.

[23] Charlotte Blindheim recalls that her aunt's voice would grow tremulous
when she read Emily Bronte's lines from "The Prisoner" aloud: "Still, let my
tyrants know, I am not doomed to wear / Year after year in gloom, and desolate
despair, / A messenger of hope comes every night to me / And offers for short
life eternal liberty."

See Charlotte Blindheim, "Sigrid Undset, My Maternal Aunt", trans. Celia
Baldwin, *Scandinavian Review*, vol. 70 (June 1982), p. 53.

[24] *Twentieth Century Authors*, p. 1433.

[25] Winsnes, p. 226.

[26] Letter from Sigrid Undset in Paris to Nini Roll Anker in the summer of
1910, quoted in ibid., p. 51.

[27] Krane, p. 45. After the divorce, Ragna Moe sold newspapers, the only
job she could find, but she could not support her two daughters and her son,
who was incurably mentally handicapped. Svarstad's daughter Ebba remained
devoted to Sigrid Undset all her life, helping her raise the younger children.
During Norway's harsh postwar period, Ebba shared her food coupons with
Undset's younger son, Hans, who had none because he had been a student in
America during the war; see Krane, pp. 57–59. When Svarstad died in 1943,
Sigrid Undset wrote to Hope Emily Allen, "It made a strange impression on me
too of course to learn of the death of the man I have been married to, even if we
did not see much of each other for years . . . I am glad to know, his daughters,
my stepdaughters, were with him when he died. They are good girls, and I

long very much to see them again" (October 23, 1943). Quoted in Marlene Ciklamini, "Sigrid Undset's Letters to Hope Emily Allen", *The Journal of the Rutgers University Library*, vol. 33 (1968), p. 23.

[28] From a letter to Hope Emily Allen, February 16, 1947; quoted with ellipses in "Sigrid Undset's Letters to Hope Emily Allen", p. 23.

[29] Sources differ on the dating of Undset's formal reception into the Roman Catholic Church. Winsnes' dates are used above, but Sigrid Undset's autobiographical essay for *Twentieth Century Authors* states, ". . . on the first of November, 1924, I was received into the Catholic Church" (p. 1433).

[30] Beyer, p. 306.

[31] Sigrid Undset, *Jenny*, trans. W. Emme (New York: Alfred A. Knopf, 1921), p. 142.

[32] *Jenny*, p. 304.

[33] Sigrid Undset, "The Fourth Commandment", quoted in Winsnes, p. 64.

[34] *Twentieth Century Authors*, p. 1433.

[35] Krane, p. 54; Sigrid Undset, *The Wild Orchid*, trans. Arthur G. Chater (New York: Alfred A. Knopf, 1931).

[36] *Wild Orchid*, pp. 14-15.

[37] *Twentieth Century Authors*, p. 1433.

[38] Bayerschmidt, p. 161. No dedication appears in any of Sigrid Undset's published books, perhaps a result of her desire to maintain the utmost privacy.

[39] Sverre Arestad, "Sigrid Undset", in *The Columbia Dictionary of Modern European Literature*, 2d ed. rev. and enl. (New York: Columbia University Press, 1980), p. 831.

[40] Sigrid Undset, *Saga of Saints*, trans. E. C. Ramsden (New York: Alfred A. Knopf, 1934), p. 150.

[41] Sigrid Undset, *The Bridal Wreath*, trans. Charles Archer and J. S. Scott (New York: Alfred A. Knopf, 1923), p. 18.

[42] The horse cult was closely related to the Norse Vanir gods Freyr and his wife Freya, and "sacred horses were kept in his [Freyr's] sanctuary at Thrandheim [sic] in Norway." When Norway's tenth-century king Olav Tryggvasson tried to destroy the heathen temple there so that he could bring Christianity to the land, he took a stallion intended to be a sacrifice to Freyr and rode it in symbolic defiance of the god. Hilda Ellis Davidson, *Gods and Myths of the Viking Age*, new ed. (New York: Bell, 1964), p. 97.

[43] Davidson, p. 121.

[44] *Bridal Wreath*, p. 19.

[45] Ciklamini, p. 1032.

[46] *Bridal Wreath*, p. 38. In *Kristin Lavransdatter: An Aesthetic Study*, Fru Ellisiv Steen sees Brother Edvin's Franciscan "lecture" as Undset's major statement in the novel, and she probes Undset's treatment of the struggle between flesh and spirit in each of the novel's major characters.

[47] *Bridal Wreath*, p. 39.

⁴⁸ Sigrid Undset, *Ida Elisabeth*, trans. Arthur G. Chater (New York: Alfred A. Knopf, 1933), p. 53.

⁴⁹ Quoted in Bayerschmidt, p. 41.

⁵⁰ *Twentieth Century Authors*, p. 1434.

⁵¹ Olav's manor lay beneath "a sheer cliff, dark gray and almost bare, facing north . . . called the Horse". "Horse" in Norwegian is "Hesten", and in a note to the novel Sigrid Undset explained that "Hestviken" may be translated "Horse-wick". The name connects the pagan Norse fertility symbol of the horse with the marauding Viking tradition, a capsule description of the plight of Olav Audunsson, dominated by his physical passions and caught up in a revenge-murder of his wife's lover. For most of the novel Olav's pagan pride prevents him from confessing and receiving absolution. See Sigrid Undset, *The Master of Hestviken*, trans. Arthur G. Chater (New York: Alfred A. Knopf, 1928), p. 300.

⁵² *Master of Hestviken*, p. 717.

⁵³ Ibid., p. 716.

⁵⁴ Whitehouse, p. 5.

⁵⁵ Sigrid Undset, *The Burning Bush*, trans. Arthur G. Chater (New York: Alfred A. Knopf, 1933), p. 265.

⁵⁶ *Ida Elisabeth*, p. 167.

⁵⁷ Sigrid Undset, *Men, Women and Places*, trans. Arthur G. Chater (New York: Alfred A. Knopf, 1939), p. 16.

⁵⁸ Jacques Maritain, "Theocentric Humanism", in *Philosophy for a Time of Crisis*, ed. Adrienne Koch (New York: Dutton, 1959), p. 202. This essay is taken from Maritain's "A Faith to Live By" in *The Range of Reason* (New York: Charles Scribner's Sons, 1952).

⁵⁹ *Moster Sigrid*, p. 72.

⁶⁰ Margaret Mary Dunn, "Sigrid Undset Seen through the Eyes of an American Woman Religious", unpublished centennial article commissioned by the Norwegian Information Agency, 1982, p. 7. Dunn is a former cloistered nun who first encountered Undset's works while studying for her Ph.D. in English literature at Fordham University.

⁶¹ *Twentieth Century Authors*, p. 1434.

⁶² Dunn, p. 6.

⁶³ Whitehouse, p. 11.

⁶⁴ Arne Skouen, *Sigrid Undset skriver hjem* (Oslo: Aschehoug, 1982), pp. 147–48. Translation mine.

⁶⁵ Undset's letters to Hope Emily Allen (pp. 22–23) record some of her losses: her brother-in-law and Arnulf Overland, one of her "dearest friends" among Norwegian writers, were both arrested by the Nazis in Norway in June 1941 (letter July 7, 1941); Overland spent months recuperating in a Swedish hospital after being liberated in early 1945, while Undset's sister's husband died shortly after his release from a concentration camp (letter May 19, 1945). Undset's dentist, another friend, was maimed at Sachsenhausen, and her niece's husband

was permanently crippled by torture (letter March 18, 1946); and her closest girlhood friend died upon hearing that the Gestapo had killed her son (letter December 6, 1945). Undset's home at Lillehammer was probably defiled by the Nazis because she had been the first European writer of stature to denounce Hitler; they had chopped to bits her father's desk where she had written *Kristin Lavransdatter* and turned her house into a brothel.

[66] Dunn, p. 10.

[67] Sigrid Undset, unpublished letter to Ingebjorg Moller, quoted in Dunn, p. 10.

[68] Charlotte Blindheim recalls that her aunt claimed that pride was her greatest sin and that this had caused her enormous difficulties; see *Moster Sigrid*, pp. 72–73.

[69] Sigrid Undset, *The Cross*, trans. Charles Archer (New York: Alfred A. Knopf, 1927), p. 420.

David A. Bovenizer

MR. LYTLE'S "KRISTIN"

On a mountain in Tennessee there lives a man who claims to know Kristin Lavransdatter, and many there be who believe him.

The man is Andrew Nelson Lytle, novelist, former professor of creative writing (whose students included Flannery O'Connor, James Dickey, and Madison Jones), and the sole surviving member of the most remarkable band of writers (and prophets) in American literary history—the Southern Agrarians. Now ninety, his unassuming witness to familiarity with the protagonist of Sigrid Undset's monumental trilogy of fourteenth-century Norway is his new work of literary exegesis, *Kristin: A Reading* (University of Missouri Press, 1992). A journey through its mere ninety-two pages is tantamount to an imaginative re-embodiment as a man, or woman, of the part-pagan, part-Christian society of the Scandinavia of a half-millennium ago, and (well, almost anyway) compels the conviction that, yes, Andrew Lytle *lived* back then, so well does he know the time, its sensibility, and its people.

How is it that a novelist who is legendary in his region but too-little known outside the South can have written, on the threshold of his tenth decade, what his admirers accept as the finest commentary of its kind on a country (Norway) and an epoch (the Middle Ages) so far removed in time and space from 1993 and Tennessee? The answer is bound up with biscuits, bourbon, and butterbeans, and an old red flag defeated in battle though bearing the St. Andrew's Cross. The answer, that is, has to do with a particular kind of society, a certain mode of being and knowing, and the American South as a place within Christendom that could be characterized (Southern style, of course) as a first cousin of the Norway recreated by Sigrid Undset in her three-volume novel, *Kristin Lavransdatter* (which, being translated, is "Kristin, the Daughter of Lavrans").

Perhaps yet one more explanation-of-sorts is necessary to retain the attention of the nearly incredulous.

The log cabin built by his ancestors at Monteagle Assembly Grounds where Andrew Lytle resides is but five miles from Sewanee, Tennessee, where stands what is arguably the most beautiful campus on the North American continent—the campus of The University of the South. Old Confederate generals are buried there, as is Allen Tate, the late great (Catholic) poet and novelist who also was Andrew Lytle's life-long friend and fellow Agrarian. Only a few miles to the north (small *n*, one must note) is Murfreesboro, founded by one William Lytle of Revolutionary War fame and defended in a later, even more revolutionary conflict by the ferocious and fearless cavalrymen of Nathan Bedford Forrest, subject of Mr. Lytle's one book of nonfiction biography. His grandmother, when a girl, the author notes, heard the thunder of hoofs as Forrest's men rode. . . . Visitors to The Log Cabin eat foods Mr. Lytle has grown—and cooked—himself, warm themselves before a fire he stokes himself, and imbibe of Tennessee whiskeys which he serves (liberally, one must gratefully acknowledge) in old and familial goblets. To the fortunate, he signs his letters, invariably short but compact of wisdom, "Your Ancient Friend", and they know that 'tis true: he *is* ancient, less so of years (though that, assuredly) than of discernment (actually, *seeing*), wisdom, and what the mystics would call a kind of hindsight/wholesight.

Thomas Carlson, a Sewanee professor of English who partakes (liberally) of these singular graces as one of Mr. Lytle's principal protégés, has masterfully limned his subject in the eloquent foreword to *Kristin: A Reading*. As he writes,

Kristin Lavransdatter is that one special work of literature which in structure, characterization, and action peculiarly stimulates Andrew Lytle's imagination and sympathy. In its depiction of rural manners and mores and in its historical milieu, he clearly finds a close connection between the pre-industrial south and medieval Europe. "I know these people. I grew up with them", he once told a startled class before discussion of the novel began.[1]

This, we must be mindful, of an author and teacher whose previous essays on Flaubert and *Madame Bovary* elicited—as we shall see—an astonishingly similar statement from Allen Tate, many years ago.

But how, many will wonder, can this be? How can it be that a man born in the twentieth century is as at home, emotionally, psychically, and spiritually, in the fourteenth century—or even, some might conclude, *more* at home in the world of the Middle Ages than in the world of today?

Mr. Lytle himself has often attempted to answer this query. "I am closer [in sensibility] to the twelfth Century than to the twentieth", he has been known to remark.[2] And he has written:

> Born the day after Christmas, 1902, like a wet firecracker, as my mother remarked, I entered a world that lived with and by other creatures. My grandchildren and their ilk are unaware that they are creatures. I am closer to the twelfth Century than to their world, for that world has money, not salvation, as its ultimate desire. . . .
>
> As I grew up in Murfreesboro, the town easily joined the country. There were horses to hitch up, cows to milk (and that twice a day), often gardens to make. In town and country both, communities had the same kind of family life, with kin and connections, the connections by marriage, not blood. Because of this, people of the same station had the same social life and, frequently, the same marriages. Farming had not lost then its prestige as a way of life, and you could live well by it. . . . [M]ost human creatures, as they set forth to work or play, dance or love, touched hallowed ground, a pond, an everlasting spring,

an old elm, a farm that generations had known and lived on and by. . . . And there was the common knowledge of the long history all creatures shared. The rat, the skunk, the fox that set out on the chilly night had most of the instincts, needs, and faculties humans shared. . . . The farm was not only the land; it composed all the creatures inhabiting it, and all the things that grew. Even Brother Rabbit. This connection is no idle matter, or the sentimentality of pride. It is finally metaphysical. The identification of man through family with physical nature measures the state of religious belief. This induces a respect for and concord with all of God's creation, and a more practical knowledge of what to expect from the world. It teaches that you often eat your meat with sorrow and that you can lose in vital ways all that is dear.[3]

Because one may safely assume that readers will be coming to Andrew Lytle's *Kristin* only after having read the 1,047 pages of *Kristin Lavransdatter*, it is appropriate to remark the amazement—the kinship—that these of Mr. Lytle's reflections indicate to the story of Miss Undset's saga. Did Kristin not live such a life in such a place, and did she not "lose in vital ways all that [she held] dear"? Indeed, she did, and in losing all she found All. For, as the old, old Story insists, only they find life who lose it—*if* the loss quickens the soul unto spiritual vision and rebirth.

Thus it is no exaggeration on his part when Mr. Lytle writes in the same breath of salvation and sassafras tea. There is, to continue the exposition, a "metaphysical" quality inherent in pre-industrial (hence somewhat premodern) societies, and specifically the societies of Norway in old Scandinavia and the Old South in North America. This is because the very encounter of human nature with the natural world (after the revelation of God in Jesus Christ) makes luminous to consciousness (and to conscience) the "connection" (a decidedly Southern term in Mr. Lytle's vernacular) among all "creatures" (ditto) and also the fundamental realities of sin and the supernatural. There naturally follows the realization that the individual exists only and always in a society either attuned or antagonistic to the Divine, and that a people's history is a matter not of mere economics or politics but of nothing less than either salvation or damnation. As Mr. Lytle has suggested in his family memoir, "a country society, which ours was and is not more, by its habits and customs discovers the identity between the natural and the supernatural, that mystery which becomes ceremony to people who make their living by the land and the sea."[4] And, as he insisted to Allen Tate, who had come to wonder if the Agrarians had not made an idol of the Old South, "I don't see how you can save the truth of God and man except in terms of the conventions of some society. You might have a private salvation, but. . . ."[5] In that *but* resides the essence of Mr. Lytle's conviction that only a traditional society in harmony with the natural world and bound by ceremonies handed from generation to generation fully reflects on earth, in time, the order of heaven (that is, God) and eternity, and even specifically, the eternal truths.

It is this understanding of the nature of history, one does well to reiterate, which for Andrew Lytle reveals the similarity of the South of his boyhood and the Norway of Sigrid Undset's rendering. He *knew* such a society, in Tennessee (and Alabama) as recently as the 1920s, so he knew girls just like Kristin. They were his cousins, so to say, you see. And the defining characteristic of both societies was what can perhaps most accurately be defined as a "second-nature" understanding that "all creatures great and small"[6] were (and always are) just that: creatures. That is, every *thing* is made by God, all living things are creatures of God, and mankind is a creature made in nothing less than the very image of God. Of course, many late twentieth-century folk still believe this, intellectually or theologically. But there is (literally) a world of difference between a society (our own at present) which purports (if now reluctantly) to acclaim "In God We Trust" and a society in which virtually everyone would know intuitively that "In God we are". Such a society has been the South, and such is the society recreated by Sigrid Undset in *Kristin Lavrans-datter*.

Which brings us to Brother Rabbit.

Societies at home in the wildwood know where the laurel grows, and what the hoot-owl hoots, where the big catfish lurk, and what may be eaten and what may not, and also what will eat you "if'n you don't watch out."[7] "It takes all kinds" may not have been uttered by Noah, but it could have been, and it is a phrase natural upon the lips (for natural to the lore and language) of every traditional society from the dawn of time (until our own—but of that sad fact, more anon). The society which takes the whole of the creation of which it is a part, and which, in its economy, polity, and manners and morals, it reflects, *knows* that hoot-owls and sweet potatoes, odd people and snakebites, cannot be accounted for but must be accommodated. That is, no system of quantification either encompasses or explains the whole wondrous vastness and variety of "the things that God has made". So such societies in their quest of self-articulation turn, not to the beancounter, but to the story-teller.

Which brings us to Brer Rabbit.

Only a generation before Andrew Lytle was born, Joel Chandler Harris was still telling his stories of Brer Fox, Brer Bear, and Brer Rabbit. The voice of his Uncle Remus is thus as old as Adam's, which is to say, nearly as old as God's. And it shares, of course, in the tradition of him "who never spake without a parable", and whose parables (naturally) were understood perfectly by those whose life was connected (there's that word again) with lilies of the field or birds of the air, with the frustrations of fishing and the futility of reform. (Thus, by the bye, the tragic and ultimately doomed attempt of black Southerners today who seek their proper identity in pre-Christian Africa, through the ideology of Afrocentrism, rather than reconnecting with the richly Christian sensibility of the admirably Southern—hence American—Uncle Remus. But that is another story.)

Do we begin to see?

Kristin Lavransdatter is a monument of the human imagination because *imaginatively* (the stress is on *image*, as in *Imago Dei* . . .) it is a story true to the whole of life in a society aware of (if not, of course—for none is—perfectly conformed to) the mysterious relationship of all creatures one to the other, of the troubled (by sin) relationship of man and God, and of the poignancy of the human pilgrimage through time unto eternity, and that an eternity of either redemption or doom. In times past, such a society existed, and it was called Christendom. It stretched from Thessalonica to Tennessee, and encompassed old Norway, too. *Kristin Lavransdatter* is about it, and Andrew Lytle was born in it (though he worries whether it will still be around when he is not).

Here and there in his earlier writings, Mr. Lytle has offered provocative images by which to contrast the world of Before and the world of Today, which is to say, he contrasts what once was Christendom and what now is merely "The West" or "Western civilization". For example: "By means of [the] bold claim that we are made in the image of God, the structure of Christendom bound all men together, from King to peasant."[8] By "the structure of Christendom", he means the customs and compacts by which a society lives according to the shared conviction that the origin of all men is in the dim, misty past, back beyond time, within, finally and originally, the mystery of God himself. Today, this structure is all but effaced, because Western societies (once knit, however loosely, as Christendom) have allowed the postulates of materialism (of both human origins and ends) gradually to displace, virtually to dispel, the old sacred mystery. (One need think but for a moment on the difference between even "Europe" and "Christendom", let alone between "Christendom" and what now is proposed as "the European Community"—that is, a European Trade Zone, as it were.) Writing specifically of the United States, Mr. Lytle has sighed, "this whole country's Christian inheritance [is] threatened. But let there be no misunderstanding.

We still are subjects of Christendom. Only we have reached its Satanic phase."[9]

By this latter (terrifying) phrase, Mr. Lytle means nothing less than that the American component of Christendom has come to manifest the malevolent spirit of Babylon of old, and Babylon he defines as "the acceptance of matter as the only meaning, the source of the mystery".[10] In *Kristin: A Reading*, which is his latest statement on the subject, he elaborates on the contrast between modern America (and, one wonders, Norway, too?) and the world of *Kristin Lavransdatter*:

> It is well to examine how the Norwegians in the beginning of the fourteenth century accepted their world. This is crucial to an understanding of the action [of the novel]. Today we take the world as the end of all action, our reward or our bane. To the Christians of Norway it was the ground for the drama of the soul, salvation or damnation.[11]

The loss, or worse, the abandonment, of the understanding that history is bound up with the mysterious "eternal purpose"[12] of God, hence that it is the "ground for the drama of the soul" unto either "salvation or damnation", leads a society (downward) into what Mr. Lytle elsewhere has termed, simply and significantly, "confusion".[13] In the midst of such confusion, invariably there arise artists who plumb to the dark heart of the matter. In Norway, Sigrid Undset was one—she wrote *Kristin Lavransdatter* in 1923, which is, one should note, but a year after T. S. Eliot published "The Waste Land". In America, Andrew Lytle is one, and though his *Kristin* came to us as recently as 1992, his first major statement on the same essential theme appeared contemporaneously with Miss Undset's trilogy, in 1930. In each case, the necessary *a priori* form of social criticism (and proffered cure) is, not some sort of political action or reform, but the story. As one of Mr. Lytle's fellow Agrarians, the late Robert Penn Warren, wrote, in a poem:

> In this century, and moment of mania,
> Tell me a story.[14]

And Warren it was who described Andrew Lytle as "the perfect teller of tales".[15]

Which brings us to the mystical fact that Brer Rabbit is a creature best to be understood, not in the woods, but in a story. That is, he exists both as a bundle of fur and a cottony tail on four swift legs and as an image in the mind of man which in artistic men and women (such as Andrew Lytle and Sigrid Undset) is a participation in the very imagination of God. Such artistry is called storytelling, and very probably it is the oldest of human crafts because apparently it is the preferred form of communication (hence creation) of God. Thus the kinship of word and Word. . . .

In ancient societies, and perhaps especially in pagan societies, the *shaman* served as the principal "medium between the visible world and an invisible spirit world",[16] and part of his purpose was to divine the meaning of things. Much of the action of *Kristin Lavransdatter* is made all the richer in the very encounter between what could loosely be called a shamanistic paganism (the old religion of all of Scandinavia) and the storytelling—of the ultimate Story about God and man—of the Christian Church in its transmission of the revelation of God-to-man-in-Man by which it had been conceived.

It is for this reason, culminating all other reasons, that Andrew Lytle's *Kristin* is so helpful a *reading* of Kristin Lavransdatter. (*Reading* itself means to "grasp the meaning of" and is derivative of the Old English *raedan*, which is "to advise".)[17]

Two contemporary critics offer indispensable insight into this quality of the storyteller shared so profoundly by Sigrid Undset and Andrew Lytle. They are Lewis P. Simpson, retired former Boyd Professor of English in Louisiana State University, and the late Paul Zweig, who taught in Queens College, New York.

Writing on Cleanth Brooks and the late Robert Penn Warren, both of whom forged life-long friendships with Mr. Lytle, Simpson has written: "we must keep the storytelling going, since the storyteller . . . is the first to envision the struggle of man to realize his nature in community, the first to know man both as subject and object, the first to experience the deliberate detachment that comes with the responsibility of telling what has happened so that it will be remembered."[18] Is this not precisely why readers love *Kristin Lavransdatter*?

In "The Adventure of Storytelling", a major chapter in his eloquent account of the foremost tales of history, *The Adventurer*, Zweig reminds:

> Civilization is an affair of storytelling. In oral cultures, the wisdom, moral standards, and skills handed from one generation to the next are kept alive in the repository of tales. For Homer, the memorable life was modeled on a story, and had as its goal to become a story. This, perhaps, is the shaman's [or, we must be quick to emphasize, the storyteller's] most profound function: to extend the clarity of words—of human power and knowledge—ever further into the realms of the unnameable.[19]

It is precisely in this respect that great literature, that is, a great *story*, is by no means an "escape" but, quite to the contrary, both a return to the past—for the truth of the origin, nature, and destiny of the human community—and a morally informed compass which at once indicates a society's present situation and the path forward, so to speak, to its rightful way.

In pondering this almost-religious office of the literary artist, and in writing on Andrew Lytle himself, Lewis Simpson has suggested that "the mind of the literary artist may be almost the last mind articulately open to history as a mystery that unfolds out of God."[20] The "last mind", that is, in our essentially materialistic epoch. It was this same appreciation of Andrew Lytle's mind, hence his gift of storytelling, which prompted Allen Tate (the reader should recall the earlier allusion) to note, in remarking of Mr. Lytle's writings a generation ago on Flaubert, that Lytle "writes about *Madame Bovary* as if he had written Flaubert's masterpiece".[21] We may extend the observation to suggest that, in *Kristin*, Mr. Lytle writes, not as though he had written *Kristin Lavransdatter*, but as though he *knew* Kristin. Which completes a goodly portion of the tale.

Literature, the great literary critic Cleanth Brooks has written, is "knowledge by imaginative enactment".[22]

Even more profoundly, and writing as not only critic but churchman, Brooks has declared, "Literature is a kind of liturgy—a symbolic action."[23] In our time, when the ascendancy of the ideology of materialism has all but driven a sense of the sacred from the mind of man, Sigrid Undset has rediscovered old Norway, and Andrew Lytle has seen to the same land and time through the still "Christ-haunted"[24] sensibility of the South, and each has told tales which are akin to the liturgies of the Church in this respect at least, that they re-mind us of the intimate connection between time and the transcendent; indeed, of time's very existence within the all-enveloping eternal.

In his deep familiarity with Andrew Lytle both as friend and artist, Brooks has not hesitated repeatedly to define as the basis of Mr. Lytle's art nothing less than "the metaphysics of Rutherford County", Rutherford County being the Tennessee bounds of Mr. Lytle's life and the particular ground of his universal vision.[25]

Within this metaphysic, which he himself does not hesitate a moment to ascribe to his Christian faith, Andrew Lytle apprehends the very nature of Norwegian society of the fourteenth century and the very heart (unto nearly the very soul) of *Kristin Lavransdatter*. In a country and age marked now by the re-emergence of paganism as the principal challenge to Christian teachings, he understands wholly the similar if reverse situation of old Norway, when Christian teachings were slowly but forcefully chasing away the old false gods. And in this old and ever-new engagement, he *reads* perfectly the symbols by which Sigrid Undset establishes her subject's saga.

For Kristin, Andrew Lytle discerns, is confronted as all of us are at one time or another by "wreaths" of opposite, even combative, allure and destiny—of either "salvation or damnation". One is the wreath of innocence and Christian maidenhood, and one is the wreath of the elf-maiden. One, he reminds, is "of gold", the other "of golden blossoms".[26] They are utterly different in nature and destiny. And—ah, but to tell more would be to spoil his tale. . . .

For *Kristin: A Reading* is, of course, a *reading* by Andrew Lytle of *Kristin Lavransdatter*, by Sigrid Undset. But just so, it is a tale about a tale which wonderfully retells "the old, old Story", and his book summons us, not only to reread the great saga of medieval Norway, but to re-engage a question of eternal importance: How can we live the life which the story of Kristin enjoins in our own now nearly pagan time, in our evermore-alien land?

NOTES

¹ Thomas Carlson in Andrew Lytle, *Kristin: A Reading* (Columbia, Missouri: University of Missouri Press, 1992), p. ix.

² From conversation with the author, Crozier, Virginia, November 1983.

³ Andrew Lytle, "A Myth in a Garden", in Lytle, *From Eden to Babylon: The Social and Political Essays of Andrew Nelson Lytle* (Washington, D.C.: Regnery Gateway, 1990), pp. 192, 195, 187.

⁴ Lytle, *A Wake for the Living* (Nashville: J. S. Sanders and Co., 1992), p. 3.

⁵ Lytle to Allen Tate in T. D. Young and Elizabeth Sarcone, eds., *The Lytle-Tate Letters* (Oxford, Mississippi: University Press of Mississippi, 1987), p. 245.

⁶ From the hymn "All Things Bright and Beautiful", by Cecil Francis Alexander (1818–1895), first stanza.

⁷ From the poem "Little Orphan Annie", by James Whitcomb Riley (1849–1916), first stanza.

⁸ Lytle, *From Eden to Babylon*, p. 181.

⁹ Ibid., p. 229.

¹⁰ Ibid., p. 154.

¹¹ Lytle, *Kristin*, p. 12.

¹² Eph 3:11.

¹³ Lytle, *From Eden to Babylon*, p. 154.

¹⁴ Robert Penn Warren, cited in Lewis P. Simpson, ed., *The Possibilities of Order: Cleanth Brooks and His Work* (Baton Rouge: Louisiana State University Press, 1976), p. xxiv.

¹⁵ Robert Penn Warren, "Andrew Lytle's 'The Long Night': A Rediscovery", in *Southern Review*, n.s., vol. 7 (1971), cited by Thomas Carlson in "Jacks Are Much Misunderstood", in *The Chattahoochee Review*, vol. 8, no. 4 (Summer 1988), p. 16.

¹⁶ *The American Heritage Dictionary of the English Language*, 3d ed. (Boston: Houghton Mifflin, 1992), p. 1657.

¹⁷ Ibid., p. 1504.

¹⁸ Simpson, *The Possibilities of Order*, p. xxii.

¹⁹ Paul Zweig, *The Adventurer* (Princeton, N.J.: Princeton University Press, 1974), p. 93.

²⁰ Lewis Simpson, "Lytle the Critic: A Further Note", *Chattahoochee Review*, vol. 8, no. 4 (Summer 1988), p. 56.

²¹ Ibid., p. 52.

²² "A Conversation with Cleanth Brooks", in Simpson, *The Possibilities of Order*, p. 48.

²³ Ibid., p. 48.

[24] Flannery O'Connor, "The Catholic Novelist in the Protestant South", in O'Connor, *Collected Works* (New York: The Library of America, 1988), p. 861.

[25] From conversation with the author at Piety Hill, Mecosta, Michigan, August 1989.

[26] Lytle, *Kristin*, p. 52.

TRANSLATIONS

ASTRID O'BRIEN

A NOTE ON THE TRANSLATIONS

In the Gray Light of Dawn (*I grålysningen*) was written in 1908, during the earliest phase of Sigrid Undset's literary activity, when she was still feeling her way among different literary forms. *Fru Marta Oulie*, a modern novel dealing with a married woman's adultery and its ethical and psychological consequences, had been published during the previous year. A collection of short stories entitled *The Happy Age* (*Den lykkelig adler*) was published in 1908. But this, her only drama, lay unpublished in her desk drawer. Gidske Anderson tells us in her biography that Undset tried to get it accepted at Fahlstrøm's theater in Kristiania, now Oslo, without success.[1]

In 1926 it was finally published in *Norrøn helf*, and in 1930 she permitted it to be reprinted in *Nordens kalendar*; however, both publications reached no more than a small circle of readers. Not until after her death, in 1956, did it become available to the Norwegian public and amateur theater groups when, thanks to Erling Nielsen, it appeared in the Danish publication *Perspectiv*.

Even in this small, early work, we meet two themes to which Undset returns again and again in her later works; the obligation of husband and wife to be faithful to each other and that of parents to put their children's welfare ahead of their personal happiness. This emphasis on fidelity is deeply rooted in the Norwegian character: a solemn oath bound a Viking to his leader as well as a wife to her husband. Neither vow allowed for any exceptions: total fidelity was expected, no matter how imprudent the leader or husband might be.

The play treats the theme of fidelity and betrayal through the restrained conversation of former spouses, divorced for a number of years, who meet at the sickbed of their now teen-age daughter. The edition from which this translation was made was published by Aschehoug in 1968.

"Some Reflections on the Suffragette Movement" ("No-gen Kvindesaks—betragtninger", or literally, "Some Feminist Considerations") first appeared in the periodical *Samtiden* in 1912. It was later reprinted in *A Woman's Point of View* (*Et kvindesynspunkt*—Aschehoug, 1919). It was written not long after Sigrid Undset's marriage, while she and her husband were living in London. While her husband was painting, Sigrid was immersing herself in English Renaissance literature and working on short stories which appeared that year in *Fattige skjaebner* (*Poor Fortunes*).

Sigrid Undset wrote this essay in the Dano-Norwegian used prior to the spelling reforms of 1919 and 1938; some of her vocabulary is Danish as well. It was perhaps written hurriedly and sent to the periodical without adequate editing, since there are a number of long and complex sentences whose meaning is not always clear, as well as some needless repetitions. The translation is based upon the original essay as it appeared in *Samtiden* (Kristiania, 1912).

The essay should be read as a statement of Undset's feminism at the time of her novel *Jenny*, published in the fall of 1911, which had established her reputation as an author and outraged many Norwegians: conservatives had found its acceptance of women's sexual needs scandalous. More radical feminists, on the other hand, opposed its insistence that women cannot find spiritual fulfillment solely in work or art, since they are far more naturally restricted by their biology than men.

"If 2 + 2 = 5" was found among her papers after her death: its original title was "Preface", but there was no indication of what she had intended it to introduce. Neither was there anything to help determine the date of its composition, although it must have been written shortly after Sigrid Undset was received into the Roman Catholic Church on November 24, 1924. It was first printed in *St. Olav*, the monthly published by the Catholic Diocese, in 1965, when it was given its title. The copy on which this translation is based was sent to us through the kindness of Rev. Claes E. K. Tande, J.C.L., of the Oslo Diocesan Tribunal.

"Catholic Propaganda" ("Katholsk propaganda"), "A Letter from Archbishop Nathan Söderblom" ("Et brev fra Ärkebiskop Söderblom"), and "Reply to Archbishop Söderblom" ("Svar til Ärkebiskop Söderblom") all appeared in 1927 in the publication *Vor verden* (Oslo: March, pp. 106–39; April, pp. 221–34; May, pp. 294–304). "Catholic Propaganda" was published separately that same year (Oslo: Some). The copy from which this translation was made was obtained from the research collection of the New York Public Library. We gratefully acknowledge the help of Sherrill Harbison, who was in Norway at the time, in obtaining copies of the Archbishop's letter and Sigrid Undset's reply.

"A Christmas Meditation"—This little reflection first appeared in German: *Und war dies Kindlein nicht geboren* ("And What If This Baby Were Not Born"), published in Munich by Verlag Ars Sacra, Jos. Müller in 1929. It was reprinted by the same publishing house in 1958. The Norwegian "*En jule betraktning*" was published in *Julehelf* (Oslo, 1950) with illustrations. The text from which this translation was made appeared in the collection *Artikler og taler fra krigstiden* (*Articles and Tales from Wartime*) edited by A. H. Winsnes, published by Aschehoug in 1952. Unfortunately, this edition did not include illustrations, although the text makes clear that Sigrid Undset was referring to specific paintings of the Nativity.

"Progress, Race, Religion" was written first in German, "Fortschritt, Rasse, Religion", in 1935, and appeared in *Die Gefahrdung des Christentums durch Rassenwahn und Judenverfolgung* (*The Endangerment of Christianity through Race—Insanity and Persecution of the Jews*), a collection of articles by Protes-

tants and Catholics published by the refugee firm Vita Nova
in Lucerne. The Norwegian version, "Fremskridt, Rase, Religion", from which the translation was made, appeared in
the periodical *Fritt Ord* (Oslo) the following year and was reprinted in *Artikler og taler fra krigstiden*, edited by A. H. Winsnes
(Oslo: Aschehoug, 1952).

It was Sigrid Undset's first direct attack on Nazism: it is
a strong indictment, written with a sense of urgency. Those
who persist in worshipping technological progress, racial superiority and totalitarian leaders are walking a road which
leads to dissolution and death. In opposition to such mythical
ideals, she maintains that real human fellowship must be based
upon honest recognition of human fallibility and the hope of
redemption given to us by Christ.

Her books, especially the medieval novels, were very popular in Germany, hence this essay, which is both an appeal
and a warning, could not fail to attract attention. The Nazis
denounced her viciously as hostile, un-Nordic in her attitude,
the spokeswoman of the Catholic Church, which they regarded as the most corrupting international power.

After the invasion of Norway in April 1940, she was ordered by the government to leave the country as soon as
possible; her attitude toward the Nazis being so well known,
it was feared that she would be forced to make propaganda
broadcasts—or worse—if she were to fall into their hands. In
America she continued to write, condemning totalitarianism
in all its forms—the title essay of *Return to the Future* (*Tilbake
til fremtiden*, 1942) contains the crux of her anti-totalitarianism
message.

NOTES

[1] *Sigrid Undset—et liv* (Oslo: Gyldendal Norsk Forlag, n.d.), pp. 169–70.

SIGRID UNDSET

IN THE GRAY LIGHT OF DAWN

A One-Act Play

Characters:
Office Manager Cato Brinchmann
Lydia Brinchmann

The action takes place at the home of Lydia Brinchmann. Lydia Brinchmann's living room.

In the middle of the back wall an open door to the bedroom. A night light is burning there.

To the right a door to the lobby.

On the left are two sets of windows, shades drawn, outside a grayish summer morning.

The living room is informally, but tastefully, furnished.

To the right, below the door, a sofa is placed at an angle from the wall, a table and two armchairs in front of it. A small lamp on the table is lit. To the left, between the windows: a desk and a chair. To the left, between the window sills and on a flower table: several vases with partly withered flowers placed around the living room.

Lydia Brinchmann sits in an armchair, she has a shawl around her and an open book on her lap, but she is not reading.

A moment after the curtain is raised the doorbell gives a quick ring. Lydia, strangely agitated, gets up and puts away the book. While she stands as if to compose herself, she straightens her hair and her dress and walks into the entrance hall.

One hears a muted conversation from there, and then, Cato Brinchmann and Lydia enter.

Translated by Liv I. Shank

He is dressed for the outside and carries a small suitcase.
At the beginning they talk softly.

CATO. I was thinking that since you hadn't wired again, nothing had happened.

LYDIA. Yes, but didn't you get my telegram last night? "Else better", I wired. I sent it to your private address, Lerberg, half past six, I think, was the time.

CATO. Oh, you see, I was away, in Sweden, on a business trip. I came home last night and went by the office first and there was your first telegram. I could then just catch the 7:30 train south and took my suitcase and went straight back to the station.

LYDIA. Poor dear, you must be terribly tired.

CATO. Oh—.

LYDIA. And now you are coming directly from the station?

CATO. I took a carriage straight here.

LYDIA. Oh dear, have you had any food? Last night or now?

CATO. Yes. I had supper at the station.

LYDIA. You must be terribly hungry—sit down and I'll get you a cup of something. Do you want tea or coffee?

CATO. Oh, no. Don't go to any trouble for my sake. I only wanted to drop by, find out how she is. Now I'll go to the hotel. Then I would like to come later this morning and hear more and say hello to Else, perhaps?

LYDIA. But can you get anything there at this time? It is no bother for me. I have gas in the kitchen and everything. Isn't coffee the best, or perhaps you'll try to sleep when you get to the hotel? It is probably better that you get a cup of tea then?

CATO (*sitting down on the sofa*). But you must be so tired. (*Lydia exits to the right. Cato gets up and walks around the living room, looking at things, picks up a photo from the desk, looks at it for a while.*)

LYDIA (*entering, continuing*). No. I'm not so tired anymore. I slept part of the night; then the maid attended. Doctor Larsen practically ordered me. A while ago I sent Caroline to bed. During the previous nights we had a nurse.

(*Pause*)

LYDIA. Take off your coat for a while and sit down.

CATO (*taking off his coat*). Thank you. Good heavens, Lydia, what a terrible ordeal this must have been for you.

LYDIA (*clenches her teeth, shakes her head from side to side. After a while she speaks*). And it happened so suddenly. We went down to Hvitsten last Sunday to look at an apartment where I thought we could stay during my vacation. I don't know whether she got wet feet or if she had been too scantily dressed on the steamer—it was rather cool in the evening as we came back. On Monday she had a fever and was delirious (*halfway in tears*).

CATO (*after a while*). You haven't been to the office then?

LYDIA (*holding back her tears*). I was there on Monday—but when it turned out to be pneumonia—It is terrible to go around blaming oneself, whether one has been careless, perhaps—

CATO. Good heavens. I try to imagine if something had happened, if you had lost her—(*Walks over and sits down on the sofa.*) It was terrible, so terribly hard on you, Lydia, that you even sent me a telegram.

LYDIA. You had the right to know—if something should happen—to see her. I know that you love her. (*Pause. Lydia sits down at the desk, facing him.*)

CATO. Does Else know that I'm coming?

LYDIA. I haven't told her yet.

CATO. What does Else think about it, about me—if she thinks of me at all?

LYDIA. What Else thinks about it—

CATO. Does she speak, does she mention it at all?

LYDIA. Never. Not now. But you know we have talked about it. We talked about it when you got married. I thought it was better that she learn it from me than hear it from other people.

CATO. What did you tell her then?

LYDIA. I told her how it was—as much of it as I thought she ought and should know.

CATO. How did she take it?

LYDIA. You can imagine that she couldn't really understand it. (*bitter*) She'll learn about it, when she gets older.

CATO. She has written rather friendly letters, I think—the letters I've received around Christmas-time and such. Is she as beautiful as she looks in the picture you sent to me last fall?

LYDIA. It is a good likeness. (*shortly after*) Why don't you go in and look at her—but be careful—she's sleeping soundly now. (*Cato tip-toes into the bedroom. Lydia exits to the right. Returns with a tray. Sets the table. She stands looking at the bedroom. When Cato enters, she only says softly*) Please help yourself. (*Cato sits down. She pours tea.*)

CATO (*slowly*). My God. How she has changed.

LYDIA. I'm sure you find her changed.

CATO. Her face is so thin. When I think of her having been so sick—and I didn't even know about it.

LYDIA. She hasn't changed much during her sickness. She is gradually changing to look more grown-up—don't forget that she will soon be fourteen. She is getting to be rather tall— Please, help yourself.

CATO. Yes, please, another drop—No, thank you . . . I'm not hungry. Lydia, I was just thinking that your vacation isn't until August—couldn't Else—it would probably be good for her to get to the countryside as soon as possible after she gets well—couldn't she come and stay with me for a while? We live on a big farm, you know. She might enjoy the stay—and now the illness just before her exam which she probably can't take.

LYDIA. Visit you?

CATO (*quickly*). You see, Nanna is leaving in about a fortnight and will be away for most of the summer with the little ones. Aunt Sophie is probably coming to take care of me while she's gone. You must know, Lydia. I would take care of her the best way I know—our doctor has girls her age —I could teach her horseback riding— Lerberg is such a pleasant old farm. I would make it just as nice for her as I could. Well, I can only ask you—

LYDIA. Yes, thank you, Cato. But you see—I had thought of arranging my vacation to start now—so we could go to the country right away, and stay at a pension outside town for the rest of the summer. You see, being without Else for a whole month—and now that she is convalescing—

CATO. I do understand. But Lydia, would you be so kind— if it could be done, and if Else herself should want it—that she come and visit me for a short while this summer, even if only for a week's time. Now that I'll be alone. Would you permit me to ask her about that?

LYDIA. Yes, of course—

CATO. That we should become complete strangers to each other—the two of us—has often caused me to despair these last years, although I am completely at fault.

LYDIA (*interrupting*). No indeed. I never wanted to separate this child from you—you should know that. On the other hand, I feel that, while she is still a child, the less she is reminded about anything extraordinary in her relationship, the better. So she could be left at peace these years. She may have enough to think about anyway— But it may be just as well that she gets used to regarding the situation as something completely natural. I'll be happy to send her to you for a visit.

CATO. Thank you, Lydia.

LYDIA. By the way, Cato, how are you? You look good.

CATO. Thanks.

LYDIA. How is Nanna?

CATO. Oh, fine— She'll be at Strømstad this year—first with her married sister, Emma Lund—

LYDIA. You have two small boys.

CATO. Yes, Finn and Leif. (*involuntarily, slowly*) How often I have been yearning for Else.

LYDIA (*somewhat at a loss*). Are your boys healthy and fine?

CATO. Oh, yes. Finn is really a sturdy fellow. Leif, the poor dear, has a harelip, otherwise a good-looking child.

LYDIA. Oh, I'm sorry—

CATO. The doctor thinks it can be operated on when he gets older, then it won't show.

LYDIA. They are able to do that now. A good thing he is a boy —it doesn't matter so much then.

CATO. Yes. I had, by the way, wished for a little girl, but now I feel happy about another son.

LYDIA. May I pour more tea?

CATO. No, thank you. I enjoyed the tea. (*Lydia gets up and cleans the table, carries the tray to a serving table in the background, re-arranges things for a while.*)

CATO. You keep everything so nice, Lydia. All the flowers—

LYDIA. Please, don't look around—it looks so untidy, all the withered flowers—I haven't been able to do anything these days. Else picked these flowers the day we were at Hvitsten. So I didn't feel like throwing them out. By the way, how did you know my vacation is in August?

CATO. I talked to Agot Larsen the other day. She visited her uncle for a couple of days—

LYDIA. Oh, that's true, she has an uncle in your neighborhood. You probably see her now and then?

CATO. Yes, I talk to her when she is visiting. (*He suddenly bends forward, hiding his face in his hands.*)

LYDIA (*in the background*). Do you know anything about this engineer Paulsen to whom she is engaged?

CATO (*trying to control himself, wants to answer, but cannot*). (*Lydia waiting for an answer—surprised. When he doesn't answer, walks forward when she sees that he is crying.*) (*Getting up, drying his eyes*) I'll leave now—(*Sits down and starts crying again.*) Oh no, let me sit here for a while—stay here. (*Cries strongly.*) (*Lydia stands quietly next to his chair.*)

CATO. God only knows what you must think of me, behaving like this, coming here to you in the middle of the night and starting this way—Now. I'll go immediately—Oh, poor Lydia, you yourself are so tired and concerned. Don't be angry—

LYDIA. You poor thing—you are nervous—tired—

CATO. Oh, yes. It was terrible last night. I didn't know what the situation was like here. Didn't even know whether I would come in time. And there were people on the train whom I knew and who talked about everything in the world to me.

LYDIA. So you haven't been able to sleep at all.

CATO. Oh, no. I dreaded meeting you too. Lydia—when I thought of meeting you again—and Else near death, dead perhaps—the only one you had—(*Lydia puts her hand on top of his. He takes it and kisses it. She withdraws her hand.*)

LYDIA (*pulling herself quickly back*). No, Cato—

CATO. Forgive me, Lydia. May I just stay here another moment? I'll behave properly—when you stood there—when you came to the door and greeted me, you were so kind, served me tea— And I was thinking that I had lived apart from all this for six years and sat here at home as a stranger who was to leave again in a short while—

LYDIA (*slowly*). You started this conversation, Cato. When I stand here and look at you, think of your coming from your home—you were there yesterday and are going back there —you have a wife—I'm not your wife—you have a couple of children with somebody else—

CATO. I'm really a scoundrel talking to you like this.

LYDIA. Hush, hush. I didn't mean it that way. I only try to remember that is the way it is. Somewhere far from here there are living rooms with chairs and tables where you are every day, and rooms with beds and everything—I have never seen it. That is the truth. And even yesterday it seemed reasonable. I had gotten accustomed to the thought, I had resigned myself to it.

Cato.   Yes, Lydia. But I have gotten what I deserved, in every way. Believe me, if you knew everything, you have gotten all the revenge you could wish for.

Lydia.   Don't talk that way. I have never wished for revenge —as you say.

Cato (*smiling lightly*).   Well you have always been a superior being to some extent.

Lydia.   Don't say such things. Of course, sometimes I have wished for it. But I wouldn't even admit that to myself. And I believe I had reached a point where I would have wished you well, if I knew you were happy in the new— (*She walks up and down.*) If you had received my second telegram, you probably wouldn't have come?

Cato.   I cannot tell—Perhaps I would only have written then.

Lydia.   For we have no right to talk about something that we want. I wouldn't ask you about the only thing I care about. I saw you one evening at the theater—three years ago: it was before you were married.

Cato.   You saw me that evening?

Lydia.   Yes. I stood near the glass door and waited for Sara and Ernst. Then I saw you as you entered the lobby. You looked terribly sad. Sara said it—she isn't very tactful, you know. "Cato looks terribly depressed", she said. God only knows everything I was thinking—but I did nothing—I was only being careful to prevent a situation where I would have to meet you. And for a long time afterward I was waiting— and trying not to wait.

Cato.   You probably feel that I am betraying Nanna? But the fact that I couldn't leave her alone that time when she returned from abroad, and I felt that she was in love—that I could have her in all her youth—such a fun person. That was treachery.

LYDIA. Toward her too?

CATO. Mostly toward Nanna, I think. She doesn't have the strength you have. I ought to have known that I wouldn't be able to finish the course I'd chosen and still be able to make a new start. I ought to have known that you can't just walk away from ten years of your life, ten years in which you've lived more fully than any other years. At least one shouldn't be like me—a coward afterward. One should either have no conscience or be able to turn it on and off. How much damage I have caused—to you and to her—but even more to Nanna. I think you would pity her if you met her now.

LYDIA. Poor thing—how I hated Nanna—

CATO. It would make more sense to hate me.

LYDIA (*laughing lightly*). Well, but the fact is I hated Nanna. Of course, you too, sometimes that; but I didn't want to admit —just the way I didn't want to admit that I loved you.

CATO. I could see very clearly that evening at the theater that you avoided having to greet me.

LYDIA. That evening at the theater?

CATO. Yes—God only knows if that wasn't the worst thing I have ever experienced. During all those long months—that whole winter—I was with her every day and came home to you and realized that you knew everything and never said a word about it. It was strange, as well as uncertain. I only wanted to take one day at a time. Any day might bring something like an earthquake—

LYDIA. What do you mean?

CATO. I expected that you—I was too much of a coward to make a decision. I expected you to force me, to demand to know—come and demand, use your rights—

LYDIA. Do you mean that I should have demanded that you stay with me?

CATO (*closing his eyes for a moment*). God only knows what I meant. It was like walking in the dark. I perceived nothing the way it was. I felt everything I came near was much larger and kind of out of shape. I was probably in love with Nanna, but I really don't know if it wasn't a kind of pretending.

LYDIA. Pretending?

CATO. Yes, Lydia. I'm not like you. I wish I could make you understand this—however much you may despise me. I was probably in love. But it was like in a dream. I think I would have snapped out of it if you had called. You must understand that I don't blame you for anything. I hope you understand what I mean. I think this is something that is beyond reach —right or wrong. There was a period at the beginning about which I don't feel responsible. I don't want to minimize anything I have done. I was unfaithful, cowardly, mostly cruel and cowardly beyond all reason, and I ought to be silent about this now. I shouldn't use this time this way, but now that I have begun, shouldn't I continue? At the beginning it was as if I didn't know the difference between right and wrong, for I was like a sleepwalker who didn't know where to put his foot the next step. I ought to have known you. I knew so well what you were like. And any time before it all started I could have said that you would never stoop to hold on to me—never ask me to stay. Then one day, suddenly, I knew nothing more about myself. I was a completely different person from what I had imagined. And by God, Lydia, I think I simply expected to see that you suddenly were a different person too from the one I knew, and that I would see you the way you were.

LYDIA (*remaining silent for a while*). I believe I understand you. When did you start thinking like that?

CATO. That evening. I probably knew previously that I had
regrets. I had attacks of nostalgia before. But I saw everything that evening—the way it was. Then I understood that
it was my home I had betrayed, that I had cut all my roots
to the past when I broke my life in pieces. That I was too
old—and too weak—to strike roots in a different life.

LYDIA (*involuntarily*). And then—

CATO. Then I married.

LYDIA. But she? Didn't she understand? She had to suspect
something?

CATO. Well, we were both singled out by the scandal. Had
started out on this. And then, you know, you don't give up
and turn around in the middle.

LYDIA. That is something I don't understand—

CATO (*fumbling*). Well—in a way—just then we loved so passionately in a desperate sort of way. You understand, we had
nothing else—

LYDIA (*shivering*). I cannot imagine Nanna— What does she
say now?

CATO. Nanna wants a divorce—

LYDIA. What are you saying?

CATO. Yes. (*He hides his face in his hands, looks up again.*) She
has said so many times. (*completely despairing*) Oh, Lydia,—
Lydia—it makes no sense to try to hide anything from you.
You know me, you have seen me naked, you know my ways,
my misery. Oh, Lydia, Lydia. I know I should have died—
(*She has walked up to him, he puts his arm around her waist, rests
his head against her lap. She puts her hands round his head; she
is also sobbing.*)

CATO. It's true, Lydia—I can't hide anything from you. Nobody else knows how I am except you. My wife—you al-

ways were my wife— (*He stands up, still holding his arms around her.*) I cannot stand it. All these things here—it seems they are screaming at me— I know everything—aren't I at home here—and to know that I never again will be with you—never again—never again—

LYDIA (*defending herself lightly against his kiss*). Please let go of me—let go—

CATO. Well, yes. (*He doesn't let go.*) (*Lydia puts her arms around his neck. They stand close for a while, swaying. Suddenly the table cloth is pulled down; the vase, a picture, everything falling on the floor with an intense, unbearable noise. Lydia quickly gets away from his grip, runs behind the sofa as if she were fleeing. Absent-mindedly she takes her shawl from the sofa and wraps it around her as though she were cold. She then walks over and closes the door to the bedroom and pulls the drapes in front of the door. Walks to the window, opens the shades and the windows, first one, then the other. Remains standing in front, pulls the shawl tighter with a shiver.*)

LYDIA (*slowly*). This is completely crazy—

CATO (*picking up tablecloth, puts everything back*). This vase—it broke— (*He holds the pieces in his hands.*) (*Lydia is silent.*)

CATO (*holding the pieces*). Where do you want me to put it?

LYDIA (*loud and angry*). Just put them there. (*She suddenly starts laughing, hysterically. He walks toward her.*)

CATO (*concern in his voice*). Oh Lydia, Lydia—My God! What have I done again—

LYDIA. I'll stop—(*laughing again*). Oh, God, it is so ridiculous— (*She gradually regains control of herself, sits down near the window.*)

CATO (*slowly*). I'm so ashamed. What should I do?

LYDIA (*slowly, friendly, in a strained manner*). I think you'd better leave, Cato—I hope you aren't angry— You can come back before noon when we both have had a chance to rest and we aren't so nervous.

CATO. Yes, I'll go. (*He walks over to pick up and put on his overcoat and also picks up his suitcase and hat.*) Good-bye, Lydia. Thank you for letting me come in and see Else. Now you probably think worse of me than before.

LYDIA (*taking his hand, holding onto it*). No, Cato. I don't want you to talk like that. And I don't want you to torture yourself. Listen, it was mostly my fault.

CATO. No, Lydia— Oh now you speak in that good, warm voice you have—You have barely changed, Lydia. Are you aware of that?

LYDIA (*smiling sadly*). I'm a completely different person. Oh, poor Cato, I wish I could help you. I feel I have also acted so wrongly toward you. I understand that very well now. But I couldn't have acted differently—

CATO. No. But just imagine if at that time I had understood what I had in you—you remained the same, always and unchangeably—faithful and good and honest and proud and true, (*shyly*) noble—

LYDIA. Oh poor Cato. No, I was none of the things you mentioned. You must believe me. It was not because I was noble, as you say, that I acted the way I did. God Almighty— When I didn't talk, didn't demand an explanation when I knew you were with her, I was afraid. I was afraid of learning that you loved someone else. I dared not say what I thought— because, believe me, it wasn't noble. There wasn't a thing, no matter how shameless, that I couldn't think of when you were with her. God, how I hated that woman. I was afraid to talk because I didn't know what I would say once I got started.

Oh, I was jealous of her even before we married. I hated the fact that you corresponded with her. I didn't say any-

thing for fear I'd say something nasty—I didn't want to
admit thinking there might be danger in your remaining
friends. I only degraded her quietly inside myself. Pooh—
she isn't as good-looking as I am—not so intelligent either
—only cheerful and flirtatious—but a goose. Don't you remember? I went around talking to you about her quietly and
shyly but in a degrading way. Poor dear, you didn't notice
because I didn't dare do it in a curt, obvious manner. And
when she returned home—every time she visited with us
—I wished that she would have an accident, die, be run
over, be maimed—

Amazing that you didn't understand—

CATO. I didn't—It never occurred to me that you were thinking that way.

LYDIA. No, because I was noble—a superior being. (*whimpering*) I felt I was so dull, so poor, had so few strings to play
on. And she had so many, knew all the beautiful tricks to
catch you. I couldn't fight against her. I didn't know how.
I was only your old wife—

CATO. And then you wouldn't admit that you loved me—

LYDIA (*remembering*). Did I say that? Oh Cato, I wanted to be
proud and noble, like you say. When I couldn't be young and
adorable and delightful like your party girl, you must remember that I had always been very much by myself—as a young
girl—had gone between a business and the guest house—
among people whom I often despised, among whom I felt
arrogant, people who often weren't particular about how
they behaved toward each other— I didn't want to beg—
I never believed it would be possible that you would leave
me and the child— You had to get tired of that show-off—
I was someone completely different— And when I realized
everything was lost, I had to take Else and leave. I did have
the wildest plans—The last time we met, when everything
was decided—When I came home, I thought of sending

Else to you. I knew you would like to see her, but I realized it would be wrong for her. Oh, God, all the ugly things I thought and wished—all the right things I tried to do—all led to the same end.

CATO (*quietly surprised*). I knew nothing at all of this.

LYDIA (*intensely*). How I wish it were yesterday, the day before —the terrible days when I was agonizing over Else—and you were a stranger far away about whom I thought quietly —and all *this* would be a far-away, dead life—

CATO. It would be a crime if I stopped believing— It cannot be over between the two of us, Lydia—

LYDIA (*despairing*). You know it is over.

CATO (*slowly, seriously*). Nanna has suffered just as much—she too wants out. Sometime later, Lydia—in years, perhaps— if only we knew we would meet again, could try if we dared to find our place in life.

LYDIA. Do you think that Nanna would want a divorce if she knew you were here today? (*Cato is silent.*) No, Cato—in years, perhaps, as you say—I have again become the way I've been the last few years. Neither happy nor sad—rather satisfied—with sorrows and pleasures, with Else—but through with life for my own part. I cannot start to live again— for I cannot dream and walk through darkness anymore like you talked about. (*brutally*) And you have your little boys— the little tyke with the harelip. (*Cato looks up with a painful, uncomprehending look.*) (*Lydia speaking tenderly*) I think of that poor little dear.

CATO. Shall I leave now? (*Lydia nods.*) (*Cato is on the verge of tears*). Good-bye then—

LYDIA (*Nods again. As he is approaching the door, she says*) Else will visit you this summer for a long while. I promise. She will learn to love you so much.

CATO. Oh, Lydia—(*at the door, slowly*) Wave to me through the window, Lydia.

LYDIA (*walking over to him, giving him a quick kiss*). Be kind to me, Cato, leave now— (*Cato leaves. Lydia takes her handkerchief, dries her eyes, walks slowly to the window. She puts her handkerchief in her bosom again, peeks out behind the curtain which she holds out from the window. Sobbing, she glides down on a chair near the window. Sobs more and more.*)

Curtain.

SIGRID UNDSET

SOME REFLECTIONS ON
THE SUFFRAGETTE MOVEMENT

Regarding *The Man-Made World* by Charlotte Perkins Gilman:

At a bookstand in one of the subway stations the other day, I found a paperback with a fine jacket and the tempting title *The Truth about Man*, by a Spinster. Of course I purchased it on the spot.

The spinster—the unmarried lady—touches only briefly on the questions with which Mrs. Perkins Gilman[1] deals in her book, *The Man-Made World*. The spinster deals essentially with men in relationships—the love relationship—to women, and she readily produces here her own experiences, collected through, I think she said, sixty-two affairs. Since she, however, presents herself as an Englishwoman of the upper—the very upper—class, she indicates that her experiences go only to a certain point. Beyond that, she limits herself to her observations. But she often presents her truths in a witty and amusing manner, which is not very flattering to men but which, from a woman's viewpoint, is no doubt very truthful. In particular, she manages in an amusing way to make accusations against men similar to those they usually reserve for women. I remember from my early youth how unbelievably depressing it was when girlfriends with more experience explained to me "how men actually were"; and the more men had contributed to their experiences, the more deplorable the report. Somewhat later, I learned that the same held true regarding men's experiences

Translation of "Nogen Kvindesaks-betragtninger" by Liv I. Shank.

with women. The more overwhelming they were in quantity, the less satisfying they were in quality. Acquaintances, whether male or female, whose company one enjoys, of course, take so much of one's time and life that there cannot be room for many of them. And people with exclusive taste do not choose to have a steady stream of people coming and going. Don Juan with his thousand and three in Spain alone surely could have written the truth about women in just as honest and sad a way.

But when the spinster points out the many deplorable conditions in the world, due to the way men have organized it, and when she prophesies about the new woman who will appear and bring order, then she has the absolute advantage in proclaiming that she is not at all the "new woman" nor does she feel called upon to take part in society's rebirth. On the contrary, she does not feel called upon to do anything but study men as buccaneers on the hunting ground of love; and she confesses that she uses make-up, is always in debt for hats and dresses and does not know the price of anything edible but candy. And thus she confesses that she, a woman created by man in his image, is the way she is and tells the truth about men the way she sees them.

With these comments, one may conclude the discussion of the spinster's book, unceremonious but not lacking in seriousness.

What is more serious, however, at least in my opinion, is what Perkins Gilman has written in her book, *The Man-Made World*, from a limited a knowledge of the world as it is and of people as they are. Her view of things is extremely beautiful, but it is inconceivable that a thinking woman can have this view, except in countries where women have not had their demand for full equal rights honored and have not met society's rightful demand for coresponsibility, which will be made of us women the day we receive what we have fought for.

Perkins Gilman's book abounds in a multitude of assertions, arguments, hypotheses, and slogans that are familiar from feminist campaigns here at home and are frequently used all over

the world among women who are still fighting for the rights
and position which they must necessarily achieve in society.

I have the deepest veneration and feel the most grateful
respect for these feminist champions at home and abroad—
however much nonsense they have sometimes produced in
speech and writing—beautiful, childlike, tasteless, and ridiculous statements—and just as much respect for whatever insane
and unappealing tactics the English suffragettes, for instance,
have adopted lately. Let me say, in passing, that conditions
here in many ways—and not only with regard to women's
position in law—are such that violent and senseless behavior
among suffragettes and other parties is very understandable
and as excusable as it can be. It is, of course, always an in-
defensible tactic when a party, wanting to overcome the anarchy—ruthlessness, plundering, suppression, mass murder in
some unbloody manner—which exists under presently insuffi-
ciently organized societies, itself preaches disorder and anarchy;
this is indeed inexcusable. Somewhat unfortunate are the effects of campaign boasts about ideal conditions that the party
in question will establish after achieving power, even though
the purpose of these boasts is understandable; it is the cause
that sweetens the appetite of blue-eyed, childish listeners and
makes them swallow the realities of these programs with a big-
ger appetite.

Let me repeat that I have the greatest sympathy and respect
for every woman who has fought and is still fighting for the
feminist cause. It must not be forgotten how often these women
have voluntarily accepted the greatest martyrdom a woman can
accept—that of ridicule. There are no walls, neither force nor
tyranny, that so hopelessly exclude a woman from any hope of
a happy life like being placed in a position of ridicule. What a
burning belief in the justice of her cause, what courage, what a
willingness to sacrifice she voluntarily takes on! These women
certainly give more than their lives for their cause—although
they may not always be aware of it.

It is unjust to argue that these women have been mainly

"upper-class". Does anyone believe that the feminist movement here in its childhood would have been able to muster
a sufficient number of working-class women, who were the
very reason the movement had to arise but who were not in a
position to develop their thinking to a point where they could
head a movement, especially one with no prospect of progress
anyway? And the fact that these forerunners for the most part
did not understand the cause of the women's movement is easily explained. For those, who at first had to start rebelling at
home, who had to fight against scorn and threats from their
families, who met with vulgarity, ridicule, and misunderstanding first from their own, who were then from all classes in
society, the cause and goal naturally appeared like this: It was
the woman who revolted against the man's thousand-year-old
tyranny. In the same way that the man had suppressed her, being
the weaker part, and kept her as a slave of his lusts, he had also
suppressed everybody weaker than himself, enslaving them in
order to exploit them. When the woman revolted against her
tyrant, she was not only fighting for herself. A mother's natural
instinct was to protect and love her little, weak, and helpless
children—therefore, one presumed that a woman's instinct in
all ways was to protect and love small, weak, and helpless creatures. Society should make a place for this instinct.

The anonymous English spinster and the famous American
writer both seem to share to the same degree this popular concept of the women's movement.

Like many other writers, Perkins Gilman daydreams about
a Golden Age, the age of the matriarch, which is supposed to
have existed prior to the period when men made themselves the
master of women. As far as I have understood the various authors who have dealt with this mythical era, the males gathered,
supposedly once a year or so, decorated themselves, danced to
please the females and fought among themselves. Thereafter
the females selected the strongest ones to father their children.
Two aspects about this seem to offend Perkins Gilman. First,
she thinks women have lost "this prerogative of the female, this

primal duty of selection"—although it seems to me we have at least some of it left; I have not been to America, and therefore don't know what the situation is there, but I did not believe conditions were inferior in that respect. And, second, "as part of our androcentric culture, we may point to the peculiar reversal of sex characteristics which makes the human female carry the burden of ornament. . . . [S]he does not fight for her mate, as yet, but she blooms forth as the peacock and bird of paradise, in poignant reversal of nature's laws." Mrs. Perkins Gilman occasionally uses images from the animal kingdom to illustrate the relationship between man and woman, a fact which does not convince me that the writer has a clear understanding of how complicated the machinery, "the man-made world", is.

I have never been able to ascertain whether it has been proved that this so-called matriarchy has ever existed among humans. But according to popular scientific writing, our original forefathers are supposed to have lived in the treetops. I would presume that a female hierarchy, a matriarchy, would date back to that period. In any case, it would make sense to me if, when our ancient forefathers came down to the ground and settled there—one can hardly talk about them as humans prior to this event—the relationship between the genders that Perkins Gilman and others have found offensive came about naturally. It seems reasonable for the physically superior male to make the female or females his property already at a rather early stage. Also, the defense of the family or tribe became his duty, whereas care for the human children during their relatively long dependency and work at home came to be hers. Due to the conditions under which Perkins Gilman's genus *homo* developed into what she calls human nature, it seems natural to me that the relative position between the genders turned out the way it did; therefore I cannot at all accept the concept of "the man-made world". I am afraid we women have to admit to having taken part in organizing it as it is—at least it has not been possible for us to organize it differently.

As long as society's order and management were such that

practically all women found their place and occupation in dependence upon a man, and as long as it was normally in his own interest to watch out for her interests, then it was just as absurd to call this relationship protection as it was to call it submission. Certainly, both took place, and some women lived happily, some unhappily, under those conditions, just as will happen during any relationship.

Only when the new cultural factor, the machine culture which the man and man alone created, became of primary importance in society did these relationships become unnatural. As the machine industry displaced the cottage industry, the upkeep of several women in a household became unnecessary and unprofitable, and it became necessary for those who had no man to take care of their interests in society to find other ways of having their interests represented. When the self-supporting woman—"unprotected" and "untyrannized" by man—nevertheless must obey the laws of society and is affected by the economical order of society in war and peace, it becomes a compelling necessity for her to acquire influence over the factors that decide these conditions.

I therefore find it difficult to talk about the injustice women have suffered through millennia as representatives of their gender. A person does not suffer from wrongful conditions as long as he does not regard his prevailing conditions in this way. Prisoners of war who were kept as slaves in previous societies did not suffer injustice, however much they suffered, as long as they would have enslaved their masters under reverse conditions. Slaves of our time suffer injustice because, in an age of modern industry and capitalism, they are slaves under conditions that they know they could not have created and which they cannot fight by creating new capital and new machinery, but only by changing the system of production and profit-sharing.

Right and wrong are specifically human concepts unknown outside our human world; and, as Perkins Gilman also notes, humanity is constantly undergoing development or redevelopment, whatever one calls it.

"Our human-ness", says Perkins Gilman, "begins with some low form of social relation and increases as that relation develops." This expression is hardly comprehensive, but I am unable to find a better one and can agree to take this definition as a basis for research as to what humanness is.

But with this starting point, the task which Perkins Gilman declares her book to have—to separate what belongs to human nature as such from the specifically male and female traits and to examine to what degree either one influenced the development of society—will be unsolvable. The lower social organization from which society developed always consisted of men, women, and children. And primary gender differences—the male's greater physical strength and the female's more intimate relationship to the offspring—made for a natural distribution of social functions. Defense against other human groups and the fight against man's natural enemies and prey—the various kinds of animals—obviously became the men's tasks, whereas care for children and the beginning and most primitive attempts at farming and industry were left to women.

It is impossible to determine to what degree the development of society has been influenced by this original and natural distribution of work and to what degree the original and natural distribution of work has developed the characteristics of the genders which one tends to call male and female.

Perkins Gilman's ideas about common human characteristics of both male or female seem almost unbelievably superficial and conventional to me. As to some of them, it would be impossible to present them except in a society like that of Great Britain, where men's and women's upbringing and position in life are so similar to conditions in Norway. When she, for instance, philosophizes about the man's greater pugnacity and need to make his personality felt and about how these characteristics are expressed in different fields of competition, one really has to believe that the writer has never come across female self-preservation except as a desire to get married and "be supported"; that she has never known women who must work and support a family, but only women who have worked for fun and because the work was of particular appeal to them. The fact that there are women who have the opportunity to work as a form of luxury and entertainment is good, and the fact that many do so is even better—but there will always be few who have this opportunity. I am afraid that of those who are able to work just for the sake of the job, many will choose some other, less appropriate, form of luxury and entertainment.

Inasmuch as Perkins Gilman regards the fighting instinct as something specifically male, then the male is supposed to take the whole blame for something called war. Well, it is true that women have not till now had executive power in their hands. The so-called lower classes have not either. Prevailing conditions have made it necessary for both to acquire political influence. But on the day when they are in power, let them see how fully they can carry out their promises to improve social conditions.

The conviction that the strongest and most virile leadership is necessary in a country like England—and that therefore a deadly danger is connected with giving numerically superior women voting rights—is the only justifiable argument one can present against the suffragettes. The fact that women, although in the majority, do not have any other rights in society, no other protection by law, than those that men, who are in the minority, choose to give them makes these rights and protections problematic and completely insufficient. However, it seems defensible that the minority should rule a majority that is so evidently lacking in understanding of the organization they want to take part in—however right the majority are in asserting that the organization immensely needs improvement.

This is manifested when those who fight for their rights start to talk irresponsibly about world peace and disarmament. A country like England, for instance, rules over millions of subjects belonging to suppressed nationals. Not even the most optimistic of political dreamers, who completely lose sight of the earth and worldly realities in their flights of imagination, could visualize England or any other European state voluntarily surrendering such a dominion. And even if we ventured into such a far-off conjecture as the white race voluntarily giving up its domination over other races, a domination which it gained only by its superior strength and through detestable actions, we could not exclude the fact that the vengeance we have so richly deserved would come down upon us. And if we had not acted in a way that deserved the revenge of other races, but had stayed properly in Europe on our own ground, which we have owned since prehistoric times, we would probably long ago have been annihilated by the Mongols.

The white race can probably never give up its defenses. Any white nation considering to do so must be prepared to be oppressed and to find its ability to defend itself exploited by any of the greater nations, which must always be prepared to defend the life and existence of the white race against other races.

Perhaps one may hope for a period when wars among the European peoples will be nonexistent. But nobody knows: the growing feeling of solidarity among the working class in all countries is a fact. But will it remain long after a breakdown of capitalism's domination? There is also unity among representatives of capitalism all over the world—against the labor movement. But not any more. It is unthinkable that the feeling of brotherhood should ever include all races. Even if we should reach out to the yellow man, do we have any idea how he would react? Just ask the worker who has visited America if he can imagine the American worker giving the Negro or the Chinese the kiss of brotherhood.

The feeling of brotherhood—human love for all mankind, which fights the same battle to understand itself, to perfect its humanity, the same eternal battle against the in-human part we call nature—is eternal and entirely human. Neither religion nor the spirit of the times is alien to it. Time and again it has poured over the world like a wave. And every time it has been followed by a reaction stemming from the human instinct to assert itself at other people's expense. The call for freedom, equality, and fraternity spread through Europe around the end of the eighteenth and the beginning of the nineteenth century. In that manifestation of humanity called politics, it turned into revolutions, and, in another manifestation called art, it resulted in romanticism. The reaction that followed gave rise to both the feminist and the labor movements.

There is no reason to fear that the feeling of solidarity will die. One may hope that man sometime will refrain from suppressing his fellow man—but I do not believe it. We are all humans—the oppressors as well as the oppressed. If people were not the way they are, the feminist and the labor movements would have been superfluous.

As it is, these movements are products of what Perkins Gilman herself calls our human-ness—some low form of social relations. In any such relationship, the drive for self-preservation—which is not unique in man alone—will dictate cooperation between several, individually weak members in order to represent their common interests against fewer and stronger individuals who have other special interests. These are conditions which will probably never change under any form of social relationship. The ability to organize a society which represents everyone's interests is highly unlikely. There is absolutely nothing in the history of man that justifies such an expectation—on the contrary, it seems that the most conspicuous and repeated line in this history is the following: man's most human actions, regulations, and inventions have always had completely unforeseen consequences.

"The nomad", says Perkins Gilman, "living on cattle . . . is less human than the farmer raising food by intelligently applied labor." It was surely development of what we call humanity when the nomad, having learned from observation and experience, settled down on unowned land to cultivate it and thus support himself. Just as human was the action of the following generations who added more and more unowned land. But the present order of landowners and landless is only a natural consequence of this and has created many complicated problems about right and wrong. The fact that human parents left their children as much as possible of their "human-ness" in the form of experience, tools, and material products is regarded as an advancement for human growth as a whole—and yet, we now protest in the interest of humanness against the right of the individual to create and pass on to his children increased and unlimited fortunes—as well as the power they have over their fellow men. This is, among other things, the result of "extension of trade and commerce from mere village market-places [perhaps it ought to be called bartering] to the world exchanges of today", which, according to Perkins Gilman, is also an extension of humanness.

This applies to everything Perkins Gilman calls humanness, which "is seen most clearly in three main lines: mechanical, psychical, and social. Our ability to produce and use things is essentially human. . . ." We use our stronger power of thinking gradually to invent a multitude of different weapons.

It applies to our inventions, to all our development—mechanically, psychically, and socially—that we have never been able to foresee the range of the inventions and the direction development will take in the future. We have often been terrified about the consequences of our own actions and have longingly looked back to the good old days, before this or that had come into existence.

Man's resistance against the feminist movement—a result of the industrial and social conditions he himself created, women's sighing and longing for those days previous to the feminist movement, when every woman was safe in her husband's (or another man's) home, taking care of her own (or another woman's) children—this does not seem a particularly male or female reaction to me but rather human.

But let us see what Mrs. Perkins Gilman finds especially female: motherhood, of course, and, besides, something she calls motherliness—a whole series of beautiful and valuable psychical and intellectual qualities, which she and innumerable other women associate with the role of propagation common to all female species and with their instinctive love for their offspring, who depend for a longer or shorter time on the mother or the parents.

I admit being personally somewhat sceptical about the above-mentioned theory that the beautiful qualities called "mother-liness" are directly connected to a woman's biology. Mother-liness, in a wider context: care for the weak and helpless in society, for neglected children and the old and the sick, has, when administered by women, been performed by mainly childless women, and not especially by mothers. "The de-voted love and unlimited tender care which is a consequence of motherhood" has primarily been restricted to a woman's own offspring. An emotional disinterest for everything else is some-times the result of motherhood. In some instances, a mother may have to concentrate her motherliness on her own children. But—.

When Mrs. Perkins Gilman, and many other women, talk about "motherhood", they seem to move in a world so far above our heads that I'm almost embarrassed to share my "back-yard gossip". Have those ladies never met regular mothers—in the real, imperfect world—whose love, devotion, sense of justice and understanding applied only to their own sweet chil-dren and never included the disgusting children on the floor above or the caretaker's louse-infected offspring or minor er-rand boys presenting bills?

I remember a young wife who told me how inexpensively she had gotten the whole outfit for her much-desired and happily expected baby. It was made in an underwear factory whose em-ployees were "such bad girls" they did not demand high salaries and only pretended to live on the income from sewing, said the young wife soon to be a mother! At that time I was very young and exclaimed in dismay: "But you cannot possibly want to make use of such clothing—and for your child at that!" Where-upon the woman answered with a smile, almost loving in its innocence, beyond good and evil: "My dear, of course I shall disinfect them before using them."

I remember another woman, an innocent young girl, whose "innocence" I would not dare guarantee. She is married now and a mother—she is supposed to have become a uniquely loving and careful mother. I doubt, though, that motherhood would have changed her view of this old story. Full of admiration for her sister-in-law, she told me how resolutely the latter had cleansed her home when one morning she discovered that the nanny had aborted during the night. She further told how she had "lectured" the sinner when the latter tried to explain away her condition and how the nanny was simply ordered to get up, pack her things, and leave that decent home immediately! I admit knowing nothing about the nanny—she may have been a person whom every responsible mother would chase out of her home. However, taking the circumstances into consideration, I think the mother in question may have deserved a whipping, at the very least.

There are good women and bad women, and I have never found that a woman's biological fecundity is in any way dependent on her human value. It sometimes happens that a woman turns into a better person when she becomes responsible for the care of a child—but she may not change at all. Does any mother deny that no other woman can be as despicable as a mother—and are not all contemptible actions committed by a woman twice as despicable and mean when committed by a mother?

Being a mother does not signify anything but a woman's physical ability. This physical fact means so much in human relations that a woman cannot achieve anything better than being a good mother and nothing worse than being a bad mother.

But more is demanded of a good mother than the instinctive affection for her own children, the impulsive pleasure she gets from caressing them, and the punitive inclination to protect them and care for their well-being—often at her own or other people's expense. All this only sums up the components that make a normal woman happy and therefore is no reason for her to expect gratitude. Nobody should imagine that a woman's responsibility any more than that of a man should be limited to being happy.

At home [in Norway] lately, some prophetesses have announced that they want to be women and nothing else, which means that these ladies want the female to be excused from any concerns except her private sex life.

It seems to me that these prophetesses will rather soon discover that they are forced to interest themselves in what we usually call society, because human beings also have to live their sex lives within society. Society has always required a framework of laws within which a person has to stay with respect to his sexual affiliations, whether legitimate or illegitimate; included within this framework is also legislation regarding the result of these sexual relations—the children. For a woman to have no interest in social laws and to surrender her rights in society to men in the legislation pertaining to the support of children, education, and exploitation of their productivity is very strange, to put it mildly, especially when this is the gender which professes to have the strongest love and understanding for children.

Some women, who, by the way, are not less intelligent than most people, have in fact told me: "I am not any happier because I can go out and vote." I don't know if there are men who regard voting as the biggest satisfaction of their private lives. We usually do not associate our individual happiness with social conditions, although, on the other hand, we do associate our individual misfortunes with them.

Every woman, according to these ladies, would rather be married and have children than work in an office or serve behind a counter or operate machinery in a factory. I am not sure about that. Anyway, I would personally prefer anything to marriage and motherhood as an occupation.

However, in spite of Perkins Gilman and the equally optimistic opinions of women, I'm afraid there always will be women who will not do anything else if they can earn their living as representatives of their gender. There have always been work-lazy individuals, men as well as women, in all societies, and work-lazy women have in any case till now always been able to earn a living in one way or another by being available as women to one or more men.

Besides, I have no doubt that many women find fulfillment in their work, especially those who have had the opportunity to select their work on the basis of interest and ability; for them, their work means more than anything—even if they have also been wives and mothers. This has been the case, even if they might possibly deny it. Likewise many a woman, at the time when her work was done entirely in her home, found her greatest pleasure in the products of her loom and her linen cabinet and her storehouse pantry rather than in her husband, even if he were somebody she liked very much. For many of these energetic and hard-working housewives, the main role of the husband was to give them the leadership of a home and the opportunity to display their special abilities—and they gladly left their children in the care of nannies, servants, and unmarried female relatives who were part of the household, while their own concern and care were directed toward the keys to the pantry and the contents of the linen closet.

There are enough men and women who are fortunate enough to be satisfied with making the most of their personal abilities —and who have never yearned to break out of their solitary life and join with somebody else in order to achieve a more challenging and rich life together. Their expectation in marriage is often for a peaceful and comfortable home where they rest after the day's chores like a cat curling up near the stove, where the children are a source of pride and pleasure, if not on a very deep emotional level and whose care and upbringing are left to servants who are often much better qualified than their mother. (I know that all mothers will protest against such a notion, even those who, indeed, leave their children's care to strangers in order to pursue their social entertainment or their dilettante social work, which does not benefit anybody but themselves. Only some grown children will agree with me.) For such people, however, it is their work or the benefit they get from it, economically or as recognition, that will provide them their greatest excitement, their highest pleasure, or their most bitter disappointment.

The new order will probably mean improvement only for those women who cannot find happiness except when being absorbed in another person and, in the abrogation of their personal self in a relationship toward husband and child. Perhaps just as many—or just as few—women found that happiness previously. As long as marriage and motherhood were the only honorable sources of income for women, it was the natural order of things to arrange support before they became too old. If a woman could not get the man she wanted or if she did not want any of those she knew, she would have to accept the one she could get. And thus an honorable woman had no right to hope for love and happiness. Yet the loneliest, hardest-working woman—behind the typewriter, in the classroom, in the store, the factory, or behind the sewing machine—has the right to hope and wait and dream of happiness as a wife and mother, a dream richer and more beautiful by far than those women can dream who are satisfied with the pleasure of having a child that may have been conceived in a man's casual or disgusting embrace.

I know that numerous women of my generation regard all of the feminist movement with indifference or scepticism. I would therefore wish for this book by Perkins Gilman to be read in Norway—in spite of everything. Its weaknesses are obvious: the writer's limited and superficial view of the social order she so readily criticizes, the naïveté displayed in her pointing out what she regards as social wrongdoing and her suggestions as to how to make amends.

But her confident eagerness—her urge to do something, to help and improve wherever help is needed, and her firm belief that this wide-reaching helpfulness is a universal feminine characteristic!—that is the strength of the book. The book's unlimited well-meant intensity and the public spirit that fills it are touching and beautiful.

Alas, was there not also a time here when good women for the first time looked beyond the doors of their homes and wondered about the structure of a society they had had no need to worry about before? They were horrified to find so many wrongs in the world. They had had no idea how bad things were and how complicated the outside world was. They came from their little domestic world—and, being honest, hard-working housewives, they rolled up their sleeves and went after the slovenly and disorganized men: here came the women, housewives, mothers all set for social housecleaning—in a jiffy they would turn the society of mankind into a newly cleaned, cozy, warm home for everybody to enjoy.

As women, they should have realized that there is no end to housework. The fact that social work is in the same category should not surprise them. The most ideal social order would soon require revision just like the clean home eventually needs cleaning again. Another similarity between the home and society: although good organization and order create individual well-being, they do not guarantee happiness. On the other hand, poor organization and disorder may cause calamity for individuals.

The position of women in society hardly makes the individual woman happy but may make many women individually unhappy. Good and sufficient pay does not necessarily make the worker happy—but workers will certainly suffer with slave wages.

In Norway, women look after their interests in society to a higher degree than in any other European country. It is touching and beautiful to read about Perkins Gilman's perception of women's interests in society. Therefore I hope her book will be widely read. We may smile about some things, laugh about some statements, but there are many statements which ought to move us to shame, and many things we should think over and keep in our hearts. Those of us who have our civil rights ought to remember that our rights also include duties, and if it is more difficult to be good citizens than the brave American woman believes, that does not reduce our duty and responsibility—on the contrary.

London, October 1912

NOTES

[1] Charlotte Perkins Gilman (1860–1935) was a socialist, feminist author.

SIGRID UNDSET

IF 2 + 2 = 5

If every single convert who returned to the Catholic Church were to tell his story, no two of these stories would be the same. It should not surprise us who have accepted the Church's invitation to man that the ways which lead to it are as many as there are kinds of men, and that all these ways meet at one point —since truth is one, and illusions are endlessly varying. This is probably one of the reasons why men cling energetically to the hope that there is no absolute truth. We convince ourselves that life would be monotonous and freedom would be lost if there really were one Truth and if that Truth were one.

At times it occurs to all of us that it is downright trivial for two and two to make four. If one first accepts this boring doctrine, then it clearly opens the way for the development of very many different human talents and possibilities—it is easier for beginners to learn their first piano lessons, and it is almost necessary to believe this before one begins to study higher mathematics or to build railroad bridges, for example. If anyone wants to maintain his freedom of spirit by thinking that two and two make five or nothing or seven, he must be prepared to take the consequences if, on such a subjective faith, he proceeds to drive a car on narrow country roads or does bookkeeping for his business. Nevertheless it is best to be prepared to find that there are people who think they have

Translated by Rev. John E. Halborg. This article was first published in 1965 in *St. Olav*, the Norwegian Catholic magazine. It had never been published before and was found among Undset's papers at her death. It was originally titled "Preface", but, to what?

been harmed as a result of this free and subjective relation to
the little table and that they take reprisals.

After all, we have all experienced at least a passing feeling, a
longing for a far distant dreamland where two and two make
whatever we wish them to make. Freedom in dreamland is almost certainly illusionary as well—in fact the types of dreams
and the combinations of dreams are not so overwhelmingly numerous, and dreams are in reality directed by laws to a greater
extent than most people suspect. But what one does not suspect, as they say, does not hurt one. In the world of reality,
where results are joined to causes, no one can gain freedom
without working forward through the web of causal connections, and there is always a danger that he will be caught in
the web. There is no other freedom than that which St. Paul
[sic] speaks of when he says "the truth shall make you free."
If one dogma is, or several dogmas are, accepted, then one
must loose hope of winning freedom by an easier way than by
fighting against the realities of existence. Thus far, it is natural
enough for "modern man" to attempt with all his life force to
escape the authority of the Catholic Church—for many years,
it would seem, we have tried to escape from any conceivable
kind of authority. These escape attempts and the fight against
a Church which has always openly confessed that she demands
authority are not unique to "modern" man; they are factors
manifested in full force in Jerusalem in the days immediately
before Easter in the year our Lord was crucified.

Very few Christians are prepared to explain how their natural reaction of fear and mistrust to one who calls himself the
way, the truth, and the life has been overcome. It does not happen without the action of the mystical and supernatural factor
which the Church calls grace. Nevertheless, in large measure
most stories of conversions fall into two categories.

One group of converts reveals that they felt drawn to the
Church long before they came to belong to her—for all that
time they thought that the Church could provide their inmost necessities of life. And this attraction for the Church

may have been awakened because they came into contact with
some particular aspect of the Catholic system—perhaps they
experienced a Catholic liturgy and were impressed by the atmosphere of it—or it is the thought that a Catholic really is
able to address Jesus' mother; or the Catholic teaching of our
relation to the dead takes hold of them at a time when it seems
to them unendurable that death descends like an iron curtain
between them and their beloved. (If these impressions are only
purely aesthetic or are sentimental, naturally they seldom lead to
conversion; in any case, I have never seen people become Catholic because they "admire the beauty of the Catholic Church"
or think that there is merit in the fact that Catholicism "per-
mits us to worship the feminine also"—despite the fact that
I continually meet people who say such things. On the other
hand, when a contact with one thing or another in the Catholic world wakes a suspicion of the spiritual reality which lies
beneath these things, it can bring a person into the way which
leads to conversion. But this is completely different from a
catholicizing aestheticism or sentimentality which causes some
soul to wander around and around the Catholic Church for
years and look at her in the manner of tourists.

In this group above all one will find converts from the different forms of Protestant Christianity; they are Christians who
return to Mother Church to find Christianity in all its original
fullness. Of course, one sometimes also finds converts from
one or another atheistic sect that is dogmatic and convinced
in its faith. But in any case this kind of convert is most often
a person who is not especially loaded down with scepticism:
It has always seemed natural to them to believe in something,
and they proceeded from the idea that a faith should feed the
hungry with good things.

There is another group of converts—and perhaps it is rather
large today—who have come to the Catholic Church because
they have been convinced that she can tell them the truth about
human origins and being and duty in the world. But they were
convinced before they were *converted*—they have studied, not

only to be converted, but also what is the meaning of conversion and why conversion is necessary after they have become members of the Church. (Surely not because they were satisfied with themselves or led by any self-contentment—if this had been the case, on the whole they hardly would have bothered to ask after the truth.) But helped and guided by supernatural powers, they have been able to experience the very possibility of a change of mind before they could begin to believe in it.

Many of us modern agnostics had, even in childhood, lost faith in the doctrine of God held by our parents or our teachers of religion in school or the priest who confirmed us and which they tried to convey to us. The fault with Protestant teaching about Christianity was that each preacher had his own "personal conviction" and his "subjective understanding". So that we came to be convinced that faith was a minor matter: they who spoke to us in the name of Christianity had in reality given up the historic Christianity as a teaching no longer maintainable, but, purely on emotional grounds, they would not give up a view of life which was colored by Christianity. But the new humanistic and godless religions with which preachers tried to snare us as we entered into the world of adults were truly even less able to overcome our difficulties as young sceptics. If we had met only *one* type of atheism, probably there would have been greater danger of our being ensnared by it. But, thank God, there were as many sects of atheism as there are of Protestant Christianity—many too many for us to take them seriously! Finally, it seemed that disbelief was also a minor matter—lack of belief proceeded from the idea that historic Christianity was completely untenable; in opposition to modernist Christians, they were only too happy about that. So far we were in the same situation as our own forefathers in far distant days, when Christianity first gained a foothold in the Northern lands. Also these preachers had come to hold the old teachings of their people about God as a poetic fiction or a kind of philosophical figure of speech—and the explanation of nature mysticism concerning everyday phenomena, which

was the real popular religion, soon became untenable for thinking, observant people and became the world of the fairy story.
More and more, adults were driven to believe only in their
"own power and strength"—and that was not much to believe
in, as adults knew. Among other things, this is a faith which
eliminated "comfort", in the religious sense. People are wont
to expect—and receive—comfort from their religion. They
are, however, ready to overlook the fact that there are other
persons who can both live and die without any true comfort.
This was how it was in all heathen groups. The proclamation
of all heathen religions is not a longing for comfort, not even
a longing for salvation, as much as a longing for clarity. The
question of first and last things has engaged mankind more
deeply than the question of their own weal and woe.

We had thought that we ourselves were washed—clean heathens—and one day we discovered that we were not that at all.
True heathens have always known that they are not alone in
the world, and they compose their myths about the completely
other, the Other, the Others—the divine, God of gods, which
they feel is there, but they cannot see. All pre-Christian heathenism has presupposed that humans were normal enough to
believe in spirits other than the human spirit—even if only in
evil spirits.

There is no way back to the old heathenism. Our part of the
world cannot undo the fact that it has experienced Christianity.
It is a part of European experience which cannot be uprooted,
and our fathers believed that God would finally meet the ques-
tioners face to face, that at last God would give the answer to
our questions concerning first and last things. And for us, the
history of the world since that time has been the history of
the human fight for and against the revealed God, who was so
different from all human myths of God and gods—who gave
what men had never dreamed that God would expect of them.

This faith is *our* tradition. But the old heathenism lived completely in tradition—and, everywhere, Christianity conquered
people's tradition, selecting some things out of that tradition,

since it had the authority to weigh, destroy, and preserve. It claimed that it came with God's solution to all the mysteries of the worlds, and it accepted all the attempts of heathenism to find solutions—it rejected many as pure error, corrected some which were almost right, and to some it said, Yes, that is a correct surmise. We cannot find our way back to the old heathenism, because we cannot return to our own pre-Christian heathenism as though the experience of Christianity had not intervened between it and us. The modern heathenism is a new thing—a declaration of war against a God who has spoken, where the old heathenism was a love song to a God who hid himself, or an attempt to *live* with the divine whose power men felt around them.

The old mythology contained poems about God and his family and personalized manifestations of his *Wirken und Weben* (knitting and weaving). The new mythology excludes God and contains stories about human work and human *Weben und Wirken*. In the old heathenism, men believed that they descended from gods. In the new heathenism, men try to believe that gods descend from men.

And we, who had smiled overbearingly at our old teachers' opinions on the God who had created humanity—because each of our teachers came only with a crazed photograph of himself and supposed that this was the genuine, real pictorial resemblance—perhaps we openly laughed, enlightened by the new teachers who supposed that they could create God and gods. But after we had laughed long and well at all the others who preached their own illusions and idiosyncrasies, we had to ask ourselves: But you, who have no trust in the subjective faith of others—what is your own faith? You think that you have seen through the naïveté in the solipsisms of others. But then you cannot believe in yourself without resigning from the brotherhood of man.

From the deepest and innermost part of us whispered a feeling—and we had the first suspicion that there was One who spoke in us, who was not ourselves, but One who dwelt in us

—the person who sees himself as an exception to the general weak human race is a betrayer. We hardly knew ourselves what we had betrayed, or wherein the betrayal was. We had heard so much loose talk about solidarity between people that we had never discovered that human solidarity really is a fact.

So it was that we discovered that there was a power in the world that taught human solidarity in one single great case— the fall into sin; solidarity as joint heirs to his gift which paid our debt. We discovered that all those who try to encapsulate themselves in their own self-created illusions were united in fearing, hating, and trying to avoid this power. If they were not united about anything else, they were united on one thing: opposition to the Catholic Church. And we discovered that there was also something in our own human nature that rose up in opposition against her claim. It was a resistance which was not like our smiling doubt in the face of all the religious constructions of other people and all the other views of life which had been offered to us. It was as if we had come to deal with an element from another world. And for the first time in our life, we felt a fear of the supernatural. We can make the word of Gertrud von Le Fort our own: "I have fallen on the law of your love as on a naked sword." About the one who would win his life but must first lose it—this we learned later. For some of us it was easy to bear this, for others it took a long time. Some of us felt for a long time like wild beasts who had fallen into the power of the hound of heaven. Others felt right away that it was our own Father from whom we had been stolen long ago, so that we did not remember who we were, but we knew him again with his first word.

There is one thing we must all be prepared to understand: the fear which lies beneath the modern world's resistance to Christ's Church. The world is no more ready for God than we were for him. In many years or in a single last second, we must hand ourselves over to him.

This fear has been our own fear. We have received faith and love as gifts of his Spirit—to the degree we are able to receive his gifts in our narrow hearts. It is little enough for most of us. But there was a day long ago, soon it will be two thousand years ago, that a young woman went on foot to the door of her old relative. And when the old housewife heard the voice of her young guest greeting her, she went to meet her and greeted her: "The Mother of my Lord!" And the young woman broke forth in a song of praise: "*Magnificat anima mea Dominum, et exultavit spiritus meus in Deo Salvatorem meum.*"

Why were the two women celebrating, and on what did they build their faith which was so sure of victory? Only on visions of angels and angelic voices and on the hope for the work which the child would do—he was not yet born, he who would create new heavens and a new earth.

Sometimes it can seem that the hope which we Catholic Christians place in the All-worthy today is just as weak and tender and destructible as the little baby in the arms of Mary, whom Joseph rescued from the small town in Judea in the darkness of night and fled with to Egypt. Our stubbornness can be seen to be as meaningless as was the apostles' when they set their faith against an empire's countless convictions and beliefs. Perhaps this is the task which has been given us, we who have doubted everything and everyone before coming to faith in Jesus Christ in his Mystical Body, the Church—that we should bear witness to the impotence of men's arrogance against his power. For our arrogance was indeed not small, and it was strong, as the arrogance of lonely men always is. And we confess that we are his prisoners, and his yoke is easy and his burden is light.

SIGRID UNDSET

THE UNDSET-SÖDERBLOM EXCHANGE

Introduction

Very often great events occur and, while we can discuss their significance, we know little of the personal factors behind these events. The present article gives us a personal glimpse into an early stage of the modern ecumenical movement.

Nathan Söderblom (1866–1931) is a commanding figure in modern church history. A man of broad sympathies and of warm personality, he wrote on subjects as widely separated as socialism, Luther, Indian mysticism, and a fascinating study of the Passion which examines the meaning of the paschal mystery from a surprising number of angles. In 1914 he was named the Archbishop of Uppsala in the Swedish church. The ecumenical movement owes much to his initiative. Concerned that the churches should take part in modern social concerns, he was instrumental in organizing the Christian Conference on Life and Work which met in Stockholm in August 1925. At this meeting, Protestant, Orthodox and non-Chalcedonic churches met. Rome was conspicuously absent. Why? Undset gives an answer in *Catholic Propaganda* and in the article which follows. The tone of Söderblom's letter is understanding and conciliatory—perhaps he was hoping that things would be different in the future.

While all of his article cannot be reproduced here, a summary of his letter of April 29, 1927, will provide the background for Undset's response.

He begins with a summary of Catholic attitudes toward Protestantism and the modern ecumenical movement, beginning with the negative statement of Pius X and moving on to a number of more positive comments, including those of a Catholic figure who saw the

Introduction and translation by Rev. John E. Halborg.

need for common work to "defend civilization and the Faith against modern dangers to the Faith". Söderblom regrets disagreeing with Undset since he had been an admirer of *Kristin Lavransdatter* and saw much in it which was "Christian, simply Christian and common to all".

Söderblom then recounts a history of Catholic reaction to Luther. Among the positive remarks on Luther, he cites those of Grisar and Döllinger, who remarked on the truly German Christian voice of Luther. He notes that freedom in a political sense developed in those countries influenced by Luther, who believed in the bondage of the will, rather than in Catholic countries, where Jesuits taught the freedom of the will.

At this point Söderblom introduces a surprising concept of God and man as being incommensurate with one another. Undset will argue that the compatibility of God and man is central to classical Christianity. Söderblom, to be fair to him, is not really speaking about the Calvinistic *non capax* but rather is trying to explain the fact that institutions, including churches, fail to be as perfect as Christ.

The entangled history of the Scandinavian state churches and the national character of those lands are discussed. Söderblom assumes that a country will have one dominant church (he rather thought that the Episcopal church filled that role in America). He was proud of the progress and orderliness of Scandinavian life (though he deplored certain aspects of sexual relations), and thought that the Protestant church had contributed to this condition even as the Catholic Church was responsible for the primitive condition of southern Europe. He ended by saying, "Our Roman brothers have one thing and another to learn from evangelical Christians, even as evangelical Christians can learn from them."

Undset's reply seems to be less a theological response than a personal statement of her feelings about Norwegian Christianity. In her time, there were bitter fights between modernists and conservatives, including some we would call fundamentalists. There was also the first glimmering of a high church movement in the state churches, particularly in Sweden, where Söderblom was sympathetic to some of its manifestations. A close reading of Undset's response provides surprising insights into her remembrances of her earlier life.

Reply to Archbishop Söderblom

May I be permitted to make a few remarks concerning Archbishop Söderblom's letter in the last issue of *Vor Verden*. Indeed, for a Catholic, the total impression given by the Archbishop's letter is that it is unspeakably difficult for Protestants and Catholics to come to an understanding, or even a convergence. When the same words disguise essentially different concepts, something is lost, even with the best of intentions.

It is illustrative that Archbishop Söderblom can propose the possibility—to begin where the Archbishop leaves off—that a Catholic convert should "sometime when he is far from the cold North, taking part in a service in Roman Catholic surroundings, . . . hear the sound of a hymn in a Norwegian church and long for home, perhaps even verify what a great Roman Catholic scholar said to me about the deep devotion in a Nordic evangelical church."

Personally I do not consider this to be true, as I haven't the least sympathetic memory of Protestant worship. It was my obvious misfortune to receive no other impression of Christianity, either from my religious training in general or especially from my confirmation training and my experience from going to church, except that it was a kind of declaration of the sanctity of prudence and practical morality. The Christian fellowship, including the priest, was a group of people who, as individuals, had many other good qualities. But not in the wildest imagination could those who were active in the church organization at the time be accused of not belonging to Caesar.

My friends among the converts who really have become believing Christians because they have also become Catholics do not complain about what they received when they belonged to so-called evangelical denominations, but only complain because they did not receive enough. I never heard such a convert be homesick for a Lutheran service, and I cannot conceive of such a phenomenon (except if the person in question has lost his faith in the true presence of Christ in the holy Sacrament of the Altar and thus for the moment is not in communion with the Church); this is because Catholic and Protestant services are essentially different. For Protestants, the service is above all a meeting of the faithful for periodic fellowship, Sunday after Sunday; for Catholics, in the deepest sense, the service means the holy Mass, the unbloody repetition of the offering on the cross at Golgotha, a mystery which has been completed on the holy day and the *ferial* day, year in and year out, for almost two thousand years, "from the rising of the sun to its setting", each moment and second of the day, as country after country around the globe receives the rays of the dawning light. (In a wider sense, of course, all of life is worship of God for a Christian.)

When Protestants compare an evangelical Sunday service with the high Mass in some Catholic church that is starred in the traveler's guidebook, they forget that these Church festivals are part of the Church's life—which is lived on weekdays just as on feast days—in utterly impoverished circumstances just as fully as in the highest display of pomp. The holy Mass is one and the same, whether it is celebrated by a lone priest and server in a palm-frond hut in Africa or in one of the new ugly churches in the working-class district of a large city, where people from the day and night shifts of the factory begin or end their day's work with a visit to the altar, whether the Mass is read in a chapel of medieval architecture, in a little hospital in north Norway, in a private living room of a family which has a visiting priest—or if it is a pontifical high Mass in, for example, the Siena Cathedral. A Norwegian Catholic who was born a farmer expresses his experience of this fact when he took part in a pilgrimage to Rome in 1925: "You know, in a way, it was like when we ate in the parlor on the great festivals back home—ordinary days we held out in the kitchen." We are Catholics in our own home, whether we enter a Catholic church in Haugesund or in Rome, Kensington, or Montreal or Dettwang—everywhere the Bread of Children awaits us on the table [see Mk 8:26–29].

When, therefore, Archbishop Söderblom writes that "God
and man are not commensurate", does this not depend somewhat on what exactly is meant by this? One could say that this
is clearly not the Catholic's concept of God and man. The same
may be said for the religion of evangelical Christians who still
believe that Jesus Christ is true God, born of the Father from
all eternity—not created, but himself the one through whom
all things were created—that the little baby in the arms of the
Virgin Mary is, not one of the secretly chosen instruments of
the Almighty, but the Second Person of the Holy Trinity. Or,
to use an expression which seems to me to be poorly chosen
but which has now become a watchword in the Norwegian
Lutheran church, those who "believe in the virgin birth" will
hardly without reservation agree that "God and man are not
commensurate." "As many as received him, to them he gave
power to become the children of God." "I am the vine, you
are the branches." When the divine life, though not without
conflict and imperfection, can flow into the human estate, it
appears from a Christian viewpoint that the planet is far from
trivial, that the power which God has given to every soul is
very great—each soul has the freedom to choose him or reject him; heaven and earth shall pass away, but mankind lives
forever.

It is most certainly true that the word of Jesus about the vine
and the branches means something, whether it is understood to
be an expression used by a religious genius or by God himself.
But I cannot accept that it means the same in both cases, or that
it relates to every word in the Gospels—that which relates to
every word is proven in the light of the Gospel. Who is he of
whom the Gospels speak? If every person on earth who thinks
he shares the faith of Peter and who sees that his only hope in
life and death is the cross of the Savior were willing to work
with all others who shared this faith, how wide would be the
cooperation between those who in the Savior adore the Word
who was with God in the beginning, who was God and those
who with Pilate present him to the riotous and wild human

race: "Behold the man!" Pilate tries to help Jesus, attempting to rouse the sympathy of the mob for the bound and mistreated prisoner. In our days it is most often sympathy with people's chains and wounds that compels those who belong to the new Jesus religion, those who see in him a man sent from God as the revealed leader of the race but not God himself, to make the attempt to get people to accept Jesus: "Behold the man."

We Catholics believe that this kind of cooperation is impossible because we do not accept the idea that some human, subjective, religious genius can assume anything but a strictly limited authority in someone else's relationship to God. We bow in obedience to the Church because we believe that she has authority handed over to her from him who said, "All authority is given to me in heaven and on earth" and because we believe that he who said that is God himself. We humbly acknowledge that he has the right to speak all the hard, frightening words to his enemies, because we believe that they were God's opponents, not less important persons who held to their own convictions against a religious genius—because we recognize that no genius has such an autocratic judgment over human souls as Jesus Christ commands. We hold that God is the Father and that God is love—something many different people who have accepted the Bible on other grounds than those of historic Christianity acknowledge because they have experienced subjectively the truth in these assertions. But how can they establish their subjective experience of the goodness of God, that God is the Father, against the claims of the unfortunate ones whose subjective experience is based on the idea that God is evil, that the world is steered by a grim and blind power, or that we cannot know anything about how the world is steered, unless they believe that their experience is derived from obedience to the command of their Creator and not the result of human inspiration, even if that inspiration came from the most brilliant and most self-confident man who ever lived.

A Catholic cannot, therefore, agree when the Archbishop cites the names of Jeremiah and Paul, Luther and Erasmus,

Pascal, Fenelon, Bunyan, Tyrrell, St. Francis, St. Brigid, and St. Teresa [of Avila] as persons who have had to suffer oppression at the hands of the institution. For us a great difference is seen in the fact that while Luther, for example, asserted the validity of his own subjective religious experience, St. Teresa cast herself completely under the judgment of the Inquisition. Teresa had wisely discovered that there was something called hysteria—she called it melancholy—and that this sickness which she apprehended and discussed very well can clearly imitate supernatural contemplation so amazingly that she did not dare to trust the genuineness of her own supernatural experiences: Other women have been deceived and have deceived, and who am I, that I dare to place myself above these? It is precisely at such points that the Spanish lady shows the basic soundness of her soul and its sweetness—in contrast to Luther, who thinks that "the great mass of people should stay under the papacy for the sake of pedagogy." St. Teresa never demands that she be treated as an exception, not for the sake of her weak physical condition and not because of her shining gifts. With her wonderful supernatural experiences of God, she counts herself as nothing but a servant girl whom God sends on his errands. She wants to be nothing but Catholic, in the most literal meaning of that word.

It is also natural for Catholic Christians who do not know from experience the religious situation in non-Catholic countries to look with less pessimism on the ecumenical movement than we do who have grown up in these lands. Indeed, as the Archbishop notes, there are believing Christians: but Catholics, obviously, if they are anchored in the best traditions of the Roman Church from childhood, cannot have any living concept of the degree to which this common Christian vision is thrown back and forth by the waves of shifting opinions in the Christian organizations separated from the Catholic Church. From rationalism and its attempt to identify Christian ethics with the ideas of the Enlightenment about civic duty and "what is for the common good" to pietism and the spontaneous outbreak of the instinct for asceticism, which when mismanaged runs to enmity with both healthy and harmful joys of life and tyrannical meddling in the relation of their Christian brethren to *adiaphora*[1] (dancing, games, alcohol, etc.) by creating prohibitions of all sorts. Above all, Catholics who come from a completely Catholic milieu can be completely disoriented with regard to what is meant when a non-Catholic church organization speaks of "spiritual freedom", from which they seek their own right to existence. It is evident that within the Catholic Church sympathy with this concept can arise along with the dream of union between all Christ's church organizations in order to preserve civilization and the Gospel from the modern dangers to the Faith, yes, perhaps actual positive help can be expected in the fight against heathen thought forms and non-Christian religions.

But it would be less natural if we converts who have grown up in "evangelical" countries were so sanguine about a gathering around the Gospel—without agreement on the content of the Gospel, dogmatically defined. One cannot escape dogmas —those who hold most firmly to dogmas today are those whose only dogma is that dogmas should be feared like the plague. Can we believe that fruitful cooperation is possible in the long run between a number of different types of church organizations that do not agree about what the content of the Gospel is—we who (in a few words) have seen that fruitful cooperation between members of the different sects living in the same parish is impossible? We who have only seen believing Christians— fanatically believing—clumped together in small intimate circles, because they are united by a fixed concept of the Gospel or in cliques of their own social qualifications! Common to the circles and cliques is most often the simultaneous appearance of humility and spiritual pride, assurance of salvation and fear of the faith of those who believe differently from them. Even so, it was precisely in these circles that I came to understand that Christianity is a living spiritual power now just as it was nineteen hundred years ago; the proclamation and prayer of lay preachers gave me an impression of the seriousness of religion which I had never suspected in any service at church. But these same people, shockingly, passionately convinced in their faith, were remarkably willing to sacrifice when it came to matters close to their heart—I would not say there was none of them who had heard about the eighth commandment, but I would say that I myself have never met one of the "awakened" who seemed to remember it when they spoke of the "unawakened". We Catholics should be the last to underestimate the meaning of the anguish that arises when one of these circles of friends that sets all its hope in the Precious Blood sees the village church handed over to a priest of dubious orthodoxy, decidedly opposed to the whole "theology of the blood". But I have seen anguish and pain in such a group take the form of an unknowing or insidious hunt for reasons to be angry with the priest and all his house. I have seen baroquely comical examples—pious evangelical personalities, grown men and women, sighing over the priest's wife who took "unspiritual walks" on country roads, and the white summer pants of the priest's son called a certain sign of damnation, and examples as unpleasant as prayer meetings where the prayer for the priest turned into divine persecution, pure and simple.

So it is, as any slightly alert person can see, that unlimited tolerance between people is impossible. One can try to set up boundaries for the areas in which tolerance is possible between people and where it is a duty. Or one can employ the idea of tolerance as a working hypothesis and give the wandering stream of intolerance free play. The example of our Lord does not encourage tolerance in all its possible meanings. One cannot, on the one hand, accept the Gospel of love, lowliness, purity, and the forgiving of one's enemies an unlimited number of times, of not judging so that one will not be judged, without, on the other hand, judging the thoughts of those who think otherwise —since there are, always have been, and always will be people who think the exact opposite. "I am not come to bring peace, but a sword."

It would be somewhat easier for Catholics and Protestants to come to an understanding if the latter would remember when and how the wedding between the so-called "spiritual freedom" of Lutherans and Calvinists took place and how freely and gladly these two denominations took over the role of being lovers of freedom of the spirit. It is true that I know only a few separate episodes in the history of the freedom of the spirit in Sweden —the actions against the Baptists in the 1850s, the judgment of the Svea supreme court from 1858 on the six women who were exiled because they had become Catholics, the action against Strindberg caused by *Giftas*—and these only from second-hand observations, somewhat after the source. But from this I gather that in Sweden little is known of what is called "freedom of the spirit" in our secret Protestant jargon.

When *Bergens Aftenblad* for May 24, 1927 (referring to the Eskeland affair),[2] wrote, "If one is engaged in a firm and later decides that he must oppose the firm, then he must leave and find another place where his views on things are held. . . . The state demands, in accord with the clear words of the law, that the religion of the state shall be evangelical Lutheran and in agreement therewith its teachers and priests should arrange their teaching whether it is of religion or history"—these are, in any case, straight words for the money. So the minister for religion, Magelsen, said in an interview (*Vestopland,* May 16, 1927): "When some journal complains about an attack on spiritual freedom, I don't understand what they want. The Roman Catholic Church practices an intolerance and oppression of spiritual freedom unknown to us." This is as clear an admission as we could wish for that, with regard to the Catholic Church, one deals with her after her own principles (understood or misunderstood) and not according to one's own— that freedom of the spirit in the evangelical Lutheran church is not a principle, but politics. Under these circumstances it seems to me that no one should wonder that not only do we not complain because Rome officially stayed away from the meeting in Stockholm but look with more scepticism than born Catholics do on the meaning of the many church bodies officially represented there.

The Catholic Church teaches us that we can separate between a person's intention and the expression that intention takes. An author's purpose (what he wants to say), only God and he himself fully know. The reader can only judge by what is written. The amount of sympathy with or antipathy for the man Luther which any Catholic has cannot therefore be obligatory, only the rejection of his theology. That he was a German Augustinian monk who broke his three vows of poverty, chastity, and obedience may be said to be a fact—whether one finds grounds to glorify, explain, excuse, or completely condemn this action. That some Germans, also to a certain degree Catholics, are gripped by Luther's Germanness is very natural. A Christian may experience that he fights against his own individual peculiarities when they conflict with Christian ethics and yet has a tendency to tolerate the weaknesses which are his own: if a person is born wasteful, it is easier for him to forgive someone who freely throws away his own money and that of others entrusted to him than it is for him to forgive a miser— he concedes that both are sinners, but, to him, miserliness is, in addition, a mean and ridiculous sin. A pampered sensualist sees mitigating circumstances for young Paris who runs away with the beautiful Helen but not for young Persen who seems to steal shabby hussies as readily as a Helen. It is no different when the question turns on the traits of one's own people which are considered national characteristics. This is no less valid in the study of antiquity, and the return to antiquity, which was one of the main causes of the renaissance of heathenism in the fifteenth and beginning of the sixteenth centuries. In Italy this movement was felt to be a national renaissance; there it was not, as in other parts of Europe, a fruit of reading and of the impressions gathered from travel. The pious Italian Christian who took part in the movement in the beginning did not suspect how different from Christianity it would be or that the stream of pagan thought and life ideals would grow into a flood, which could have carried the Christian Church into the abyss if the Church had not been built on rock.

Through my father's connections with Italian priests who were also archaeologists, I know some of the difficulties they went through between 1850–1870. Their hearts burned for a united Italy, even as they understood that the head of the international Church could not be the subject of a national state. To some extent this same problem applies today in Mussolini's Italy, with his dreams of a Roman empire.

But for us Norwegians, ur-Germanness is not fashioned to arouse our sympathy. On the contrary, I think that if here in Norway knowledge of Luther and his own writings had been greater, he would never have been so popular with us. The Luther whom the common people place together with St. Paul (!) is a folktale—he is credited with, among other things, having given us "the Bible in our mother tongue". Few of our national folktales contain so little historical fact; anyone will be convinced of this if he compares the different editions of the Bible in Germanic Danish with attempts in the native tongue (Norwegian) by, for example, Kleiven or Skar or Landstad. The first Protestant Norwegian translation of the Old Testament was issued in 1851–1876, and the New Testament in 1904. On the relation between the Christian III Danish Norwegian Bible and Luther's German, see Dr. Lis Jacobsen, *Dansk sprog* (Copenhagen, 1927). Of course I do not mean to say that this peculiar "Bible language" was incomprehensible to the Norwegian people, for the clergy who here, as in other reformed lands, were mostly recruited from so-called "priestly families", this was a precious family tradition.

There is much that we admire about the Germans, and there are even more things which we ought to have the intelligence to admire or respect or learn from; even though we act differently, there is much about the south German people with which we feel at home. It is true that now we Norwegians do not feel we belong to middle Europe but to Western Europe. German *Ungestum* [violence] and *Inbrunst* [fervor] in large

doses seem foreign to us. I willingly admit that my antipathy
to Luther dates entirely from the time when I read his writings purely from linguistic and historical interest—but I think
that many Norwegians would have the same impression of his
"frighteningly powerful voice", which resounds at full volume,
whether he is speaking with religious pathos and inwardness
about sin and grace or flaying universities, German peasants,
the Pope, the curia, the Jews, or what have you, interpreting
Scripture or explaining what women may be used for. Above
all, Luther's view of women is perhaps indirectly inspired by
his social principles, clearly as a reaction against the high Middle Ages' spiritual liberation of women which, not the least in
Germany, was expressed in the number of nuns in the endless
line of gleaming convent figures. It would be natural for a man
of Luther's spiritual constitution to be brutal in his determination to drive women under male domination again—in the
bedroom, in the nursery, in the kitchen as their home. For a
decidedly heathen view of life, it is rather natural for the sex-
ually (as lover or wife) less attractive woman to be considered
less important on the whole—Christianity has claimed that
she is not. The glory of holiness is the same for the sick, the
ugly, or the crippled woman as for the healthy and beautiful
or for the crusader or the intrepid missionary. The virgin who
devotes her life to prayer and intercession or to works of love
and all that is associated with that is just as worthy as the good
housewife and mother. The unchivalrous picture of the old
virgin which Lutheranism has found to be incompatible with
Christianity is one of the stains on Lutheranism.

However when I, in some newspaper articles which have
come to the eye of the Archbishop Söderblom, introduced
among a number of Luther's sayings on different matters some
dicta probantia concerning humanity's unbreakable slavery under
sexual desires, what prompted me was an Oslo priest who, in a
lecture which was reported in a journal, cited some of Denifle's
strongest attacks on Luther but did not say what Denifle was
disturbed about. I permitted myself at that time to point out the

comical aspect of Lutheran priests who today rejoice over the fact that Luther did away with compulsory celibacy for men and women—most of whom had chosen to be priests or monastics —and instead opened the door to the married paradise of evangelical Lutheranism for everyone. They seem less concerned about the forced celibacy which modern conditions impose on a much larger number of youth than, in comparison, the Middle Ages ever imposed on monasteries and Beguines. And these are keen young women who never considered following any inclination to celibacy—and who freely discuss how they should choose between a chastity which is impossible because of nature or in any case useless torment and a normal marriage which is impossible because of social conditions or because they are too old. I direct the Archbishop to the discussion which was carried on in this journal at New Year's time and, if it interests him, the discussions published in magazines for women and the home, discussions on weekend marriages, birth control, and the duty of engaged couples to try each other out with respect to the libido. Before this choir of youthful voices, the old Lutheran foundations fall in a rather peculiar way, even as we hear again the old song about the frightful consequences of vowing chastity. The vow is made by men and women who dream of emancipating themselves from this drive with God's help in order to fulfill special duties in his service, even if this drive in itself is just as natural as, for example, the drive to escape mortal danger. But the same priest who knows all the possible fallacies of the monk's fantasies and the nun's hysteria seems often hardly to have discovered that right in our midst we have eremites who live in lodgings and nuns who live in the enclosure of a ticket window, and he has difficulty conceiving any kind of a situation which would be more attractive than their life in a cell—and many young girls find bookkeeping at least as destructive to the spirit as breviary prayers and a great many young people love their work in the firm or the factory about as warmly as Fenja and Menja loved King Frode's mill.[3]

It is unfortunate that even in these circles what Dr. Harry

Fett called Luther's sexual-romanticism has not been discovered. This is our Lord's purpose for us, but ordinary persons
are not to be overwhelmed by erotic experiences—at least not
today—because the right one will come along, and then they
will awaken from their enchanted slumber, and Providence will
supply someone they can marry. Most people still believe that
monogamy is more natural than celibacy. History, beginning
with the fall into sin, does not seem to provide clear evidence
that people have found it so natural unless the need for support
made a virtue out of necessity—there are exceptions. As a tradition from earlier times in Catholic Europe, quite a few people
thought that the desire for a monogamous marriage was the
ideal—n.b. if it works out that way, one is happy with the lot
one has chosen. If it doesn't, there is now a broadly held opinion that it is neither a right nor a duty to bear a monogamous
marriage as a cross. I don't know if Archbishop Söderblom ever
reads stuff like illustrated magazines—railway literature? They
have their great sympathetic appeal. Films do also, for those
who are able to go to the cinema—I go only when necessary.
Neither celibacy nor monogamy is natural in the sense that it is
possible if a person does not assume control over his nature—
just as it is necessary to take control of the wooden piles when
one is going to build a stave church or of a stone in order to
carve a marble pillar.

   An example of this is what was said to me in a "radical" organization: a true believing, free-minded person in his eighties
who had been "saved" discussed the reshaping of marriage into
a freer relationship and the new creation of an erotic trial relationship with limited bonds. He said this was the way things
were developing, "and if we thought that young girls would
have trouble adjusting themselves to this new condition, to the
point of committing suicide out of shame over their dissolute
state, etc.—it was too bad about such out-of-date girls who
couldn't be helped. Women must learn to live their girlhood
days like men live their time of bachelorhood."[4] The only thing
that could slow down this development, if not stop it—would

be if ten to twenty young priests chose celibacy for the sake of young people—but, as said, no one in the group thought that in Denmark, Sweden, and Norway put together there could be found twenty theological students who would renounce ministers' wives and Sunday midday dinners for the sake of the Lord.

This last is far from true in my opinion. I think, moreover, as some hope, that we will see Protestant convents and monasteries arise here, too, and that we will hear of a brand new concept of priestly celibacy. This is already the case in the English church and, as far as I know, also in Germany. The increasing interest which can be observed in certain non-Catholic circles in Germany in the medieval mystics, not least for the Dominican mystics in South Germany, is striking. There are a growing number of people who have learned to value the religious life of nuns as being, not a surrogate for erotic experience, nor hysteria or sickness, but as the response of completely normal, strong women to a special calling. The asceticism of Henry Suso is no longer considered to be the tasteless aberration of a half-mad individual but rather his conscious fight against the causes of the World War at the one point where he can put his hands on them—in his own flesh. If this interest should develop into a direction in German theology, we would soon see that willingness to sacrifice was not lacking here at home.

When the Archbishop cites the old phrase, *naturalia non sunt turpia*, I must honestly confess that I do not completely agree with him. It seems to me that this is often cited by people to excuse the *naturalia* which belong to their own nature— the *naturalia* of others they are very willing to judge as perversities. Cancer and tuberculosis, vitriol and World War— are not all of these natural phenomena? Nakedness is neither good nor evil—the heathen mindset in Renaissance paintings of naked women is not so much revealed in what the women have taken off but in what they have on, most of them have stripped themselves of everything but a pear necklace. When trustworthy persons use old figures of speech about light and dark powers, of the evil and good in human souls, they are too much inclined to think of this image as a pattern of stripes; they do not notice that evil and good do not lie in stripes in the mind but are blended, as red and blue blend into purple. And so often it is this purple that the natural man longs for secretly and willingly falls down and worships when he finds it.

Lillehammer, June 12, 1927

Respectfully yours,
Sigrid Undset

NOTES

¹ Undset's term indicating that which is indifferent in the eyes of the Church and the theologians—TRANS.

² See *Catholic Propaganda* for further discussion on Lars Eskeland's controversial conversion to Catholicism—TRANS.

³ The giantesses Menja and Fenja ground gold for King Frode—TRANS.

⁴ There are no closed quotation marks in the Norwegian text—TRANS.

SIGRID UNDSET

CATHOLIC PROPAGANDA

Well-known cases show that the normal and expected result of evangelical "conversion" is the feeling of safety. Catholic "conversion" results in a feeling of repentance. If a thoroughgoing Protestant is asked, "Are you saved?", and he has experienced a "conversion", he will without hesitation answer affirmatively. But no Catholic would dare to say more than that he hopes for salvation. These two answers do more than express dogmatic propositions: they have their own psychological value. The Protestant feels himself saved. He is assured of a condition of safety and trust. He theologizes over the cause and purpose of this safety and trust; the interpretation is moot, but he feels and is intensely assured of what his feelings confess. Psychologically, he is "saved" because he feels he is safe. With a Catholic, on the other hand, the most powerful feeling is one of sorrow and hope, the warp and woof of repentance.[1] Completely aside from dogmas,[2] he is unable truthfully to answer the question "Are you saved?" affirmatively, because his sins are ever before his eyes. No reader of the lives of the saints would dare to deny that this is the normal psychical experience of the truly "converted" Catholic. St. Teresa does not speak of herself as a great sinner in any dishonest or conventional way: to the irritation of many good, lukewarm Catholics. She who had led a singularly spotless life made herself one in perpetual penance with the life of a great penitent, St. Augustine.[3]

"Is not considering these two types of conversions identi-

Translated by Rev. John. E. Halborg.

cal a game of words? They are clearly two different kinds of psychosis."[4]

However, it is true that the Catholic feeling of insecurity is not directed toward God but toward oneself. There is no room in the Catholic Church for different concepts about the being of God or about the divine-human nature of Jesus Christ or about the motherhood of the Virgin Mary; because Christ himself is the way to God's kingdom and because his death on the Cross is the secret which opens God's kingdom to the descendants of Adam, his blood truly cleanses the sinner from all his sin, his body is truly the food which is the life of believers. He who does not believe this is not Catholic but something else. If he is a priest, the Church says he is not her priest; if he is a layman, the Church denies him the sacraments, because she is convinced that they harm rather than help the one who does not believe; the Church excommunicates, that is, she breaks her relationship. And if one is a Catholic, one thinks that this is her right and duty. If Jesus Christ is the incarnate Word who was in the beginning, the way, the truth, and the life, who has promised to be with his own every day to the end of the world, who said to his messengers: who hears you, hears me —the inner being of the Church is as infallible as that of God.

But redemption is a drama which is played out between two parties. Floating in the infinite personality of God, the human personality rests, an infinitesimal speck in infinity—just as the earth is a speck in the part of the universe which our knowledge can comprehend. The earth, men, atoms, become almost equally small when measured against infinity—and each person is as complex as a planet or an atom. With the same understanding, one understands the distance between the heavenly bodies and his own littleness in relation to Sirius, the age of the earth and the relative nothingness of his own lifespan, and he sees, even if he does not understand, concepts like eternity, the infinity of space and time. Seen from the standpoint of matter or biology, his body is an animal body with senses and desires like an animal's. But seen from our animal standpoint, the senses and desires of man, by some baroque complication, can be the cause of things. That is one of the difficult questions here on earth: What is the viewpoint of the animals, have they any? They have eyes and we have eyes—but we are alone in our mania to reproduce that which we have seen with all kinds of additions of unseen things which we seem to find in ourselves or nowhere; cave paintings, stone carvings, the Eidsvold monument. Apes have ears and hands, but they have neither harmonicas nor philharmonic orchestras (when I was a child I used to think, when I heard the ape theory, that if there were anything to it, the apes might become angry and do something to renounce this relation; as long as they are not bothered, we do not need to be either). Animals feel the temperature as do we, but only we have lit bonfires in the forest and installed electric fans in hotel dining rooms. Animals mate and we mate, but how have we not managed to complicate our sexual life—even going to such peripheral phenomena as jokes and anecdotes about mothers-in-law. The animals must have food and drink and we must have food and drink, but so far no animal, as far as I know, has thought of getting food in order to arrange an exchange of food products, for example, to organize an agency to take the leftovers of factories and wine bars and banana boats? Mankind itself has often explained its tragic isolation from the animal kingdom by conceiving of a supersensual world, peopled with invisible beings, bodiless but yet with personalities of the highest degree. And it is this world which has never left mankind at peace, and men have never been able to leave it in peace.

I

Christianity explains—in unity with other religions—that the invisible infinity is God. He has created all things visible and invisible out of himself and all rests in him. By a special act he has created man in his image—in Catholic theology that means, as white light is broken up by a prism, God's uncompounded being is broken into human properties. (This picture is incomplete; as St. Thomas bids us remember, all attempts to explain God are limited by the limitations of our being. To speak of the finger of God, the shadow of God's wings, the anger of God, is to use inescapable anthropomorphisms. Had the poor Christians in *On God's Way*, which builds its faith on independent Bible study, stood in direct or indirect contact with the great scholastic master, they might have been spared many shocks, as the young Kallem frightens them with the revelation that the Holy Spirit began by being feminine—in some Semitic language—in Greek he is neuter. As St. Thomas reminds us, all gender language about God, with the exception of the Son becoming man, is grammatical gendering.)

Therefore, the first human couple, created in the image of God, may certainly have looked more like a pair of chimpanzees than like Michelangelo's fantasy picture of Adam and Eve. That we find "development" attractive reflects our own taste. Christianity by nature is somewhat sceptical about "development" on the whole. Had the fall into sin not taken place, development would have proceeded in another manner in any case. Perhaps the pyramids would still have been built, but they would not have been built by slaves. Gunpowder would not have been discovered—nor the first stone axe or the latest explosive material: God knows, what would they have been used for?

"*Minuisti eum paulo minus ab Angelis*"—you have made him a little lower than the angels, you have crowned him with glory and honor, you have set him over the work of your hands; you have laid all things under his feet, beasts great and small and the wild animals, human self-assurance says about humanity. On the other hand, in the storm-driven Psalms 94–96, God shall come to judge the peoples: "*Tunc exultabunt omnia ligna silvarum a facie Domini . . . Flumina plaudent manu.* (Then shall all the trees of the woods rejoice before the face of the Lord, because he comes to judge the world; the streams of the sea shall clap their hands.)" This is because at last they will be rid of us and our lordship. Abel's blood cries to heaven from the whole earth. "In former ages, at many times and in many ways God spoke to our fathers through the prophets; in these last days he has spoken to us through the Son whom he has made the heir of all things, through whom he has also created the world."

"He came to his own, and his own did not receive him. But as many as received him, to them he gave power to be the children of God." This is Catholic faith, that an act of the will on the part of man is unconditionally necessary before he can be saved. The will is the center of the person; with the accompanying properties such as the intellect, feelings, and fantasy it is a unity, as the glowing interior of the earth and the mountains and soil and water and vegetation make a globe. By his will, man turned from God; with his will he turns back to him. God pours out his saving grace for us because of love alone and not because in the least measure we have deserved or earned it— the Catholic Church teaches nothing else. If you want to find confirmation of this, you can, for example, open a Missal and find the prayer "*Nobis quoque peccatoribus*" in the Canon of the Mass, and you can also examine the different Offices.[5] A person may "receive" this grace of God in Jesus Christ, as St. John expresses it. In reality, the fight between the Church and the "reformers" concerned this: What is human will? What is its worth? Free will, says the Church; the will in bondage, says Luther. God knows beforehand who shall be saved and who shall be lost. He knows this, says Calvinism, because he has predestined some to the eternal light and some to eternal fire. The Church says, God does not will the death of any sinner, but he knows the will of each person from eternity better than the person himself knows it. It is true that this is a cross for the man controlled by our time; why did God create men who would be lost? Scholasticism answers bravely: being is a good in itself. In reading Dante's *Inferno*, what scholasticism meant becomes more understandable: in hell, Farinata degli Uberti is still Farinata, the proud. Here thoughts collide: the business of indulgences was mostly a pretext, the fight with the papacy a consequence. And the countless sects which have developed out of the work of Luther and Calvin have forgotten what the fight was about to begin with; Rome remembers and stands where it stood: None is condemned unless he wills it; none is saved unless he himself wills it—rather, lets his will be in harmony with the will of God.

From these presuppositions, Luther claimed that human nature with its inherited sin was so lost that man lies like a decayed stick of wood; he becomes as if wrapped in grace. The merits of Christ cover his sins with the forgiveness of sins, if the sinner merely believes. Moreover, what Luther has uttered about the power of the grace of faith automatically causing good works in the poor will-less being—even as he warns against scrupulosity and uses the less well-chosen expression admonishing people "to sin boldly"—is something else again. To find any consistent, well-thought-out principle in Luther's own writings other than his fight against the teaching regarding the freedom of the will and the divinely instituted teaching office is a difficult puzzle. And Catholics and Protestants never find the same solution.

The teaching of the Church on inherited sin is that it is a kind of innate eye disease of the soul. Man was created for blessedness—the vision of God as he is. With the fall into sin, man loses the ability to see supernaturally. In the supernatural world, which has become an invisible world to him, he proceeds like a blind man, using the sense of touch. Not everything he feels is wrong but only imperfectly understood. When "the morning star visits us from on high", it shows a person what he had his hands on when he was in the darkness: poisonous monsters and flowers, and stones which become jewels in the light— that explains the relation of Catholicism to heathenism, that is, as the non-Catholic expresses it, it has taken to itself heathen elements. In the countryside around the newborn Rome, the parents worshipped the good powers which they sensed, watching over their children—they could not know what kind of powers they had felt in the dark before our Lord told them the shining answer: it was their angels. Our fathers made offerings to their parents in the grave, as most other men have done; the Church answers, this is right. Death does not break the fellowship between friends and relations, but it is a fellowship in prayer and the worship of God; the dead have no use for food and drink. The Norwegian-born Bishop of Skalholt, Jon Halldorssøn, proposes the custom in one of his tales that the *De profundis* for the dead should be learned by all as a table prayer said for the dead.

Since people are blind to the supernatural light, it not only follows that they pick up poisonous snakes or go into the bog or over the cliff; fear of darkness is also a consequence and so is a perverse pleasure derived from forcing others downhill, from hurting others and themselves, so that they become moral cripples.

Through grace, man receives back his supernatural vision—inherited sin is really taken away. But the power of sight which now should teach us to endure the full strength of the light of God is still weak. God may give his children both tempering and purgatory, here or there or both places. It is becoming morally adult, more or less; there are men who have so much natural moral strength and thought that they are good enough from a natural standpoint, but even they, when they have gained their supernatural vision and begin to discern God, find what a poor empty picture they had of him. For Catholics, grace is a medicine which sinners may ever inhale and bathe in, that they might grow up rightly—become saints,[6] be perfect as their heavenly Father is perfect. Only when we are as good as God are we good enough.

Because "renewal" in the Catholic sense is a renewal to activity—to work with God and not against him—no Catholic can be at peace because he is "saved". He cannot comfort himself with the thought that sin is human nature, unless he becomes faithless after his "conversion". He cannot understand concepts such as sin and punishment for sin and the vengeance of God in such a human-juridic sense that God becomes like a judge of criminals who gives sentences of a certain amount of suffering proportionate to the crime, except that, for the faithful, Jesus has paid, so he escapes the punishment—or the punished one snarls and it seems that God's sentencing to punishment is not reasonable. For the Catholic, after "renewal", sin is clearly not natural but a weakness after an unnatural life; each faithlessness shows how much he falls short of coming to full health —the wholeness of sanctity. He not only continually prays to God for forgiveness, for more of his medicine, that God may never loosen his grasp on his soul—even if there comes a time when the soul involuntarily struggles to be free—because the physician's hand touches such sore wounds that it, seemingly, is more comfortable to let the sickness take its course than to treat it. He must, in any case, have a proper will to subject himself, to do as God says; as God himself has spoken, he shall gain his sight. And with this we come to the dogma that, for a person to be saved, good deeds are of absolute necessity.

The inclination of man's mind to create idea associations, to gather perceptions into complexes, to push down frightening or disgraceful desires or concepts into a kind of dark cellar of the mind, or to deck them out as modern and pleasing if one wants to keep them up—the Church has always acknowledged this inclination, and she has worked on the basis of this knowledge of humanity, which she has expressed in different ways through the ages. Richard of St. Victor (c. 1140) expressed it, for example, sometimes in hopelessly tiring allegories, sometimes in passages where each phrase shines like a naked blade. We think that it is natural for the Church to have this breadth because we believe that in a mysterious way she is one with him who created us. But it is rather strange to see how modern psychology occupies itself with the laws of the creation of a complex—it was on these laws that St. Ignatius built his Spiritual Exercises —or how psychoanalysis accepts phenomena which every confession manual at least from the twelfth century to the present is directed against. (I don't understand how anyone can confess to another person comfortably, whether the matter is small or great, unless one is convinced that he is not confessing to another person but to a priest in the place of God. That someone can trust a doctor in that way, to surrender part of his soul to attain physical benefits—I have never been able to understand.)

For the Catholic Church it is important always to find the center of each complex of feelings which react against the grasp of Christ. Weakness and sensual enjoyment can join together in spiritual laziness just as in sensitivity before the experience of pain or in the desire to be admired; sensitivity or love of gossip can join in a lack of courage or in misplaced self-criticism or in unrighteous overestimation of other poor sinners. It is worthwhile, then, to grab hold of the tallest weeds; afterward it is relatively easy to pluck away the small weeds from the loose earth. And then it pays to plant one of the "theological virtues" which, with its complex of ideas, is most capable of smothering the weed as it grows. Obviously, there is no Catholic who believes he can do that without an unceasing influx of supernatural grace—through prayer and the sacraments. Using the image of St. Teresa: for the silkworm to become the butterfly, it must continually work and spin the case in which the mystical development will take place, but the silkworm gives itself the ability to spin no more than it created the world of leaves in and from which it lives.

When therefore, for example, Friedrich Heiler calls scrupulosity a sickness to which Catholics are especially prone, to some degree that is true. However no Catholic dreams of considering as a criterion for a religious truth something which is pleasing for a life of sensation and pleasant impression or spontaneously strange or pure secular energy or is felt to be especially fitting for a certain type of people. Religious rationalism was a fiasco because it was not rational; the great mass of people who have contact with the unpleasant realities of life turn their backs on false religious optimism—they are tempted to jump the ship of any such Christianity and by their own strength, to drag themselves away, in any case, from evil which is materially felt, or they run after fire-and-brimstone preachers. Lacking a religious system that reveals wider and deeper perspectives, people will at least listen to a person who has discovered the fact that we all are in danger of being damned; and whatever else our Lord is, "reasonable" in the human sense he is not.

Naturally it also happens in the Catholic milieu that scrupulosity degenerates into real sickness of the soul—in any case priests theoretically are familiar with a general oppression which is sin, essentially different from faint-heartedness before concrete difficulties. Still, we believe that while, for example, mental illness as a consequence of "renewal" occurs so seldom in the Church, it occurs rather generally in sectarian revivals, and this was also true in the Middle Ages with heretical movements like the Fraticelli. Nothing like this was depicted in the story-spinning craft of the priests or in the Church's treasury of human experience, but only that the Church teaches and acts according to the law of normal religious life. Fear and hope drive the soul forward; they teach it to watch and pray and thus gain a growing knowledge of God—and as a consequence more and more to lose its egoistic concern for itself and to become unselfish, with adoring love for God: this is the fruit which the soul may bring forth at last, so also the saints confess in choir. Love cannot be inactive; if the soul has not discovered the relation between our good deeds and the reward which God has promised us for them, it understands it now; would any father or mother drive away a little child who comes and gives them the stalk of a plant which has lost its flower or a fist-full of sand? Their concern and love is not a reward for the funny little gift, but the gift is received, as is proper, as a reward for love. Thou shalt love thy neighbor as thyself—the soul discovers that it is nothing and becomes loved, and no other soul can be a more complete nothing than the soul which is without God; it ought not to doubt that it is possible for anyone to become what it has become. God has given us various commandments to do certain things for our neighbor—now we see that what he said is literally true, that everything we have done or neglected to do for one of these very small ones, we have done or neglected to do for him.

This is the unceasing energy of Catholic Christianity—there is no peace in the Catholic sense in salvation—but deep anguish about defrauding oneself, an audacious hope that it is going to persevere after all: "I will lift my eyes unto the mountains, from whence my help comes", as it says in the Breviary, an intense and burning knowledge that the Lord whom we know will conquer. And, having a burning sorrow and shame in thinking of the price he has eternally paid for the victory, the Church ever holds the crucifix before our eyes—on which he fought for our salvation against each one of us.

We do not want to be impolite in directly contradicting Archbishop Söderblom when, in the book about the schismatic church organizations meeting in Stockholm, he declares, "If we compare the Church's hymns and prayers with the Bible, we see, if our eyes are open, the extent to which the thought of eternal salvation has devoured Jesus' proclamation of the kingdom of God and the New Testament concern for the neighbor and common life. Really, the kingdom of God has first gained its rightful place in Christian teaching and interpretation in our time."[7] But one can point to many explanations and excuses for the rather striking lack of initiative on the part of the different church organizations through the years, when it comes to work for the victory of God's kingdom here on earth. It seems to me, *inter alia*, that it might be hard to know what should be done when it is hard to know what one believes. For most of the church organizations that are direct products of the "reformation" in the sixteenth century, it is also true that they have taken a position between that of a protégée and a housewife in relation to the power of the civil state. It is not easy for them to protest when the power of the state takes purely material viewpoints and, from these, attempts to solve the tasks which the Church until the "reformation" had worked at solving. But it should be understood that the Church was successful in getting rid of the problems of the world, or she as much as promised that she would someday do so forever. It is a fact that poverty, need and illiteracy can cause people suffering —but worldly wisdom has a tendency to want to attend to these things by getting those who are better placed materially to look after the unfortunate, the enlightened to teach the ignorant. The Church has wanted to point to the fact that, just as a man can be a criminal because he is poor and oppressed, he can be the same because he is rich and powerful; he can be repulsive because he is poor, but he can be even worse if he is rich; he can be superstitious because he is uneducated, but enlightenment can make him many times more superstitious. It was the Church's program for the unfortunate rich to be helped by the unfortunate poor, and conversely; the taught and the untaught should help each other to become wise. She has ever and always looked sceptically at do-gooders who do not perceive that at times her own consecrated and sworn servants did not take care to steer clear of the danger of riches. The "reformers" in their anger over this kind of an arrangement nevertheless gave the *patrimonium pauperum* to kings and rulers. It can never be easy for the state church to resist the economic system of a government that threatens to return some part of the people to near slavery. When the Stockholm Conference suddenly discovered that these state churches are now strongly interested in the worker question, it caused both Catholic and free churches to remark, in human terms rather than Christian, on what the inheritors of Luther and Cranmer have become at last, they who once were "mighty lords and hereditary rulers". The state churches have often attempted to find a *modus vivendi* in which they could adopt much that was originally foreign to them but, even more, that which they used to strive against. Even the "spiritual freedom" which afterward they learned to praise is not completely Lutheran or Calvinistic but more than anything else a fruit of the spiritual currents of the eighteenth century whose most dramatic representative in our area was Streuensee.[8]

Also, speaking in human rather than Christian terms, Catholics have muttered that the "reformed" churches first took a serious interest in sending missionaries to countries when, because of the colonization policies of the great powers, there was relatively little danger of martyrdom. The Catholic Church has had missions to the heathen continually since St. Peter and St. Paul lived on earth. In the time of the "*volkswandring*" and the raids of the Vikings, which harassed Catholic lands, the Church replied by sending missionaries out among the ravagers; if convents and churches were burned, monks and nuns murdered, the Benedictines set out to convert the murderers.

Tollak Mathiesen wrote a letter to *Gula Tidend* that was printed February 2 of this year. He said that the introduction of Christianity into Norway was not carried out without blood witnesses to the old faith. I believe it is true to say that our fathers found this not so horrible: the modern type of whimpering girl who cries when someone wants to do to her what she had done or promised to do to someone else has had the help of the "reformation" spirit in her development. From the Protestant side, it is certain that there has been infinitely more praise for the courage of Luther when he traveled to the Diet of Worms—not without the purpose of finding powerful protectors there—than has been spoken from the Catholic side for the courage of all the English Catholics who, from the time of Henry VIII to Charles II, sacrificed their goods to the last penny and their lives and the lives of their dear ones for their faith—without the least shadow of a hope of finding a protector on earth. In a desperate adventure, young and old men fled England by the hundreds to the seminary for priests in Douai, that they might be competent to fight for their faith. With the weapon of learning, they underwent intensive studies; then they sneaked home again. Daily they practiced their priesthood in danger of their lives, fully knowing that it was probable there would be only one way out of the struggle—sooner or later Judas would whisper, and there would be a trial in the torture chamber, while all their members were stretched out in pain, to be loosed on crutches only to be dragged to the public hearing, with its ridicule of all they held holy. And at last the place of execution, where the "mass priest" was hanged on the gallows but then cut down before he lost consciousness and stripped so that the executioner could eviscerate him—and his body was divided up for its last resting places, stakes and the wheel. And they endured this torture with prayer for the Church and the enemies of the Church; they turned the public hearing into a disputation, so that the room was cleared of people for the sake of the poor reformed priests who came off so ill; at the gallows they made sharp and serene ripostes. When the executioner in his roughness tried to stop their prayer because it was time for the slaughter, the brothers kissed the hand of the executioner, for the sake of the blood of martyrdom, when their turn came. But I am not at all sure that, for example, any Norwegian paper would print the presentation with enthusiasm, if I decided to translate a handful of the most thrilling and dramatic eye-witness accounts of the fear of God and courage displayed by English Catholics. From the school in Douai alone there were more than 150 priests killed in this way—and that is only a small portion of the martyrs of the English "reformation".

Some of the medieval missionary orders to the Muslims still exist as general mission orders. When they began, they had the task of redeeming Christian prisoners; young and strong monks gave themselves in exchange for sick and exhausted slaves or for men who were fathers of families.

St. Francis Xavier came to Japan in 1549, and there were 300,000 Catholics in the land around 1590. Six years later, the Japanese persecution of Christians broke out, the worst known in the entire history of the Church. Mass crucifixions of monk-priests in Nagasaki took place in 1597; in 1622, fifty-two martyrs were burned. Also in Nagasaki, some years later, 37,000 Christians were massacred in the province of Arima. Then Japan was closed to Europeans, and during this time, which lasted two hundred years, a number of persecutions of Christians occurred. Some Jesuits and Dominicans had the courage to push into the closed land, and they received the fate they expected. In 1859, when Japan was opened again to Europeans, they found that there were still about 50,000 Christians there; as in China, the Church has always tried to transfer the priesthood to natives as soon as possible, because the sacraments should be offered continually, independent of political situations. Protestant missionaries came to Japan in 1859. The position of the Church during the French revolution can be discovered in Brandes: *Reaction in France*; for the martyrs in Mexico, refer to the daily papers [in 1927]. The Church never grows wiser. But when the worst is said that can be said about the fanaticism and cruelty of Catholic Christians to other religions, the Church is able to answer in every case: We have not done anything to others that we did not will that they should do to us, nothing which untold thousands of the Church's own children have not joyfully accepted. And we do not believe that human nature has changed, and we know that the Church cannot become wiser. We can each have doubts about ourselves, about what we would be able to do, but we do not doubt that there are enough of our sisters and brothers who can do all for our Lord.

We are invited to doubt ourselves but to believe in God and in all other persons, to judge ourselves but not others. The Church refuses to deal with human opinions when she accepts a revealed dogma, and she forbids us to call by any other name what our Lord has called sin. At this point she is exclusive and unbowing. But she refuses to have purely human opinions about secular things—such as constitutional matters or foreign affairs—making them dogmas; there we have been given freedom to do and take counsel in a given situation as it seems wisest, to the extent that what is done is without sin. And she forbids us to judge the nature of any individual, the inmost part of his hidden being. She cannot solemnly bury heretics or suicides, partly because she can help only those who believe— and simply in human terms, it is not customary to bury troublemakers or deserters beneath the regimental colors. But this does not bar priests or laymen from hoping and praying for all, for none knows what can happen between God and the soul even if it happens in the very last second. Her saints have never felt sure of victory before the last minute of death, and she gives the same comfort to the sinner who prays for grace at the last second, purely out of fear of hell, as she gives to one who has all his life grieved over his difference from our Lord with the eternal warmth of love. She is as full of paradoxes as the so-called "simple gospel" of the New Testament itself, as full of seemingly unresolvable contradictions as the Creed of St. Athanasius. She came into the world in a society which seemed to rest immovably on the foundation of slavery —the Church said not a word to the slaves about organizing and bettering their lot or about it being unworthy for a person to be unfree—just the opposite. She pointed to the lack of freedom of the slave owners, and they were seized by a longing for freedom which made the foundations of slavery crack and crumble. She claimed that suffering and the cross were necessary for salvation; rightly understood, sickness and poverty are special graces, and people ran after the poor with gifts and built houses for the sick.[9] She claimed that one thing was necessary, and no learning was necessary to learn what that was—God has not made human salvation dependent on practical skills like silent reading—and monks and nuns became teachers. In the English "chantries"—privately established chapels—the chaplain was to read free of charge with all who asked him for this in God's name. Plundering these chantries brought 180,000 pounds into the treasury of the "reformation" kings. Yet, in 1645 there did not exist a single free school beyond what remained of the "chantries". The Church celebrated her worship in dungeons and cemetary chapels where the dead one himself was the altar boy, beneath God's open sky and in churches with complicated ceremonies having the formal beauty described by St. John when he attempts to use human language to describe his heavenly visions—and everywhere she has fed her children with bread.

And out of this forceful activity, restlessness, unease, and striving, out of the hard commandment to consider one's own sins and not the sins of others—confession becomes sacrilegious if the one confessing, directly or indirectly, is tempted[10] to tell on others or set forth excusing circumstances—springs the deep peace in Catholic churches, idyll and feast in the Catholic popular life. We can agree that life on earth is a vale of tears; the Protestant should feel that he can slip out of it— the Catholic cannot be too sure of that; in fear and trembling he is to work out his salvation. But he must work! And also, or therefore, the sourness and tearfulness which one so often meets in the Protestant "revival" circles is as good as unknown in Catholicism.

Is it strange that we think that beneath the perspective of other Christians and non-Christians with their seeming reasonableness and connectedness lies a deep unreasonableness; they are simply far from life. Catholicism's unreasonableness, contradictions, and problems point to a fundamental, organic connection. The Church is built on a rock. Catholicism does not explain all the problems of existence, but it explains more and goes deeper than any other philosophy of life. If the world is a battleground where God and Satan fight and there is no hope that the battle shall be finally over before judgment day, not even on that day will it become more humane; on the contrary, it shall become more grim. As St. John prophesies, we should be prepared for the worst. The best soldier is not the one who hasn't the sense to be afraid, but the one who is braver than he is fearful. And each joy, each victory, each good thing becomes wonderful—a surprise, an experience and extra delicious—*À la guerre comme à la guerre.*

II

In reality, consequently, the religious life of many Protestants develops in just this way. Protestants experience those stages which a Catholic psychologist calls the way of purification, the way of enlightenment, and the way of union, or heat, *calor*, as Richard Rolle calls it. Here the danger, from a Catholic viewpoint, is, on the one hand, the fear of acknowledging that a sinner may will and work, even if he knows he is very weak and miserable. As the teaching of *sola fide* was in reality unnatural, so life has opposed it in many ways. A sinner sins, trusting that he can be washed clean in the blood of Jesus, when it pleases him. Jesus pays the sinner's account on the day it comes due, whether the person is insolvent because of an honorable inability to pay or from speculation. These ideas are more common in anti-Christian novels than in life, but I have met Protestants who reasoned in this way. In our time, the rationalization often is that God is not so little and narrow-minded as people want to make him—the basic meaning: he is exalted enough to see the thing the way I see it myself. "Our Lord is a reasonable man."

Another consequence of the general fear of the Protestant sects to point to perfection as the distant goal of humanity is that the sin, from which conversion must first take place, is seen not as an inescapable infection but as sins—against other persons or the criminal law or civilized drinking habits, etc. In Catholic countries one often meets men who probably have not committed a real sin since, at seven or eight, they celebrated their first Holy Communion; hardly have they been heard to speak a word which should have been left unspoken: they have never wanted to do anything but to serve God and to live in God. They are, least of all, persons tempted to rely on themselves. St. Teresa pictures the water which looks very pure in the wooden cup stuck in the corner, but put it in a clear glass and hold it up to the sun! In Protestant lands one often meets both young and old persons who say, Why should they be converted? They are not worse than others. For them, civil propriety is the same as righteousness. As Bjørnsson said, right after he had presented a fine cast of people, "Where good people go, there is God's way." The state church has certainly played a large part in shaping this kind of thinking because it has always tried to go hand in hand with civil morality as expressed in the law. It has avoided such situations as, for example, the Church created for herself in medieval Norway: murder was punished as a sin at a time when private revenge was the enforcer of the law, and she considered engaged persons who lived together as having a valid marriage, even when the woman's relatives demanded a fine from the bridegroom because he had not waited for the day when it was proper for them to deliver to him the right to be her guardian.

A very funny result of this attempt to unite civil morality and the ideals of the Christian ethic may be seen in much of the newer spiritualist writing.[11] From an understandable wish that all men might be saved—a wish that Catholics share with all their hearts—they portray the "other side", above all, as bridge parties and lectures and fellowship, conceived as at least as materialistic but undeniably much less amusing than Valhalla or the paradise of Australian natives. And all are educated there, until they are "good and wise"—if there is anyone who is so desperately self-willed that he won't let himself be educated, they do not say. I think that this perspective with compulsory education and babysitters is more unpleasant than Dante's *Inferno*.

The reaction against "faith alone", a reaction which demands life and work, results, then, as it should, in the demand for life and not dogmas. It should not be forgotten, however, that the very concept of holiness demands certain dogmas, if it is going to claim to be essentially different, not just different to a degree, from the demands of pre-Christian and non-Christian religions moral purity, endurance, honor, and prudence. The danger is that one may turn back to the worship of the one, true God toward which all religions are finally directed—the Catholic Church has always known this—but then reject his answer, his work, Jesus Christ, God's only Son, "*filius unicus*" or "*unigenitus*", as is said in the creeds. One may turn away from the morning sun toward the twilight of the gods, go still more wild because one is going from light to dark and is feeding, instead of from the sacraments, from the warmed-over pot of the mixture of religions which has gone on simmering for thousands of years. That was why St. Peter and St. Paul and their converts were martyred—because they could not put their faith in the great common kettle into which, even in that time, new religions were continually added. None in our time believes that the world had anything essential against the newborn Catholic Church other than that she taught that she was infallible and unique. Jahve-Ammon or Jupiter-Jahve, Kristus-Apollo or Jesus-Mithra would have been received with full honors into the hospitable Roman pantheon and no one would have done anything to the Christians, if only their convictions had permitted them to respect the convictions of others enough to offer a pinch of incense to the genius of Caesar or to the principle of motherhood in nature. If the Church had not always known what Mary, the Mother of mercy, is, many controversies would have been avoided. But—"Hail Mary—blessed is the fruit of thy womb, Jesus", who has sweat blood for our sake—therefore, "pray for us sinners"; she is great, loving and at the opposite pole from the grim mothers.

A special modern phenomenon is the deistic and Jesus-istic readiness in religiosity to work together with all possible idealistically and altruistically colored forms of materialism—the view of life which claims that this is Rhodes, and here we shall dance. Religion has the right to exist only if it will serve this life—it can be allowed to dream about a life after death, but only if it does not demand that there be suffering and sacrifice here on earth in order for the soul which pretends to be immortal to gain the kingdom of God which is not of this world. It is true that consistent, correct materialism often demands bloody sacrifice and patient suffering from its confessors, and faith beyond all understanding—in the possibilities for human development and in the ability to love and to will. For us Catholics, it remains the case that even the act of the will that is needed to stop one's ears against the whisper of the other world when, once in good faith, it is considered to be a siren song—to harden oneself against visions which can be considered hallucinations—even this costs a great deal. Although we know that between materialism as a worldview and Catholicism there is a life-and-death struggle, and there is no work of giving or receiving pardon—yet it is in these camps that we have seen enemies whom we can really love, the persecutors we can pray for. And this not only out of obedience—what we do for everyone, since God does not demand of us more than we are able to do—the subjection of will and deed—we humans are not masters of our feelings and moods. But there is a kind of modern, confused deism, more or less Christian sounding, colored by a kind of Jesus worship that is not worship of God but of a hero. It is prepared all too willingly to enter into company with whatever king of altruistically colored materialism, without understanding that the Christian and materialistic ideals are incommensurate, even when outwardly they look exactly alike. Every idealism is first and foremost directed toward the temporal—to get the most spiritual and material goods for the largest possible number here on earth. This idealism lets it stand as, at best, an open question whether or not there is a "hereafter"—and sooner or later, but seldom later, accustoms itself to believe that these ideals cannot be realized unless the majority are persuaded or forced to obey a minority. Neither can people be led forward to material salvation without lords who command and chiefs who keep discipline. But this is just what we Catholics will not subject ourselves to—we do not agree that a man has the right to rule over other people. In purely secular matters, we want to choose our own leaders; we will not accept dogmas beyond the supernatural revelation; human ideas can be more or less valid and worth fighting for, but they can never be claimed as dogmas—political dogmas, for example. This is really the crux of the Holy Father's response to *Action française*; the monarchy cannot be made into a dogma for French Catholics, even if they have good reasons for their position that the monarchy is the form of government best suited for the French Catholic kingdom. We do not want to hear of more than one papacy, the papacy of the immortal St. Peter, to whom our Lord gave the keys of the kingdom of heaven with the instructions that whatever he bound or loosed on earth would be bound or loosed in heaven. Where one person rules over others by right of might or right of wisdom, or with the —humanly speaking—right of being better, there society built on slavery has been raised again. We do not want to be part of this—as much for the sake of the lords as for that of the slaves. We who believe that the Church of Christ shall stand until judgment day and that the gates of hell shall not overcome her—we choose to fight for all that entails. Decimation, exile to the ends of the earth and under the earth, the Church has been through all this so many times before. We fight for the freedom of the Christian person, not the varied freedoms from military discipline, from the regime of the great camp, which the "reformers" complained about—for a person's freedom to obey God alone and in the manner which he ordained when he said to his disciples: "Who hears you, hears me. And lo, I am with you until the end of the world." Finally, there is only one who will be able to evaluate and judge a person—he who has created mankind and knows it better than it knows itself.

Does anyone really believe that the feeling of freedom is especially alive in our time or in our country with the Lutheran state church, to which 97 percent of the population belongs? The state's encroachment on the rights of parents should suffice as an example in this regard, as it practically forces almost all to send their children to state schools whose direction and goal are set by party politics. It has been rather peacefully discussed in the papers—with only one woman[12] protesting, as far as I have seen—whether the state should take over the regulation of population growth. This means that whoever is in power at the moment in the state could decide on the basis of his own standards which men and women should live naturally as man and wife and which should be condemned to some unnatural form of marriage. Against the Manichaeans and Albigensians and the Cathari of the Middle Ages, who taught that the devil had created human beings as men and women, the Church claimed that creation was God's work and that the right to live as man and woman in marriage within the limits given by our Lord was a human right. Against Luther she claimed that man is not a slave, living in the bondage of the will dominated by his drives, and whom God would not want to help were he to renounce his inheritance of a natural good in order to serve God or humanity in a special way. Against the Renaissance worship of the body, she claimed that man was fallen and his original drives perverted, so that force, deceitful buying and selling, infidelity, and meanness affect even the relation between man and woman; she has reminded spouses that one's spouse is neither more or less than a redeemed partner, equal as a Christian and that they should pray as they remember this, both when they are inclined to mutual idolatry and when they are inclined to scream at each other "You skinflint", "You squanderer".

She has fought against the devil and hexes because of their effort to paralyze the human faculties. Now it looks as though the Church is going to fight a battle against all of these old enemies.

Here is a rather illustrative little example of the Protestant feeling for human freedom and dignity: a year ago the National Theater presented an English drama that was called something like "The Journey to Radioland". That isn't accurate, but the title was something like that. A group of men and women come aboard a remarkable ship without knowing each other, but as the ship sails the group guesses where it is going—yes, isn't it blasphemous to use the old expression the "land of life". They learn that there they shall be placed before, not a judge, but a censor. After the journey they meet the censor; he is a deceased English gentleman who received his training at one or another of the earth's reputable institutions of learning. He begins with judging his neighbors and asks if he has gotten to their *privatissima*! With good reason, the censor avoids going into their inner life. There is no testimony of witnesses either. When it cannot be thought that the deceased doctor or detective—whatever the figure was when alive—has found out all this about his captives with the help of some kind of immanence or transcendence, Sjøl finds out where he has dug up all the stories he has confronted them with. Unfortunately, the piece illustrates only by intimation how gossip is carried about in the other world. Some of the Oslo priests were invited to see this edifying piece—but I never heard anyone, priest or layman, protest against its main theme, which is the coarsest kind of blasphemy against God and man: that even in eternity man will judge man!

Protestantism has been so bothered by the relation of Catholicism to heathenism—that the Church has made the sign of the cross on some heathen relics and confirmed some heathen thoughts about the hidden God—that the 'reformed' churches have not bothered really to look at what Catholicism received as flowers and what it tread under foot as poisonous snakes. And all around the country, Protestant sects open the door to let in the most poisonous aberrations of heathenism—people's worship of what they have created instead of the Creator, and mankind's worship of itself.

III

I am certain that many will think that the words I am using about the Protestant "freedom of the spirit" unnecessarily harsh and critical. However, I will ask these persons: without prejudice, think a little about the point in many of the stories about the fools of Mols. What people from outside this village took for dumbness, from the standpoint of the fools is seen as an example of the need for independence, the will to build everything on one's own experience, the will to the free and unqualified, subjective solving of life's problems. When Archbishop Söderblom's book about the Stockholm meeting made

me involuntarily think about the basic mood in the classic stories of fools, it may have been due to the peculiar style of the
Swedish Archbishop—in that throughout all of the 926 pages,
it is essentially he who is the speaker in this long work. If the
different participants at the meeting had been quoted verbatim
at length, perhaps the impression might have been different.
But it is a fact that many Catholics, especially converts, look
at the whole concept, of which the Stockholm meeting is an
example, with great impatience—they consider it as a fools'
council of war in the middle of the battleground, while the
battle is going on between Christ and the ruler of this world.
Truly, it is not that we doubt that the men who took part in
the ecumenical meeting desire to see God whom Jesus Christ
calls our Father in Heaven—even if they are not quite united
about how our Lord knew that God was that; either Christ is
God's incarnate Word or he is a man who spoke from his own
subjective religious experience, different from us in degree but
not in substance. There was something in the meetings' discussions about how the world should be made more Christian
which reminded us—at least in the Archbishop's account of
it—of the fools' discussions when they wanted to get fish in
their pond. It was decided to put in two salt herring who would
reproduce. And if they were so lucky as to lay hands on the
opposition which unceasingly works against the kingdom of
God on earth, we are not certain that they would not do as
the fools did with the eel—they sailed out into the fjord with
it and drowned it. To us, it is remarkably naïve for the Archbishop to speak as if he were somewhat hurt that Rome had
commented on the meeting in a manner not deserved, because
the meeting said nothing at all about Rome. We believe in
complete seriousness that the peace of Christ cannot be advanced in the world unless we confess with Peter, literally and
without interpretations: "Thou art the Christ, the Son of the
living God" and, therefore, accept all his words as the word
of God, including the word in which he appointed St. Peter as
the shepherd for his sheep and lambs. As we well know, it is

not immediately pleasing to humans to be called sheep, but we proceed, knowing that our Lord also knew this, and he knew better than we know ourselves that naturally we all prefer to be individualists on an adventure rather than sheep in a flock, and, further, that, in a certain quarter which he called the world, sheep is anything but a flattering nickname. And if we cannot take comfort in the fact that our Lord has conquered the world, so truly I know of nothing else which we poor Catholics can take as comfort.

Another matter is that we believe that the peace of Christ is attainable for each individual who has a good will to serve God, presupposing that he really is outside of the Church not by his own will and not because he doesn't want to be called a sheep or because he doesn't want to admit that his Lord has the right to set a shepherd over him.

It is possible, naturally, for a temporary peace to be reached in the world by mutual work between all or most of the religious organizations which count themselves as disciples of Jesus from Nazareth—whoever he was. Either he is the one who has created us, the one to whom we pray, when we pray as he has taught us, since he and the Father are one: "I am the ground of thy beseeching",[13] or he is a human, hopefully for us a superman, who spoke from a self-assurance so superhumanly audacious to the invisible Almighty, as we Catholics say: *Si non est Deus, non est bonus*, or one believes with the Arians and all the Gnostic sects from the first to the twentieth century that he really belonged to a completely different sphere of the cosmos than ours and appeared here on earth as if he were wearing the costume of a human body. We Catholics believe in a gathering together with Christ as a program, because we are at one as to who he is, because we are at one about the Gospels, whether they are words about the Word or a hero saga—which can, in any case, not bring the peace of God which the world can neither give nor take a single bit nearer to us. We are afraid that such a peace would soon appear to be peace without freedom or freedom without peace.

We think of dogmas as formulae for revealed truths in contrast to human discoveries which we can evaluate for ourselves.
Dogmas reproduce the content of revelation correctly but not
completely (they are like photographs: as photographs of the
same scene can be more or less clear, dogmas can be formulated
so that more or less of their content is distinguishable). Between
accepting the dogmatic teaching of the Catholic Church and
experiencing the spiritual reality of the content of the dogmas,
there is the same difference as there is between a photograph
of Rondane and a foot trip through it. Or between studying
the map in a general's office (if the map is completely reliable)
and walking out in the terrain. First of all, one has accepted
the map because it seemed to be reliable as far as the terrain
was known. The freedom to discard a dogma because a person was not there and perhaps never will go right there, is a
freedom which is worthless to a Catholic—about as valuable
as the freedom not to believe; there are bogs or viscous seas or
a field which the map does not show because none has been
in that area, or it has been covered over today, or one is near-
sighted. In a pleasure trip, it can be fun to go on an adventure
without a map. But if the world is a battlefield where King
Christ fought for the world against the enemy and was slain,
then young and fiery Catholics can look at different Christians
and Christic [*Kristicistiske*] sects in no other way but as so many
regiments of fools. And in answer to the chattering about the
Catholic Church being the refuge for tired souls, they answer
somewhat impatiently, "Yes, we are tired—not of battles, not
of the defeats we have suffered and shall suffer, for we know
that our Lord shall finally conquer and we with him, if we
endure to the end. But we are tired of the small talk about
freedom which costs freedom, and we are tired of nonsense."

IV

With such a view of existence, it is self-evident why all Catholics want to be propagandists for the Church. And when the

editor of *Vor Verden* asks me what I believe will be the future
of Catholicism in Norway, I can answer at once: sooner or
later there will be no other Christians in Norway—taking the
name in its historic sense—but Catholic Christians. That is
not to say that Catholics will ever be in the majority in the
country. It is not completely certain that Trondheim Cathedral will ever again be used for the purpose for which it was
built.[14] It may become a concert or festival center, or a lecture
hall, a temple for one or another human cult. The majority
of our people may join a completely different materialist confession which claims that the goal of existence is this present
existence and the human spirit is the spirit which should be
worshipped in spirit and in truth. Therefore one can worship
the manifestation of the human spirit in the form of leaders—
that is, people cannot very well keep themselves from doing
this—Buddhas and Christs. One can call oneself a follower
of the Jesus of the Gospels in the same way that people have
been followers of Plato and Karl Marx. And, from the puzzle
of paradoxes in the New Testament, one can choose a line
and emphasize Christ or Jesus in the same way as people have
been Platonists or Marxists. And such a development of the
religious condition does not in any way mean a lowering of the
level of material culture, at least not in the foreseeable future.
Quite the opposite—it is conceivable that the modern type of
person could organize a slave state where the slaves are well
taken care of. I am pleased to point to a little pamphlet by
Haldane and Russell, "Daedalus and Icarus", which was translated into Swedish in the series *Mutid och Framtid* [Present and
Future]. It is probable that things will not happen quite as the
authors have predicted, but can anyone say they won't go that
way? When I was little, whenever I got a new doll head, my
mother used to cut up newspaper and stuff it, so it would stand
up better when knocked around. Nevertheless, it always got
broken and the bits of paper always showed. I must confess
that I remember these catastrophes rather often when I hear
about the type of modern man who has his head stuffed full of

clippings of learning. It is also a question of whether man at length can get people used to not thinking at all—with respect to religious questions as well. The Gospels with all their paradoxes cannot be accommodated in any simpler thought system than the theology of the Catholic Church. All other attempts to systematize the contents of the Gospels have been more or less unsuccessful.

The reformers shared the Renaissance's somewhat puerile concept of humanity, which had absolutely no experience of how people would respond to book learning, when everyone was to be forced to be educated, for example, to read and write. People today should know that everyone simply cannot learn to read and write. There are people who have gone for six or seven years to the public school and read only the papers and movie billboards, write letters with abortive dependent clauses and no orthography, and have no ability to understand a printed or written phonetic picture. If anyone wants us to believe that showing this type of person a printed authority is useful—then too much is being asked of us Catholics. Our ability to believe just copes with what the Church expects of us, not that supernatural signs are more fantastic than those of the Church. I won't even name all the tragedies of lost childhood faith which proceed from a kind of "Bible" faith. I saw this illustrated best in an anti-Catholic pamphlet which was sent to me, anonymously, of course. (I don't want to insinuate that there is something about Protestantism itself which causes a moral leprosy with a loss of feeling of honor, but it is amazing how many Protestants write anonymous letters; perhaps 97 percent of them.) On the one side stood the poor Catholic, blindfolded and led by some priests on a kind of dog leash; on the other side, the freed Protestant stretched his hands out toward the Bible, which came descending from heaven, ready set, nicely bound in one volume with a cross on the cover. In Luther's time, in an emergency, one could accept his assertion that every person had a reliable guide in his own conscience. A modern person with a tiny bit of psychological knowledge who reads Luther's own writings wonders if Luther himself was able to distinguish conscience from mere thoughts and idiosyncrasies. And each day one is constrained to admit that there are quite a few of one's own fellows who do not have any conscience discernible to the human eye; one, it is hoped, may even be willing to admit that perhaps the decisions of one's own conscience need to be confronted a bit with a supernatural teaching authority. This is clearly one of the central points in the struggle between the Church and the sects. When there is someone who needs to be taught, corrected, disciplined—if only by the police for the sake of civil order—anyone should understand that there are some persons who do not want to be taught, corrected, or disciplined. And does anyone dare to take it on himself to teach, correct, or discipline them or to take this on only out of self-confidence or with a merely human mandate? This is the shortcut back to tyranny and the slave state—and the worst thing about our age is that those who have the best chance to become tyrants are those who say and believe that they will only tyrannize their neighbors for their own good. We are threatened with submission to tyranny by a kind of babysitting—somewhat different from Well's fearful fantasies about a future with men who are like gods. When parish priest Kløvstad in an article in *Tidens Tegn* for January 26 of this year speaks of human opinions as "holy", we Catholics can only answer that we simply do not acknowledge human opinions as holy—only One is holy, and not as long as we live do we consider ourselves as completely identical with him. But for Protestants, the latent danger, clearly, is that they can easily make the little blasphemy of Falk their own:

I or the lie—one of us shall decide.

V

Propaganda is also part of the nature of the Church. But non-Catholics' ideas about the nature of Catholic propaganda are certainly very completely wrong, often misty and not seldom crazy—as are their ideas of Catholicism as a whole.

For the most part, only one thing is taught in schoolbooks: that the Church is fundamentally demented. This goes back to the reformation period's lying and tendentious portrayal of the teaching and the state of the Church. Our Protestant historians portray the facts from an interpretation based on lies and slanted history—Lange's, Keyser's and Munch's use of our historical sources swarm with examples. Or they imagine that they know something about Catholic teaching and practice and do not bother doing the research to find out whether what they have convinced themselves of is true. For example, in Nordahl Rolfsen's reading book, part three, the late Bishop Bang has an article, "A Day in Hovedøens Convent". We are told about the benefactors of the convent: "Every year on the anniversary of their death, a soul Mass was held for each one of them; it often happened that a few monks were busy from morning to evening with this tiring and spiritually deadening work." A priest fasts, that is, he does not even take a sip of water, after midnight when he is going to say holy Mass; the last Mass in a church or convent must be celebrated not later than noon. Besides this, only under exceptional circumstances can a priest say more than one Mass a day. The nonsense cited above is written by the author of *Den Norske Kirkes Historie under katholicism* [Norwegian Church history during Catholic times]. The Jesuit debate in parliament last year and the discussion in the media of the Eskeland case revealed the most fascinatingly arrogant ignorance of the essence of Catholicism, about the nature of its case and of the Church's relation to the state in those countries where there is cooperation between church and state. In no place in the world is the Catholic Church the "state religion" in the same sense as the "evangelical Lutheran" church is the state religion in Norway. In all countries, both state and Church understand that the Church cannot bow to any demand from the side of the state which would harm her nature as the Church of Christ, as she conceives this. Whenever the political division of power in the state makes demands on her, she may refuse them—even if the Church is willing to be as accommodating as possible for the sake of peace, this possibility is limited. As to schools, the Church cannot accept a ruling which, based on purely human ideas about how other people's children should be raised, prescribes how she should fulfill her own responsibility in teaching children the faith into which they have been baptized. No Catholic priest, father, or mother could be content with a non-Christian teacher of religion for their children who merely does not tell them that he himself does not believe what he is teaching. It is completely different [from Norway] in a country where the Catholics are in the majority—as in Belgium—or where they constitute a sizable minority—as in Holland where one-third of the population is Catholic. There the state supports all public schools: secular, sectarian, or Catholic. The chairs for special disciplines at the universities are often given to professional people who profess something other than Catholicism.

When parish priest Kløvstad in *Tidens Tegn* for January 26 of this year points to a number of actions of the Catholic Church which illustrate the constraint of conscience in the Catholic Church and concludes "so, when Mr. Eskeland says his being driven out was done in the name of Luther, it can be answered with full right: 'It was done in the name of the pope' ", the parish priest is completely disoriented. The papal decrees which Mr. Kløvstad mentions are directed against modernism and are meant for persons who *with the mandate of the Catholic Church and in her name* want to practice spiritual responsibilities or occupy theological teaching positions. If they want to work in the *service of the Church*, this stands as a guarantee of what they teach and confess—they must recant, for example, whatever they say contrary to the teaching of the Church. If they cannot, they must leave their position or join another church organization. Anyone who wants to teach something else besides the specific Catholic Faith may not teach in the name of the Catholic Church or disseminate his teaching as Catholicism.[15]

For many years it has been known that Lars Eskeland stood close to the Catholic idea of Christianity; his teaching of history has been colored by this. If Eskeland had been content to catholicize within the spacious state church, which takes care that the populace is supplied with orthodox and christic and rationalizing and gnosticizing priests—would this have been all right? If Lars Eskeland had, as a teacher in a school of confessional Lutheran character, taught Catholic theology and at the same time claimed he was a good Lutheran, demanding the right to share his views, unbound by any old confessional writings, then the state church would have been dealing with him in precisely the spirit of the papal Church if they had thrown him out. The spirit of the state church seems to be horrified and offended when someone really believes that there are religious issues which do not belong within it.

The Catholic Church cannot cooperate with the state unless it can remain Catholic. It cannot be like the state church, allowing her priests to marry the divorced contrary to the word of the Lord, which "reformed" priests ever since the days of Luther, Melanchthon and Cranmer have jumped over like a goat—I think the expression is Fernanda Nissen's. Or receive in the Church the corpse of a man who claimed, almost with his last breath, that he did not want to belong to the Church, merely because the Church can "honor" the dead by burying him—this contradicts both the idea of the nature of the Church and her dignity—as well as the dignity of the dead resister.

Therefore, when Bishop Bjørnes-Jacobsen, in an article dated January 26 and printed in *Nationen* and *Akershus Amtstidende*—and perhaps other places—speaks of "Catholic countries" in the same sense as there are "Lutheran countries", he is completely befuddled. Forget that he builds his considerations on purely inconsequential and shallow considerations. Certainly, natives and foreigners can find lovely playgrounds where they can "amuse themselves" in, for example, Vienna—but doesn't the Bishop know the reputation Oslo (and Copenhagen) have among foreign naval officers: one of the worst towns in Europe for young men to visit, because in no other city do loose women swarm in that way and in no other city are they so forward. Or what kind of reputation do young Norwegian girls have in Paris? It is accurate about the loose morals in Vienna —there are certain elements of the population which parade down all the streets—like Tordenskjöld soldiers. It is very true that a part of the population begs in the street, as they do in other places in Catholic countries, while in Lutheran countries they are largely cared for by the state. But, "when concern for the poor has permeated our laws and our civil life to the extent which it has", everyone knows that this depends fully as much on non-Christian idealism as it does on impulses from the state church. It is very true that the Church has not worked against beggary because she claims that it is honorable for a needy person to ask for help; and as for the person who gives, he is merely doing his duty. But he does not have the right to give something which is not his. If most of the Norwegian people were to become Catholic again, we would stop being the pioneer state until we could afford it. To bless towns with electric power plants and folk schools and old peoples' homes and then send the bill to the next generation—for Catholic morality, that is just as laudable as taking money from a young person doing an errand on the street, for example, and then giving it away.

In this country—as far as my personal experience extends —sacrifices are required for the special Norwegian concept of savings: debt and repayment are asked. The daily snowfall of letters I receive seldom contains fewer than one request in each delivery from someone who asks for help because he has bought land and small factories and his own home and pianos and dairy stores and suits and temperance cafes and installation firms and I don't know what, often for fantastic prices a few years back, and then there is a stereotypical expression that it was "perhaps" foolish when they had nothing, but. Or he asks for a loan to do one of the above things. Then all the hundreds who are in need come, pure and simple: they have only enough

from the community barely to keep alive; they work at one of
the industrial plants which now lies down and dies. It wouldn't
occur to me to blame the state church for the economic development which has caused these daily, monotonous cries of woe
—except to the degree that the Lutheran-ecclesial ideas about
religious freedom and these state economic ideas spring from
the same lack of ability to distinguish between that which can
be wished and that which is possible. I am willing to believe
that the inner circle of the church—the real church people—
have been tempted to put on the brakes or at least to be a little
more careful in their own affairs—but 97 percent of the population belongs to the state church! Also, we are the same people
as we have always been: jaunting off to foreign lands is our
proudest ancient remembrance. We have been out in a stream
of ideas which has promoted in our people all the elements
which counteract self-help, and those in Norwegian society
who are able to help themselves have worked and kept quiet.
The Italians are defiant beggars, as can be seen there, but they
are also the same people who have cultivated whole provinces
of land as a single field, where they reap three crops a year, build
up the fields in terraces from top to bottom, and plant in dirt
which they have borne up to the terraces in baskets. The family life (not in Catholic countries, for they do not exist, but in
Catholic homes) is more beautiful, warmer, cleaner, and more
loving than in any other place in the world. I have never heard
this denied by people who have been lucky enough to see it.
In Catholic settlements—that is, where most of the population
are really practicing Catholics—childbirth outside of marriage
is very uncommon. Divorce with its resultant remarriage is
completely out of the question—the Catholic who enters into
such a thing excommunicates himself; he cannot receive the
Sacrament. In countries with a mixed population, it is not uncommon for them to go over to one or another Protestant sect.
Moreover, the Bishop should know a little about statistics on
births outside marriage, for what it is worth. In Norway I have
known more unmarried women who have been lovers with-

out having children than I have unwed mothers. They viewed this, not as a sin or a shame, but as a little secret that they were proud of. At least twenty women whom I remember individually have confided to me: of course they were unmarried and old, or they had for other reasons lost hope in having a home and husband and children, but things weren't so bad that they deserved the nickname "old maid". One or another man had been interested in them for a period of time, and then he separated from them, leaving them with "wreck" stamped on them. They were not at all loose women; they were very serious, many of them very religious in their way—confident that God was not so narrow as people; he was happy that they had "lived once".

That is not as bad as what an exasperated woman wrote to me some years ago. I had replied to Mrs. Katti Anker Møller's piece on "The Politics of Women Giving Birth". I was called medieval, and the projected educational institute of Mrs. Anker Møller ought to be called "The New Luther Foundation".

The bitter and narrow-minded, disturbed, eccentric, unthinking, comic old maid figures in very serious psychological novels about "unused eros" and the syrup-and-water stories for young girls: Do the priests of Lutheranism suspect in the least what our having imported this kind of thinking from Luther's homeland means? That a being who unites femininity, virginity, and maturity must be a thing of humor and that her life must be a wasted life?

We have youth who are not afraid to give witness, even if they are so few and so against the stream—not with chatting and idle talk, but with their lives, in their prayers and intercessions. It has been said so many times, and what is said is true: preaching plays a subordinate role in the Catholic Church, in comparison to what the Protestant experiences. This is also true of the Catholic witness. Every one of our young Catholic boys and girls who lives a good Catholic life, every one of our sisters in orders, every brave and faithful Catholic mother and father and every one of our small children who receives First Commu-

nion with a heart of love, a little soul which is still so pure, and
who has a good will to let himself be led and taught of the Master—they are obviously of much greater value for propaganda
than we can be with wordy writing and educational lectures.
Does anyone think it would have profited the missionaries of
St. Olav to come and invite the heathen Norwegians to hear
a lecture? The Fulda monks did more preaching in Germany
with their lives than with their preaching. St. Olav converted
more of Norway to Christianity with his fight against his own
warlike and rash mind than with all the outer institutions he
organized, no matter how energetic they were. No one in the
Church wants Lars Eskeland to go around like a roaring lion
and see how many of his students he can talk into becoming
Catholic. He will be good propaganda by being a good Catholic. And there are some of our Catholic youth in any case who
cannot repress a certain happy expectation.

Slowly the determined Protestants will succeed in making
Lars Eskeland's conversion to Catholicism into strong propaganda—now that they have driven Eskeland away from the
school which he himself created. And they will see, when Voss
high school comes under other leadership, that it was this man
who made the school what it was.

Heaven knows what they have deluded themselves into
thinking Catholic witness is. As is well known, no one can
be received into the Church without basic instructions—it is
not enough to have "everyone who wants to be saved, raise
your hands", as I have had the experience of hearing at a revival meeting. The Church does not receive capitulations who
only join, after having been momentarily stirred either by in-
toxicating feelings or emotional worship services; she demands
that the convert should know what she teaches and understand
what she says. The convert has months, years if he will, to think
things over before he takes the step. People talk about the cun-
ning of Catholic priests which no one can resist. Yes, a Catholic
priest must go through a strict school, learn both to teach himself and to teach others, as a candidate for the priesthood he

is sifted and tested. Then he accepts ordination—giving up his birth-right as a man to call some other person his nearest one. He shall be all-in-all to others and find that they often expect the impossible of him. He must go where he is sent, without seeking another call because his family is growing or trying to move to town for the sake of the children. No one doubts that most Lutheran priests are as sacrificial and zealous as they should be, when they must consider their family as a gift which Christian men are also pledged to, but the double bands to which he is pledged limit him. It is to be hoped that these men are more knowledgeable in other areas than we get the impression they are when they speak of Catholicism.

Obviously we reserve to ourselves the right to correct when obvious nonsense and misunderstanding is presented about our Church. The danger is, however, that, after these last demonstrations against the Church, all too many of our young men have become very angry, having studied and joined in the work of education—it does not matter if only they remember that this is not what is most important: the important thing is Catholic life itself.

Finally a word: It is not the Catholics who have caused trouble, both concerning Lars Eskeland and my conversion, buzzing around with rumors beforehand and reflections afterward, both in time and preferably out of time, with public statements by bishops and the suspicions of journalists as to why and wherefore we came to enter into the Roman trap. Finally, their ears rang with their own chatter, talking about Rome in a way which advertises its celebrated trophies! Whether this talk is accurate or not, the Catholic Church is accustomed to having converts from all denominations find their way home—God be praised —but she does not know the Protestant snobbery which is often manifest in a naked enthusiasm every time, for example, a noted author honors religion with his interest. And now Protestants, and not we, in discussions of the Eskeland case, have drawn in the word "martyr". We understand completely that this seemingly endless discussion must be unspeakably painful for Lars Eskeland. He has already attempted once to separate himself from the school; he besought his fellow teacher of thirty years, Olav Holdhus, to take over the leadership. He was asked to stay on; the Minister of the Church, Tveiten, among others, had asked him to stay on. Eskeland let himself be persuaded; it is reasonable for a person to want to remain with the work of his youth and his manhood, most of all when otherwise he would have to hand it over to others who would probably slowly take its life. No one could say to Eskeland, I want to be your successor. Also, if Lars Eskeland were canonized, it would be under the rubric of Confessor. We do not call a man a martyr even if he undergoes large and small unpleasantries for his convictions. We say this because there will be attempts to replace the talking martyr with a good old Norwegian word, "blood witness"! That word was used by our Catholic fathers just as we use it and not as modern whining girls use the word "martyr".

Lillehammer, February 28, 1927

NOTES

[1] "Repentance" is used in the Catholic theological sense: the sorrow of the conscience which drives the will to arise and make its way forward through existence in a new direction—in contrast to the unfruitful sorrow of conscience which does not change the course of life but only causes loathing, bitterness, self-abandonment, and desperation.

[2] St. Thomas Aquinas, *Summa theologiae* I–II, q. 112. It is impossible to have metaphysical assurance of God's friendship. On the other hand, from certain signs we can have experiential assurance: in feeling joy in God and in divine things, indifference in the face of worldly things, and in that we are not conscious of mortal sin.

[3] St. Francis is another case in point. He knew no "assurance of salvation" in the Protestant sense. St. Francis is very popular with Protestants.

[4] John Howley, M.A., *Psychology and Mystical Experience* (London, 1920).

[5] It is, moreover, curious that people who discuss Catholicism and the teaching of the Church have hardly ever looked in a missal. Missals with Latin and German, French or English texts can be had in any bookstore, a new edition of the Latin-Danish Missal has recently been published; it had been out of print some years, the last edition of it having been burned at Louvain. We hope for a Latin-Norwegian missal one day.

[6] By saints, the Church denotes all the dead who have come to the point where they can see God as he is. For some of these, God has made known by miracles that they have run the course to its finish—Catholics, who have not known them in life, ask for their intercession and choose them as examples. But in all Catholic families, parents and children, for example, ask their deceased small children to intercede for them.

[7] *Kristenhetens mote i Stockholm*, p. 237.

[8] Johann Streuensee was the Minister of the Privy Council under Christian VII of Denmark. He was a typical apostle of the Enlightenment but was so corrupt that he was condemned to death in 1772.

[9] Professor Ehlers estimates the number of lepers in Europe at the beginning of the thirteenth century was around nineteen thousand; after that there was a steady decline in the sickness until the reformation.

[10] Note: Although the translator has verified that "is tempted" follows the original, Sigrid Undset is theologically in error here. A temptation itself is not a sin—Christ himself was tempted—ED.

[11] Sir Oliver Lodge, *Byfoged Dahl*.

[12] Mrs. Martha Floer in *Tidens Tegn*.

[13] Julian of Norwich, ca. 1373.

[14] Editor's note—Catholic Mass was finally celebrated in Trondheim Cathedral in the summer of 1993.

[15] For a more thorough discussion of the Kløvstad statement, see *St. Olav*, no. 6 of this year; it was submitted to *Tidens Tegn*, but they did not publish it.

SIGRID UNDSET

PROGRESS, RACE, RELIGION

It is often said in our time that Christianity is an enemy to the joy of life. Perhaps a special reason for this is that it has tried to insist or to persuade the powerful ones on earth to take less of the world's goods for themselves than they have the power to take. We are tempted to forget that true heathen joy in life was always strongly colored by one form or another of pessimism. Christianity has always refused to admire Lucifer, the rebellious archangel, his pride and his despair. This, in the eyes of the pious heathen, has always been one of the most unattractive traits of Christianity. Christianity will not accept the human drive toward the joy of destruction and the pleasure of death.

It is only natural that the anti-pessimism of Christianity irritates anyone who is not pure by nature and simple of heart, or who has not received the gift of supernatural grace. He can only be driven to oppose this anti-pessimism. Anyone who looks deeply into human nature cannot easily be an optimist unless he can set his trust in something beyond what we see in life. Equally, optimism about development—the concept that even as more complicated forms of life rise from simpler forms, so it follows that the continuous progress of the human race steadily unfolds itself toward a greater perfection and value of life—has arisen under the influence of Christianity. Heathens before Christ, Greeks or Romans, Nordic peoples or American Indians, happily portrayed the golden age as having been once in the past. The present was hard, the future dark and threat-

Translated by Rev. John E. Halborg.

ening. Christianity challenged the deepest human convictions when it proclaimed that the kingdom of God was yet to come.

If we have surrendered this faith—that finally the Absolute God must conquer because the Absolute God is a Person, who is living and almighty—then it would be more rational to turn back to the wisdom of our heathen forefathers. The golden age may have existed long ago at some point in time in prehistory when people had learned to control their environment to the degree that sometimes they could enjoy their rest and be safe in their hard and dangerous toil. The conditions of primitive life were harsh enough, but they had the ability to enjoy the animal level of existence profoundly and peacefully when the sun returned and warmed them after they had suffered through the time of frost and dampness; when they had been fed sufficiently and their young human consciousness displayed itself in games and camaraderie within their tribe. Considerations of the future hardly destroyed their joy in the present moment in the way that our enjoyment of the certain and uncertain goods of our complicated civilization is destroyed by our experience that all earthly things are transient.

It would seem that other forms of animal life developed to a stage where what they needed for life was perfectly adapted to certain conditions of time and space. And when they had developed to this point, the conditions of existence changed. Their highly specialized organs no longer had their primitive ability to adapt. Some kinds of animals managed to survive for a time because, when conditions in one part of the world changed, they were able to migrate somewhere else where the necessities of life were available to them. But many animal species disappeared, and all of them go that way sooner or later. So it is reasonable to believe that the relatively short section of human history which we call historical time precisely represents this part of our development—our development toward extinction —that is, if one does not believe that a personal God created man in his own image so that he might live in company with him forever. But all the other things which he created are destined to have their time and then depart. It is easy enough to understand people who say that they do not believe that. It is easy to understand those who say that they do not believe in a personal providence. It is not so easy to understand people who believe in a kind of development which is friendly to humanity but is minus God—something like natural providence or a provident nature.

If humanity is only a variety of animal which has developed away from other animals in a highly unusual way, it is an animal gone astray. Our peculiar capacities, the human soul and human intellect, we have used first of all for the destruction of our own species and to develop and give grounds for the human fear and mistrust of other humans. In other kinds of animals, the individual fights for booty; males fight for the same female. They do not bind themselves in military formation to fight about ideologies, for the possibility of booty, or out of fear of imaginary alarms to come. Our mind is eternally and always visited with fear of the future so that we even fear our own offspring. We have enough animal health in us to take pleasure in sexual relations, but we find means to make our physical activity fruitless.

It is certain that the white man—the European people—have had the leadership in this last phase of human development. Our racial pride has more or less certainly developed from the triumph of the European racial groups. The purpose of development so far has been to develop the European person. The English officeholder or soldier who established the law of his own type of civilization for the colored subjects of the British empire, the German Biedermann "delighted" with the order and prosperity of the Hohenzollern kingdom, the American citizen who piously thought that he lived in the promised land of freedom and knew with certainty that the most complete knowledge had been domesticated to play its new role as the handmaiden of the power of money—yes, even the Nordic schoolmaster who looked over whole nations with a smile because the children had received such a worthwhile

formation in school that it would be heretical to question it—
each of them could rejoice in their secret conviction that just
his people and race were the branch on the top of the family
tree of the human race. And then came the World War. And
something began to dawn on us who lost the World War. It
was the white man. We have gained a premonition that we
have lost our supremacy over the colored peoples of the world
—or we are doomed to lose it because we practice racial suicide and are incapable of turning our path away from new and
deadly European wars and sinking percentiles of birth. We can
no longer play the fool of benefactors and supporters of the
other continents while we use their natural resources and make
them into markets for our production. We have taught them
our highly developed techniques for making war—we cannot
hope now for much more than to hold an edge on them when
it comes to finding ever more perfect material for killing and
destruction, and furthermore continue to fight—fighting as
determinedly against persons of yellow, brown, or black color
as we fight between ourselves to exterminate the white race. It
may be said that finally the history of the world will be above
all the history of the white races, because we are headed into
the last phase of human development, the phase where humanity can no longer adjust to the changed conditions of existence
and will go the same way as the extinct species of animals. And
the pale races of people from the North—German and Slavic
—ought to praise themselves because they are the last bearers
of this part of progress. As a sort of phagocyte, they devastate
the races which are farther behind in progress and yet have preserved richer pigmentation and more of the animal capacity for
cheerful enjoyment of life. We had convinced ourselves that
we, ahead of all other races, were the builders and creators.
Now we begin to see that everything we have built is built so
that it quickly collapses and all that we create bears the seed of
dissolution from its beginning. And in the most secret depths
of our minds, desire for death lurks—the desire to kill others
and ourselves.

For the Christian there is the ancient explanation: the fall into sin. God willed to bring the human beings he had created into his own splendid home, to himself, in ways which would be a crescendo of life and life in abundance. The created being forgot that it owned nothing that had not been given to it by a generous Creator; it wished to be sufficient unto itself and to choose its own ways. There was a warning: these ways end in death. But mankind did not think about death while it was in Paradise, or it fooled itself into going its own way to a paradise after its own taste. It persuades itself to believe that the matter of death is only an empty threat made by a begrudging God who is afraid that mankind may become his successful rival. And when it occurs to people that the way they have chosen for themselves ends in death, they become bewitched and enchanted with death. They dole out death as if in ecstasy —they are afraid and want to confess that they have become slaves of desire, which finally shows itself to be a desire for death.

As God became man, Christ pointed to himself—he was the only person who could break the slavery of death: "I am the way and the truth and the life." The fall away from Christianity is, at its deepest, the fall away from life—the neverending life which gives to our short time on earth a meaning so decisive that it feels life to be an unbearable burden. The great majority of people have no doubt experienced periods of fundamental tiredness, when the tempter whispered that it would be delicious if one could believe that there is no personal immortality but that each person had permission to live his own life after his best judgment and his own wishes, without consequences or responsibility for eternity. And, because we cannot conceive of an absolute nonbeing and also because we ever retain a little love for mankind's beautiful and despicable world, we also dream of its future after we are gone. One person hopes for human progress in the direction in which his own ideals and ideas point, another dreams of the coming greatness of his race or some such thing, dubious comfort though that may be, if

he draws his conclusions from what history and sober understanding show to be probable.

Put into practice, these ideas lead to results which are very
different from what their first proponents had expected. All the
races consist of separate individuals, each with his own convictions and subconscious, his virtues and vices, his vanity and
cowardice. It is true that blood and race mean a great deal, even
if there is scarcely any pure race on earth today. But the earlier,
different mixtures of perhaps more homogeneous races have
nevertheless so much common inherited material—physical
and psychological characteristics, memories, and experiences
—that when they become stabilized to the point where they
have existed for some time as a people, nation or race, their
view of life gives them a certain common coloration. There
comes a rhythm and tone to their lives which separate them
from neighboring people. They lay a decided accent on the
common elements which make up human life. Lies and decep-
tions, for example, are practiced by people all over the world,
but there can be a subtle distinction in the manner in which
people lie and deceive, even if we are speaking of neighbors so
close as southern and northern Europeans. For the most part,
an Italian or Frenchman lies to deceive others, an Englishman
or German or Scandinavian seeks above all to deceive himself.
When a Frenchman wants to fool around in coarse sexual enjoyment, he does not customarily take pains to find excuses—at
most he tries to keep his moral lapse hidden because it might be
unpleasant for him if it is reported. A German or Scandinavian
who gives in to the same pleasure tries hard to convince himself that he is fighting a brave fight for some kind of morality.
The American robber barons of the nineteenth century were
in their own eyes the men who built up the new world—and it
was only the sharpest of their fellow countrymen who did not
see them in that role—even as they used the natural resources
of a part of the world for their own purpose and for a way of
life and health among themselves. The special Nordic way of
looking at life's problems is in its own way neither moral nor

immoral; in some individuals it can express itself as high voltage idealism, in others as hypocrisy. In the same way, the Northern people's penchant for working on concrete, practical matters rather than on intellectual problems makes them pioneers in the exact sciences and in the use of scientific results and fills them with worrisome concerns over what their neighbor does and how he appears. The Nordic people are by preference creators both of the miracles of the machine age and of all methods for developing gossip clubs and coffee klatches and all possible men's and women's associations, the sensational press, and the art of advertisement.

Race is neither a moral or immoral quality but is a special coloration which imprints a whole mixture of moral and immoral feelings in each individual being. To put trust in race, that is to say, to be unreasonably in love with one's own prejudices and biases without critically judging their value, is the sure way to let the least valuable elements in the race develop unchecked, simply because they are stained with our favorite colors. Races and nations are doomed to stagnate or degenerate when they become self-satisfied; that is equally certain for the individual person.

The medieval hatred of the Jew, at any rate, had a basis in understandable thought: for the medieval Christian, the Jews were a chosen people, the only race which had been chosen to fulfill a mission which was higher and more important for the world than the missions entrusted to other people. The almighty God and the Creator of the human race had chosen a people, the Hebrews, and of that people a family, the kingly house of David, and of David's house a young girl, for his instrument when he entered into blood brotherhood with human nature. His people rejected him, they rejected the handful of men and women of their people who had acknowledged him; they rejected his mother. The fisherman Peter and the Pharisee Paul died in a foreign land because they had understood who the flower was that their people should bring forth. But in place of the dead Israel, they and their fellow apostles had raised up a

new Israel, the inheritor of the promises which God had given
to Israel's patriarchs, but born "not of blood, and not of the
will of the flesh, nor the will of man but by the will of God";
brothers of the firstborn of the Jewish virgin Mary. For the
medieval Christian, it seemed clear that the Holy Scriptures,
the work of inspired Jewish authors, which Jews and Christians
alike considered holy, dealt with nothing other than the coming
of Jesus Christ. Christianity was the true Israel, the inheritor,
the freeborn "son of the free woman", and they who were Jews
and of the same lineage as the patriarchs and who read the same
Scriptures but who did not discern their true meaning must be
hardened, causing their will not to understand. On the other
hand, for the Jews, Jesus from Nazareth stood as a traitor to
the traditions of God's peculiar people, his apostles as fallen
away, and his mother's spiritual offspring as a foreigner who
persecuted God's chosen people.

It was a spiritual warfare, in any case; it was nothing so horrible and sinful as anti-Semitism. As a race, Jews were separate
from the populace of Europe; they were the result of a mixture
of Semitic and Anatolian races, while the European ancestors
were the Iranian-Mongolian and, perhaps, African races. Their
ancestors were the bearers of old and complicated cultures,
village farmers who cultivated small arable plots around primitive country settlements in the forest. In reality, the medieval
European mistrust of the Jew was, *inter alia*, a case of the peasant's mistrust and loathing of capable townsfolk and men of
affairs. The one certain reason was understandable: the religious conflict between inwardly incompatible understandings
of the eternal problems of humanity. And, moreover, when the
Jew entered into Christendom and in Christ acknowledged the
Messiah whom God had promised the Jewish people and who
was also the Savior of the whole world, then the racial conflicts
could be overcome—and to a great extent they were.

The old war of ideas has degenerated into a war of feelings (although naturally the impassioned elements were always
present); hate for the Jewish ability to accumulate wealth in a

peaceful and quiet manner in contrast to our noisy rapaciousness, hate of Jewish sensuality, since he had learned, through the millennia, how to build up a holy family life and a deep sense of blood kinship while our sensuality cast us out in comic or grotesque or tragic-romantic complications. But now, the Christian as well as the old Jewish view of life is breaking down in millions of souls.

The Jewish vices could be just as dangerous for the future of the world as those of the European peoples, and the Jew who has lost faith in the God of his ancestors is no doubt just as useless in helping humanity on its movement forward to chaos as the dechristianized inheritors of Christianity. But the hope of salvation for the human race is anchored in something deeper than variations in humanity which are determined by race and time. It is anchored in our common human nature which became united with divinity in Jesus Christ. His royal kingdom went beyond the borders of the Jewish world, went beyond the white man's world to collect persons of good will from around the world, whatever race or folk type they came from. They only need to want to receive faith in the Divine Life and be humble enough to desire union with their Creator, instead of the isolation of fetishism, the worship of things they have made themselves. That is basically self-worship, and because human nature cannot continue to exist without supernatural help, it means dissolution and death.

SIGRID UNDSET

A CHRISTMAS MEDITATION

The old masters were not afraid to make a completely realistic
portrayal of the newborn Christ Child. The sweet head of the
Child, with wavy hair, is large in proportion to the body; his
limbs are woefully thin. The Child has his finger in his mouth
and sucks on it while he rubs the shiny soles of his feet together
in reflection. The poor nursing Child lies on the cold ground
—at best there is spread a handful of hay or a little white cloth
beneath him.

Like the shepherds in the old nativity plays, it is tempting
to give the mother some advice on proper bedding for babies.
But the slender, lovely Virgin Mary kneels, deeply rapt in meditation and adoration. She looks at her little Child which she
bore in her womb and to which she gave flesh from her flesh,
and she sees her God and Savior—the Creator who has chosen this world as his royal throne. The night sky over them
with its starry host is his cape, which he has thrown over his
mother and himself. St. Joseph, the faithful and righteous one,
stands as a watchman—near him are the angels, the faithful
counselors of the carpenter. They have taken visible form and
are richly decorated for a feast—they bear well-folded white
linen cloths as servants at a festal mass, and round their beautiful red cheeks fall the luxurious locks of their hair. In order to
keep their hair in place, they have bound it with gold crowns

In Scandinavian popular belief, Christmas eve is the darkest night of the year and
all kinds of spooks are abroad. The ghosts ride their 'asgardsrei' and are known
to take people captive. Today more dangerous fliers abound in the sky above
us—TRANS.

and wreaths of flowers. Only their Lord and King can come to such a feast without this kind of ornament. To him belong heaven and earth—he has established the round orb and all that exists on it; now he has come as the last and least of all to serve mankind in accordance with the will of God from all eternity—God's secret decree which in our powerlessness and smallness we oppose and are offended by.

"Let not your heart be troubled", Jesus says to the disciples, and "Fear not"—that is one of his last words. He says just that by coming to earth—more clearly than with words. Who can be troubled by a sucking babe? The half-crazed Idumean ruler in the castle in Jerusalem—but he has been a prisoner in the kingdom of his wild dreams for so long that he has lost his senses and his taste for the simple and sweet everyday things of life. The gang of wild hunters who rage in the storm clouds on Christmas eve—they are afraid. But for men of good will, the prince of peace has come as a newborn babe in a crib, and he wanted to come, wanted to be poor, so that we could do something for him.

Is not this the final and most secret cause of the joy of Christmas, that the world has been turned upside down? The Almighty has laid aside the marks of his honor and receives our gifts if we wish to do something for him. The mystery of salvation is introduced by a Christmas play, and the seriousness of the play far transcends our ability to portray what is happening; for almost two thousand years the cries and joys of children when they come to visit the crib have echoed through the world in midwinter; and people have grown warm as they play and are full of laughter because of God's Son who became a Child for their sake.

In the writing and the dreams of the Middle Ages, there wanders a figure, the Antichrist. When he comes, he appears as a full-grown man. He cannot make himself little and humble and the son of a woman. He who for so many ages has brooded over his plans of rebellion and destruction for the world, for him it is impossible to find time to play in the streets with other children in a little corner of the world. Only the Almighty, who has created and sustains all things, is ready to sleep among the carpenters' tools of Joseph's workshop and hang on Mary's hand when she goes to the well at the city wall to fetch water.

The devil, as is proper and fitting for him, appears disguised in one or another human form. The important thing in tales of the devil is that they always turn on his disguise. The tempter, the spy, sneaks in everywhere in any possible costume. Of course it is possible that he, for reasons that we do not know, has some preference for appearing as a man with goat feet and with a clever horn on his forehead, but he can just as well appear as a beautiful woman or an honored brother in the monastery—or as a black poodle or an ardent little pig or a headless chicken, if those disguises suit his purposes.

But God comes to us, forever faithful and loving, and binds himself to us with flesh and blood to fight for the human race together with that human race, as God and true Man among men. His heart, which contains the whole fullness of divinity, has beat beneath Mary's heart; his mouth, which John saw with a sword proceeding from it, has drunk at Mary's breast. Mary has lifted up her adored Son, she has wrapped him in a cloth, she holds him in her arms. Jesus leans his head toward his mother's breast—in back of Mary's supporting hand, his serious child eyes are looking down on all of us. He snuggles even closer to his mother and lifts his right hand in the air, now raised in blessing over the entering shepherds. Mary must sit down with the Child so that the guests can properly see him. The old ruler from the Eastern lands creeps on his knees to the two of them and proffers a golden censor—perhaps it would amuse the Jesus Child to have it as a toy to play with—listen to how the chains on it rattle: For a second the Child's hand reaches out and his feet kick contentedly—then the little hand is lowered as a caress on the old man's head.

People have made pictures for themselves of goddesses and divine children in order to worship them—Egyptian, Babylonian, and Chinese goddesses. Not one of them was able to display the blessing of peace upon a child at play. They were wild and vengeful, cruel and capricious, like the nature of which they were the visible images. Then appears a human child, a woman. A gentle virgin, full of grace, gently answers the angel who brings her tidings from the One who created both the angel and her: "Behold, I am the handmaiden of the Lord. Be it done unto me according to your word." And the Word became flesh and dwelt among us. Mary lifts up her Child before us—as true God and true man, he has come into the world for our salvation, because each individual immortal soul is worth more than all the departing glory of the earth and the stars. Mary's Son says to us that all we have done or not done to one of the least who belong to him, that we have done or not done to him.

The pictures of goddesses crumble, abandoned and forgotten, the memory of orgies, the bloody rites of their cultists and their dirges sound forth in erratic myths and tales for children who, playing and smiling, gather around the Mother of mercy, wherever she shows them Jesus in her arms.

Where she is driven away, there Herod slinks on his way back and people are seduced by the Idumean's dreams of power and pleasure, of feasts in newly built palaces and blood in dark cellars, and in their hearts Herod's hatred for his own descendants and his fear of children awaken. And the old visions of the goddesses of material change, gods of birth and decay, rising and falling life, again spring up.

Each of these goddesses presses her child to her breast, ready to fight for her child against others' children. Leto's child stretches his bow again and there is no mercy for the sons and daughters of Niobe. Let us then follow the children who sing with full voice:

> Adeste fideles
> Laete triumphantes
> Venite, venite in Bethlehem.

And when we give each other Christmas presents in his name, we should remember that he gave us the sun, the moon and stars, the earth with the forests and meadows, and the sea and all that moves, and all that leafs forth and bears fruit—and we have fought over these things and misused them. And he came to save us from our foolishness and our sins, and he gave himself to us as our Savior.

Venite adoremus, Dominum.

ABBREVIATIONS

KL   Sigrid Undset. *Kristin Lavransdatter*, 3 vols. Trans. Charles Archer and J. S. Scott (New York: Alfred A. Knopf, 1988).

LY   Sigrid Undset. *The Longest Years*. Trans. Arthur G. Chater (New York: Alfred A. Knopf, 1935).

MH   Sigrid Undset. *The Master of Hestviken*, 4 vols. Trans. Arthur G. Chater (New York: Alfred A. Knopf, 1952 or New American Library, 1978).

MWP   Sigrid Undset. *Men, Women and Places*. Trans. Arthur G. Chater (New York: Alfred A. Knopf, 1939).

SR   Sigrid Undset. *Stages on the Road*. Trans. Arthur G. Chater (New York: Alfred A. Knopf, 1934).

SS   Sigrid Undset. *Saga of Saints*. Trans. E. C. Ramsden (New York: Longmans, Green, 1934).

WITHDRAWN